More Praise for Dr. Kathryn Cramer

"The six steps and practical tools in this book not only make it easier for successful leaders to increase their own creativity but, more importantly, to help bring out the immense creativity and passion of others. Because Dr. Cramer lives what she writes, this book hums with truth."
—Pam Caraffa, Vice President, Organizational and Management Development, Monsanto

"The title grabbed my attention. This book is a quick, compelling, powerful read. The six steps, which focus on moving from a reactive mind-set to a creative mind-set, are magical."
—Christine Chadwick, Executive Director, FOCUS St. Louis

"With all the demands that face your organization, it's often difficult to get the best from the people you count on the most. Dr. Cramer's six-step process can help you inspire your people and provide them with the tools and optimism they need to perform at their best under all types of rapid-fire conditions."
—Peter Corr, Senior Vice President, Pfizer, Inc., Executive Vice President, Pfizer Global R & D, President, Worldwide Development

"For anyone who's been continually frustrated by trying to control the daily production of ever-better answers, Dr. Cramer offers an effective opening to discovering more meaningful questions about the global issues that matter most."
—Joe Eschbacher, Senior Director–Marketing, Self Funded and Carrier Division, Express Scripts, Inc.

"On occasion, we all approach work as if we were boarding a routine flight—we think only the destination matters, that the journey is nothing more than awkward, idle time. Kathy insists there's a better way. She shows us how to make sure we've selected the right destination (as in destiny)... and then invites us to wake up and enjoy the ride!"
—Jim Epperson, President, Oklahoma Southwestern Bell Telephone Co.

"Dr. Cramer has identified a major problem of many at midlife—they've succeeded in becoming overwhelmed. She then uses her own creativity, experience, and wisdom to show that the solution lies not in 'cutting back,' but in the wonderful paradox that, by thinking broadly, we can find calm and exhilaration in focusing our energy on what we really care about."
—Edwin Fisher, Ph.D., Professor of Psychology, Medicine & Pediatrics, Washington University

"These six steps are a must for anyone who wants to make it big in today's world."
—Alan Heller, Senior Vice President and President, Global Renal Baxter Healthcare

"Dr. Cramer has a winning concept—everyone wins when we are congruent with who we are while we are acting in concert with who we want to be. Her six-step process requires:
1. A desire to be congruent
2. A desire and ability to take responsibility to change
3. A desire to dig deep and honestly determine our current reactive patterns
4. A desire to be positive
5. A desire to be successful now and in the future
6. A desire for applauding and appreciating our success
It will be must reading for my management team as we triple growth in three years. Yea Kathryn!"
—Laura L. Herring, M.A., SCRP, President and CEO, The IMPACT Group

"I would sure like to meet 'John' one day, as I think we'd have a lot to talk about. Kathy is doing for me what she did for John, and it truly is an adventure and a journey. There's no 'quick fix' in the leadership business, but there is a methodology and a discipline. I'll keep learning until I drop dead!"
—Jim Holbrook, President and CEO, Zipatoni

"Slow down, read this book and accelerate personal and professional outcomes you want."
—Sean Maloney, Vice President, RehabCare Group

"Dr. Cramer has created a practical and very powerful guide that is a 'must read' for everyone that is serious about achieving much more of what they really want out of life! This book is guaranteed to inspire everyone to adopt a more focused, energized, and ultimately successful life strategy. As they say, 'This is no dress rehearsal.' Go for it!!"
—Curt McIntyre, Senior Vice President, MasterCard International

"Creativity is the magic necessary for individuals and organizations to breakthrough to new levels of performance and success. However, many of us struggle to unleash that creativity. It is a messy process. This pragmatic book is designed to assist leaders, through practical tools and models, to systematically provoke the creative spirit."
—Robert G. Porter, President, SSM DePaul Heath Center

"Dr. Cramer's third book is a must read for anyone seeking a quality personal and business life."
—Pat Whitaker, IIDA, President, ARCTURIS

For readers, leaders, and high achievers: Use our questionnaire at www.fasterhardersmarter.com to determine how to set the goals you need to determine the next, best version of yourself, your results, and your relationships. A separate questionnaire on the same site can help you assess your current degree of competency in executing each of the six steps.

When Faster–Harder–Smarter Is Not Enough

Six Steps for Achieving What You Want in a Rapid-Fire World

Kathryn D. Cramer, Ph.D.

McGraw-Hill

New York   Chicago   San Francisco   Lisbon
London   Madrid   Mexico City   Milan
New Delhi   San Juan   Seoul   Singapore
Sydney   Toronto

To my husband, John Stephen Davis—in celebration of his richer, deeper, wiser presence in my life and in the world.

1 2 3 4 5 6 7 8 9 0 DOC/DOC 0 9 8 7 6 5 4 3 2 1

ISBN 0-07-137671-2

Book design by Robert Freese.
This book was set in Baskerville by Patricia Wallenburg.

Printed and bound by R.R. Donnelley & Sons Company.

This publication is designed to provide accurate and authoritative information in regard to the subject matter covered. It is sold with the understanding that neither the author nor the publisher is engaged in rendering legal, accounting, futures/securities trading, or other professional service. If legal advice or other expert assistance is required, the services of a competent professional person should be sought.

—From a declaration of principles jointly adopted
by a committee of the American Bar Association
and a committee of publishers

 This book is printed on recycled, acid-free paper containing a minimum of 50% recycled, de-inked fiber.

Library of Congress Cataloging-in-Publication Data

Cramer, Kathryn D.
    When faster-harder-smarter is not enough : six steps for achieving what you want in a rapid-fire world / Kathryn Cramer.
        p. cm.
    ISBN 0-07-137671-2 (alk. paper)
    1. Success—Psychological aspects.   I. Title.

BF637.S8 C695 2001
158—dc21

2001030888

Contents

Contents

How to Read This Book

Congratulations are in order! In making the initial investment of time and energy it takes to really look at who you are, where you are, and all the roads that diverge from those starting points, you have taken the first steps necessary to creating the next, best you.

Think of this book as your coach—your very own personal guide, companion, and voice of reason. Like a coach, this book speaks to you directly about your hopes and dreams, talents and efforts. Like a coach, it guides you toward fulfilling and expanding your potential, and faithfully supports your attempts at success. Just as a coach offers perspective and encouragement amid the clamor and confusion of a game, so does this book offer strategies, wisdom, and inspiration as you contend with the demands of a rapid-fire world.

No matter where you are when this book finds you, you can find yourself in it. You may be exhausted from trying to use the same old faster, harder, smarter techniques to keep up, and wondering if there is a better way to live. You may be aggressively pursuing long-term goals, or you may be standing at a crossroads. Perhaps you've hit a bump in the road, or your energy has faltered. You may be wishing you could imbue your life with deeper meaning, or you may be looking for a way to make a significant contribution to the greater good.

When Faster-Harder-Smarter Is Not Enough will show you how to attain all you yearn for and more, using a six-step process for achieving what you want. My advice to you, in whatever stage or place you may find yourself, is to first read this book from cover to cover. In doing so, you will get a feeling for the flow of the six steps, and an awareness of the kind of help available to you. You'll also find your starting point when you go back for a second, more focused reading. If you need all six steps, use all six steps. If you feel comfortable picking and choosing the steps that make the most sense to you in your journey, do that. This is, after all, your adventure.

Please do not hesitate to refer to the questionnaires on our web site, www.fasterhardersmarter.com, for more support in setting the goals you need to determine the next, best version of yourself, your results, and your relationships.

Acknowledgments

In pursuit of worthwhile goals, achieving what you want in a rapid-fire world depends on the creative genius of many committed people. Bringing this book into existence is no exception. It is with deep appreciation and admiration that I acknowledge the contributions of each of my collaborators.

Applause for Denise Marcil, my dear friend and brilliant literary agent. Denise provides the drive and determination that any book project demands from its inception until it lands in the hands of its readers. She has faith in the promise of operating in deeper, richer, wiser ways. Denise will not rest until the last detail of sustaining the life of this book is completed. I am the luckiest author I know to have Denise leading the way.

I savor the incredible learning experiences I have enjoyed thanks to writer, editor, and mentor Nellie Sabin. Professionally she calls herself The Book MD. Personally she exudes the wisdom and compassion that belong only to the most gifted teachers. My wish is that everyone can learn from a teacher like Nellie at least once in a lifetime. Nellie brings her amazing intellect, empathy, and imagination into her process every step of the way.

Thanks to Judy Dubin for her generous gifts of insight, encouragement, and humor. Judy is my business partner and closest confidant. With her as a thinking partner I was able to navigate my way through the inevitable episodes of confusion and frustration that plague any writing project. I am blessed that Judy is in my life no matter what Level 3 Agenda I might be pursuing.

A special round of thanks to my business partner and treasured friend Terri Goslin-Jones for inventing ways that leaders, teams, and organizations can use this six-step process to achieve greater levels of effectiveness, creativity, and personal fulfillment. I value Terri as a masterful coach and consultant who is a true ambassador of this work.

Acknowledgments

The highest praise for enthusiasm and energy goes to Amy George, resident journalist and researcher at The Cramer Institute. Amy devoted many late nights and long weekends to making sure this manuscript emerged well written and arrived on time. Without Amy's tireless effort and editorial talent, the birth of this book would still be in process.

Colleen Moore is a consummate project manager and welcomed cheerleader. During the initial states of forming this concept, drafting the chapters, and creating the proposal, Colleen's unwavering confidence in the subject matter and her willingness to produce revision after revision was the investment that paid off in finding this book the best publishing home possible.

Without the talent and diligent efforts of Russell Cole, the design of this book, its web site, its workbooks, and collateral materials and products would not exist. Russell's creative genius never fails to captivate the imagination of everyone who ventures in to explore what's possible when faster-harder-smarter is not enough.

Several other individuals have gone to great lengths to help bring this book to life. I am particularly grateful to Allen Tamaren and Peggy Guest for sharing their insightful wisdom; to Lainie Neiman and Larry Kendall for their practical applications; to Heather Needleman and Jean Lopez for their design magic; and to Lynnda Green for her creative research when deadlines were short.

Mary Glenn, senior editor at McGraw-Hill, is a truly kindred spirit. Like me, Mary has a passion for introducing millions of people to the secrets of turning the pressures of rapid-fire living into fuel for leading a rewarding life. Mary has been an inspiring editor and champion for this book from the very beginning. I applaud her for her energetic sponsorship of this project and her belief in its worth and value to the world.

Finally, I wish to honor in a special way those who helped bring this book into existence by inviting me into their lives to share the secrets of their hard-won success. I have spent my whole professional career as a psychologist seeking out and working with people who refuse to give up, who strive for excellence, who dedicate themselves to advancing the greater good, and who use every challenge they face as an opportunity to learn and grow. It is out of my encounters with these clients, colleagues, friends, and family members that the messages in the book have been born.

Richer, Deeper, Wiser

Do you ever feel like you are whitewater rafting through your day, just hoping you can make it to evening without capsizing? Most of us use familiar faster-hard-er-smarter techniques to manage our challenges and attempt to reach our goals, but today's rapid-fire world calls for more—more stamina and strategies, more creativity and cooperation. We need a better way to shoot the rapids of life. That is the reason for this book.

> *Do not believe that it is very much of an advance to do the unnecessary three times as fast.*
>
> Peter Drucker

What awaits you, just beyond the horizon of today's rapid-fire realities, is yet to be fully imagined. It is vast, alive, dynamic potential. It is a future open and ready to be shaped by your desires—what you are willing to go for, what you put yourself on the line for, what possibilities you have the courage to act on.

In order to achieve what you want, you must mentally and emotionally register whatever is happening deeply enough that you become aware of hidden variables and novel solutions. This deeper focus guarantees you will be able to craft your future by tapping into a wide array of possibilities, making it a vivid expression of the hopes and intentions most vital to you. When you are creative, not reactive, under fire, you uncover opportunities hidden in your challenge and bring them one step closer to fruition.

When Faster-Harder-Smarter Is Not Enough will show you how to turn stress into success by activating your inner creativity and resilience. You will interrupt your reactive, rapid-fire habits that

1

contribute to exhaustion and stress, and replace them with an entirely new way to live your life. You will find out how to treat everyday demands as opportunities to further short- and long-term goals, and you will learn how to capitalize on mistakes—to reveal unexpected alternatives. You will discover how to maintain your energy and stamina, how to stay optimistic and creative during setbacks, and how to tap reservoirs of resilience during periods of intense pressure. Most important, you will learn a six-step process you can use to streamline your obligations and reinfuse your life with meaning. Once you determine your most important priorities, you will learn how to pursue them—day to day and year by year—with optimism, ingenuity, and stamina.

> *Daring ideas are like chessmen moved forward. They may be beaten, but they may start a winning game.*
>
> Johann Wolfgang von Goethe

This six step creative process is infinitely adaptable. I have taught it to CEOs doing strategic planning, to work forces caught in a business merger, to the dispirited employees of large, established companies, and to successful entrepreneurs who wanted to take their businesses to the next level. I've shared it with working mothers, freelancers, professionals who were downsized, and junior executives looking to make a bigger contribution. But it isn't for everyone.

This book is not about using a Palm Pilot more efficiently ... and it is not for the self-absorbed or the faint of heart.

When Faster-Harder-Smarter Is Not Enough is not for those who need efficiency tips, or who are ready to throw it all away and move to a ranch in Montana. It's not for those who set their sights on achieving what they want at the expense of others or to the detriment of the greater good. It's written for successful executives, professionals, and individuals who want to be energized instead of drained by the pressures of life. Those who want to "radiate," not "react." This book is a practical guide to staying fully engaged and in the moment; using pressure to our advantage instead of running away from it; recognizing synergistic relationships and learning how to replicate their power; and gaining benefits when none are apparent. Achieving what we want requires a series of psychological processes and inner somersaults that are awkward at first, but well within reach. This book leads us out of the reactive traps of faster-harder-smarter and into the profoundly rewarding world of richer, deeper, and wiser.

Get ready to meet your new life.

The Premise

I am constantly amazed by how much we are willing to take on. My plane lands at 10:38 P.M. I'm in bed by 12:30, but I toss and turn for hours, rehearsing how to rescue a failed proposal. My first appointment is at 8:30 in the morning, so I rise at 6:00 A.M. to make sure I have time to review some figures beforehand. Between dressing and downing my strawberry lite yogurt, I leave two voice mails in different time zones. I get to the office early in order to catch a colleague, but find several faxes on my desk that need attention right away.

Sound familiar?

Do you hear that ticking? It's the sound of talented, successful people on the verge of implosion.

In today's rapid-fire world there is *always* something else we should be doing or could be doing. We all have "to do" lists a mile long. Whatever tasks we don't accomplish today we add to tomorrow's list until that happy time when we can cross them off—but somehow the list is just as long as ever. When we have trouble getting everything done, we go into overdrive and try to work faster, harder, and smarter. We use our best time management skills to cram more productivity into each day, and stress management techniques to deal with our growing sense of desperation. To have it all, we think we have to do it all.

This work ethic needs to be updated. Faster, harder, and smarter just doesn't cut it anymore. You cannot put 100 percent of your effort into 100 percent of the things on your "to do" list 100 percent of the time. You can play with the equation any way you like, but something, somewhere, has to give. Too often what we jettison first is our future.

Riding the carousel that never stops

In our fast-forward, exhausting existence, we are too *busy* to think about new opportunities or long-term goals. Who has time to be creative? As we concentrate on handling the day-to-day necessities of life, we ignore the less urgent, but more important, imperatives of our growth and learning. We are so busy that we have become separated from our creativity, and deprived of experiencing life as rich and rewarding. Without this connection, we can't see ourselves as the vital, future-shaping individuals we could be. If we keep using up all our energy and determination in daily skirmishes, one day we'll wake up and discover we never had a life.

> *I laugh when I hear that the fish in the water is thirsty.*
>
> *You don't grasp the fact that what is most alive of all is inside your own house;*
>
> *and so you walk from one holy city to the next with a confused look!*
>
> *Kabir will tell you the truth: go wherever you like, to Calcutta or Tibet, if you can't find where your soul is hidden, for you the world will never be real!*
>
> From *The Kabir Book: Forty-Four of the Ecstatic Poems of Kabir*, translated by Robert Bly

Each day the demands on our attention exceed the amount of time and energy we have available to cope with them. Life seems like an Olympic endurance event—the Everydayathon! In order to accomplish more, we try to do things faster, harder, and smarter, but our responsibilities, like water pouring into a boat, accumulate faster than we can bail. Ironically, the very survivor skills that have brought us this far are not enough to maintain our momentum. When we pin success on ever-increasing speed, intensity, and efficiency, we run the risk of burning out, both personally and professionally. As one executive wryly told me, "I can't work any harder or faster. I can already feel my clutch burning."

Sometimes being on automatic pilot is good enough, but faster, harder, and smarter techniques will never take us where we want to go. Even if we manage our time better, establish priorities, work more efficiently, delegate certain tasks, try to maintain a positive attitude, and calm our anxiety, we still do not approach the benefits we can derive from a deeper, richer, and wiser relationship with the challenges of a rapid-fire world.

What we need most is to enlarge our capacity to be creative under fire. This requires that we engage pressure as if it were a force worthy of respect, not domination. Stressful life events, whether routine or cataclysmic, can be managed in ways that promote health and personal effectiveness, rather than harm. It is possible to turn stress into strength and to make it a positive, life-giving force.

Courage and perseverance have a magical talisman, before which difficulties disappear and obstacles vanish into air.
John Quincy Adams

In my professional life, I have seen over and over that modern problems call for creative solutions. However, this is easier said than done. Creativity applied to any endeavor cannot be reduced to technical skills. Creativity comes from releasing the inner resources that reside deep within your mind, heart, and spirit. This book will show you how to unleash your inner resources—such as curiosity, optimism, courage, resilience, empathy, and ingenuity—under rapid-fire conditions, to produce an amazing positive combustion that benefits everyone.

We are the Transition Generation.

As a society, we are in transition between the Industrial Age and the Age of Technology. We all grew up with the Industrial Age expectation that we would memorize and master whatever information we needed to handle our challenges and demands. Today the parameters of success have completely shifted. Now we need to be able to use the latest technology to slice, dice, and deliver the information we need as we need it. We have novel problems that require creative and collaborative solutions. And the whole horse race has sped up, making it ever more difficult to stay out in front.

Our rapid-fire world has us bound up in seemingly irreconcilable demands that will confuse and defeat us unless we unleash the hidden power of creativity. In the Industrial Age paradigm, life is either/or. Faced with a contradiction that demands resolution, we usually take a position on one side or the other and try to win at all costs, or we walk, maybe run, away. Instead, we need to learn how to embrace the power of paradox in order to creatively handle rapid-fire demands. We need to be able to slow down while speeding up, to be reflective while being spontaneous, to be logical *and* intuitive at the same time. Sounds impossible? Well, it isn't. To become masterful at creating what we want, we must recognize the opposing forces that barrage us. Only after we have fully understood the importance of both sides can we mine the beneficial aspects of each opposing force, blend them, and ultimately shape a positive future for ourselves.

> *Let this be an example for the acquisition of all knowledge, virtue, and riches. By the fall of drops of water, by degrees, a pot is filled.*
>
> The Hitopadesa

When we don't know how to respond constructively, and can't imagine how to reconcile opposing forces, we are drawn into win-lose or no-win interactions. Right when we need to be creative, we fall back on faster, harder, and smarter. There is a better way.

Six steps for achieving what you want in a rapid-fire world

For over 20 years I have studied how successful people respond to life's challenges and demands. I have gained an inside look at the minds and hearts of leaders in business and science, in medicine and government; of athletes and entrepreneurs, mothers and mystics. Through my research and my professional experiences, I have distilled a *six step process for achieving what you want in a rapid-fire world*. People who are unusually resilient and creative in responding to the complexity and challenges of our rapid-fire world all use these six steps, whether they are aware of it or not. You can apply this process to your personal quandaries, large or

Experience is not what happens to a man; it is what a man does with what happens to him.

Aldous Huxley

small, and you can implement it in five minutes, five days, or over five years.

Rather than being stunned and confused by the curves life throws, you need to discern the best possible use of your time and energy. The six-step process on page 9 will help you shape a creative agenda that does not force you to sacrifice long-term goals to meet short-term obligations. It will give you the creative edge you need to be effective, and it will help you build strong alliances with others. Although each of us is responsible for the life we are living, none of us is able to create it alone. Growth comes not from "you" or "me," but through the alchemy of "us."

How would you like to take your agenda to the next level?

As a psychologist, corporate consultant, and leadership coach, I am on the cutting edge of business solutions every day. I help businesses and individuals see the Big Picture and set their priorities so the essential tasks are accomplished even as progress toward long-term goals is being made. I've found that it helps my clients to sort their goals and obligations into three categories:

* Level 1 is for daily stresses, the generic pressure we all experience.
* Level 2 is for sudden, unanticipated situations, good or bad.
* Level 3 is for long-term personal and professional goals.

Most high achievers will not rest until they have taken care of the demands of Levels 1 and 2. They are extremely skilled at using faster-harder-smarter techniques, and they see all problems as challenges that must be

Only the curious will learn and only the resolute overcome the obstacles to learning. The quest quotient has always excited me more than the intelligence quotient.

Eugene S. Wilson

Six Steps for Achieving What You Want in a Rapid-Fire World

STEP ONE: Take Your Blinders Off
How to See What You Don't See

Before deciding what to do, your first steps are to see the big picture (externally) and to be aware of your emotional land-scape (internally).

STEP TWO: Be Outrageously Optimistic
How to See Potential, Not Problems

Now it's time to imagine the best possible outcome, goal, or solution, and to become energized by how excellent it is.

STEP THREE: Make the Future Happen Inside You
How to Walk Your Talk

Next you need to make a concrete yet flexible plan for achieving your goal, and to give up any counterproductive ideas or habits that might sabotage your efforts.

STEP FOUR: Get Others on Board
How to Speak and Act from Your Heart

Alone we cannot accomplish anything worthwhile. Now you involve in your plan those you love and those you need.

STEP FIVE: Stack the Odds in Your Favor
How to Build Your Momentum

This is the follow-through. Here you implement your plan, watch your progress, overcome the obstacles that present themselves, and learn to capitalize on conflict.

STEP SIX: Celebrate Every Victory, Large and Small
How to Leverage Your Success and Wake Up
to What's Next

Enjoy your achievements ... and do it all again!

overcome. They learned their Industrial Age lesson very well: If you want to be successful, you have to work faster, harder, and smarter than anyone else. The problem is, we aren't in the

Industrial Age anymore. Using an Industrial Age mind-set in the Age of Technology is like writing on clay tablets when a fax machine is available.

The demands of Levels 1 and 2 can easily drain all your energy before you even start on your long-term goals. So how can you screen out the nonessential tasks and distractions? You need to use what I call your "Level 3 Lens." When you triage your Level 1 and Level 2 demands, you use this lens to decide what is truly important in achieving your hopes, dreams, and long-term goals. Anything extraneous you get rid of or ignore. This way you are always making progress toward the best future you can imagine.

Your Level 3 Lens ... don't leave home without it.

So where do you get your Level 3 Lens? You make it yourself, following the six steps on page 9. They will guide you through the process of creating more of what you want in a rapid-fire world. As you proceed through this book, you will refine your goals and learn how to align your thoughts, emotions, and beliefs with what you are trying to make happen. You will learn how to consistently choose to undertake activities that enhance your competence and advance your life agenda. By the time you reach the last step, you will know exactly what you want to accomplish. Then your long-term agenda becomes the lens through which you examine the demands that are made of you.

My emphasis is not on telling you exactly how to behave, but on helping you to stay creative. You can never anticipate the exact results that will occur, so unpredictability is built into the process. Some people thrive on this freedom, while it makes others feel very nervous. If you're the kind of person who wants a written guarantee in advance, have faith. You will be surprised (from pleasantly to ecstatically) at the eventual outcomes of this process.

Composing a life involves a continual reimagining of the future and reinterpretation of the past to give meaning to the present, remembering best those events that prefigured what followed, forgetting those that proved to have no meaning within the narrative.

Mary Catherine Bateson

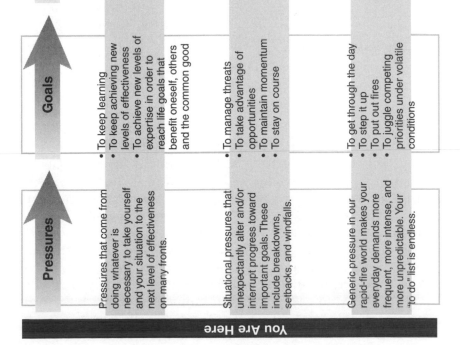

You Are Here

	Pressures	Goals	Faster, Harder, Smarter Techniques	Richer, Deeper, Wiser Perspective
Level 3	Pressures that come from doing whatever is necessary to take yourself and your situation to the next level of effectiveness on many fronts.	• To keep learning • To keep achieving new levels of effectiveness • To achieve new levels of expertise in order to reach life goals that benefit oneself, others and the common good	• Faster, harder, smarter techniques will not get you there	• Use six step process to determine priorities • Develop "lens" based on long-term personal and professional goals • Use this lens to filter the demands from Levels 1 and 2 • Use six step process to reach new levels of excellence in achieving priorities • Forge new connections
Level 2	Situational pressures that unexpectedly alter and/or interrupt progress toward important goals. These include breakdowns, setbacks, and windfalls.	• To manage threats • To take advantage of opportunities • To maintain momentum • To stay on course	• Take short-term view • Focus on damage control • Use windfalls to accelerate progress toward established goals	• Take short-term and long-term views • See context of bigger goals • Capitalize on opportunities to reach new goals • Tap creativity and resilience to find new rules of engagement
Level 1	Generic pressure in our rapid-fire world makes your everyday demands more frequent, more intense, and more unpredictable. Your "to do" list is endless.	• To get through the day • To step it up • To put out fires • To juggle competing priorities under volatile conditions	• Focus on controlling outcomes • Take on everything • Rely on self • Over promise, then fail to achieve the mark • Improve time management	• Use discretion about which goals to pursue • Collaborate with others • Pace yourself to ensure stamina • Under promise, then overachieve the mark • Delegate tasks

As you polish your Level 3 Lens, know that you are responsible for creating a strong sense of the direction in which you want things to move and the benefits you hope to achieve. In order to create what you want, you need to know your heart's desire. Then every step you take is in the right direction.

Start with the Big Picture,
then connect the dots.

As you read, all of the six steps will come alive for you, as they do for me, for the clients I coach, and for the audiences at my seminars. You will cultivate a new set of capabilities, skills, and attributes that are essential for leading an effective and fulfilling life. I am certain this book will touch you deeply enough that you will want to change. In fact, you will actually be able to see yourself change in the process of reading this book. As you apply the six steps, you will shape an agenda that is thrilling for you day by day. Yes, believe it or not, thrilling!

Because life is complex, your proactive agenda will have several dimensions. Each facet will be in a different stage of realization, but taken together they will form a coherent and cohesive life plan. Usually people focus on three areas: their professional goals, their leadership or management skills, and their personal relationships. Many people add a spiritual quest. Some need to redeem a failure or tragedy. Your plan should accommodate all your priorities and provide a place to process all your experiences. The only ground rule is that your life's agenda must do good in the world and for others, as well as for yourself. The last thing we need is more people feeding their own egos.

It is one of the most beautiful compensations of this life that no man can sincerely try to help another without helping himself.

Ralph Waldo Emerson

All of us are creatures of habit. Usually it takes a crisis—say, divorce, illness, or getting fired—to get us to change our ways. But most people are in a silent crisis right now without realizing it. This book is your wake-up call, a reminder that life, as they say, is not a dress rehearsal. I urge you to use the six steps to shape a rewarding and exciting life that is meaningful on *every* level.

The Promise

Everywhere I look there are successful people drowning in their obligations. Day after day they keep treading water, getting more and more tired but not getting any closer to shore.

Jeremy left me an urgent message. He heads the Eastern Sales Division for a company that manufactures medical equipment. His company just pioneered an upgraded device for use during laparoscopic surgery. Hospitals are so eager to replace their obsolete equipment with the new device that the company's sales have soared. Recently Jeremy received 120 voice-mail messages in one day. That's when he called me and asked, "How am I supposed to answer them all?"

Logan was a guest when I went to dinner at a friend's house. Logan makes unusual earrings from tiny little gears and other pieces she scavenges from old watches she gets from a supplier who has connections with jewelers across the country. She recently received a letter from her supplier explaining that he was going out of business because dealing in secondhand parts was no longer profitable for him. Finding a new supplier would take weeks, and Logan had an order due right away. She was distressed, to say the least.

I met Ben in a hospital waiting room. Ben's boss prepares financial reports for prospective investors, and he had entrusted Ben with doing the research for seven reports by Monday. On Friday, Ben learned that his grandfather was gravely ill. Where was Ben going to find the time to see his grandfather *and* research seven reports?

Because time was of the essence, Jeremy, Logan, and Ben all began to apply the kind of faster-harder-smarter techniques that had worked for them in the past. Jeremy was able to delegate some of his phone calls. He answered some on his cell phone during his son's soccer game, and a few more after the game in the car. Logan got her supplier on the phone and tried to reason with him. She ended up yelling at him—didn't he realize what his decision meant for her? Ben had brought his laptop to the hospital so he could keep working, but discovered there was no place where he could get on-line.

What could Jeremy, Logan, and Ben have done differently? When faster-harder-smarter is not enough, it's time to get creative.

> *God gives every bird his worm, but he does not throw it into the nest.*
>
> Swedish proverb

Jeremy, Logan, and Ben could have tapped into their deeper, longer-term commitments and desires in deciding how best to respond to their rapid-fire demands. As I talked with them about their short-term crises and their long-term goals, we shaped better solutions for them to use next time—knowing that there is always a "next time."

Jeremy could have checked with others on the sales team and his vice president to determine whether his 120 voice messages were part of a bigger pattern. If so, he might have called for a meeting so everyone could decide how to resource the windfall of sales. In the meantime, he could have delegated some calls to someone else in the company who was ready for a stretch assignment. For the rest, Jeremy could have left short, positive voice-mail messages during evening hours letting the prospective clients know when they could expect a response. This way, when Jeremy was with his son, he could have concentrated on being a father and a fan.

Let's say Logan still tried to influence her supplier, and maybe she even had her flash of temper. But then, in her moment of defeat, she could have stepped back to get a better perspective. Instead of panicking, she might have seen how this short-term crisis gave her the push she needed to fortify her business with more suppliers and a wider array of products to sell. She could have reminded herself of how meaningful her business is to her. With a more creative approach, she would have been free to research new sources to create her next line of custom-crafted jewelry.

Ben agreed to tackle his boss's request as energetically and effectively as possible. But when he learned that his grandfather was ill, he neglected to renegotiate with his boss about how much it would be humanly possible for him to accomplish. Ben should have told his boss about his family emergency immediately, and requested either assistance or a longer deadline. It's possible that this request would have hurt his chances of progressing in his career as quickly as he had planned, but at the same time, Ben would have respected himself for honoring his own commitment to family. Because of the strength of his com-

> *An inconvenience is only an adventure wrongly considered; an adventure is only an inconvenience rightly considered.*
> G. K. Chesterton

mitment, he would be prepared to deal with the consequences. He might even feel optimistic that this situation actually could increase his boss's confidence in him. If not, Ben could consider searching for a job elsewhere.

Got a lemon? As they say, make lemonade. But how?

If you asked Jeremy, Logan, and Ben what they needed most, they would say "more time." But they'd be wrong. What they really needed was ingenuity. Instead of feeling overwhelmed, angry, and backed into a corner, they could have been enthusiastic about creating ways of capitalizing on their debacles. No, it's not easy to be cheerful about setbacks, but it is more a matter of choice than we realize.

Faster-harder-smarter approaches yield stopgap solutions that often backfire in the long run. Sometimes they even make the immediate situation worse. Faster-harder-smarter maneuvers cost Jeremy special moments he might have had with his son, sent Logan into a temper tailspin that accomplished nothing, and set Ben up for a series of short nights and a fight with his boss.

What they all needed to do was innovate solutions that would create more of what they wanted—in the short run and in the longer term. Jeremy is committed to earning a six figure income *and* to being a loving father who shows up for his children in mind and spirit as well as in body. Logan aspires to expand her line of jewelry and to be as savvy about operating her business as she is about her craftsmanship. Ben is a person who places a high value on work *and* family. He has promised himself that as he builds his career, he will never allow himself to get stuck in a job that jeopardizes his relationships with the people he loves. These kinds of dilemmas can be positively dizzying—but only as long as we hold on to either/or thinking that compels us to believe that we can only do one at the expense of the other.

This book will help you set your priorities so you are always moving in a meaningful direction. You will learn how to envision lifetime goals that will guide everything you do. Instead of using a machete to hack your way blindly through your jungle of rapid-fire demands, you will find the perfect path for you—one that was nearly obscured by distractions but is now illuminated by the promise burning within your greater goals.

How can you tell the dancer from the dance?

As you can see from the examples of Jeremy, Logan, and Ben, it is possible to treat life as your dance partner. Sometimes you lead, and sometimes life leads you. It is futile to try to control everything. When you fight with reality, you are too busy to create something new, and if you can't create anything new, then you are not working on the next best version of yourself. Once

> *The best educated human being is the one who understands most about the life in which he is placed.*
>
> Helen Keller

you know your greater goals, you are able to capitalize on life events and channel their energy to the future you envision.

Each time you encounter demands and distractions, there is a deciding moment when you must ask yourself: "How important is this in my life? How close is it to my Level 3 goals? Can I make this fit into my larger plans? Is there a creative way of handling this situation so it has meaning for me?" If there is, then this challenge is your friend. If there isn't, then it is not a priority for now.

Being vigilant like this makes you better able to handle your Level 1 and Level 2 tasks. It also ensures that all your actions will increase your competency and nourish your life goals.

Apathy is your enemy.
Go for exhilaration and reward.

In the chart below, you'll see there are two zones—Zone A (Frustration and Anxiety) and Zone C (Apathy and Boredom)— where you do not want to be. When a challenge is well within your capabilities, you find yourself in Zone D, the Comfort zone. This makes a nice break, but eventually would put you to sleep. In the center is Satisfaction, which for high achievers is rarely good enough. But in Zone B, the fourth zone, is Exhilaration and Reward. By putting the six step creative process to work, you can ensure that each day will put you in the zone where you challenge your abilities, increase your competence, and add meaning to your life. No one can be thrilled with life all the time, but I promise it is possible for you to pursue your life goals hour by hour and day by day. You will experience both the fundamental shifts that promote change, and the small, subtle movements of life that help us attain wisdom.

Challenge/Compentency Zones

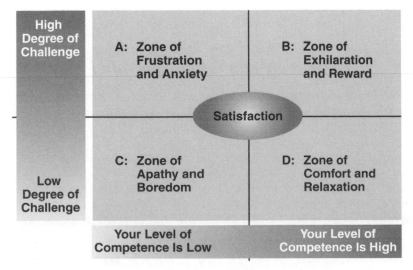

17

The Prescription

We are given the chance to make progress on what's most important to us innumerable times every day, and usually we don't even realize it. We deal with our challenges and demands in a way that just makes them go away, instead of approaching them creatively to see how they can benefit us most. Are we going to try to conquer each challenge with faster-harder-smarter techniques, or will we engage it with ingenuity and resourcefulness? In that moment of decision, we choose to be either creative or reactive, to move forward or to jog in place.

Life shrinks or expands in proportion to one's courage.

Anais Nin

If you want to make changes, start by changing your mind.

Consider some of the differences between the states of mind I call the Reactive mind-set and the Creative mind-set:

Reactive Mind-set	*Creative Mind-set*
Faster—increasing the *speed* of your efforts in order to catch up, keep up, or get ahead	Richer—expanding your levels of *awareness* to unleash hidden potential in yourself and your situation

continued on next page

18

Reactive Mind-set	Creative Mind-set
Harder—increasing the *intensity* of your efforts in order to control, fix, or dominate	Deeper—extending your *depth* of appreciation for relationships to foster progress and synergy
Smarter—increasing your *know-how* in order to outwit, outmaneuver, or finesse a win	Wiser—expanding the breadth of your *understanding* of how and why the world works the way it does to create new possibilities

We can easily grasp how each of these mind-sets establishes a very different set of objectives, and consequently a different relationship between us and the rapid-fire challenges at hand. Reactors and Creators experience life differently. Reactors always have a sense of being in a power struggle to control outside forces that suggest an uncertain possibly dangerous future. They have no unifying agenda, so they just wing it. High-achieving Reactors don't worry as much because they can always pull a rabbit out of a hat if they need to. While it's good to be ingenious, arbitrary decisions create conflicts and contradictions as their effects overlap.

Creators, on the other hand, are powerful enough to partner with outside forces in shaping a future worth living. No two Creators will respond the same way, but all Creators consciously pursue how their inner and outer realities are linked. They consciously shape their goals into a coherent network so every decision they make contributes to their effectiveness and their larger goals.

The Reactive mind-set

When we are in the Reactive mode, we make quick decisions, act rapidly, function on autopilot, and tear into life with dogged, determined effort aimed at achieving certain predetermined goals. Adopting a Reactive mind-set works best in well-defined situations—when we know where we are going, how to get there, and how to deal with the predictable problems and setbacks that might occur along the way.

However, when challenges are too big, too difficult, too rapid, too complex, too new, or too formidable, continuing to rely on the Reactive mind-set backfires. *Faster* turns into harried, hurried, frazzled, and busy-beyond-belief. *Harder* gives way to frustration, exhaustion, and even resentment over time. *Smarter* spawns overload, confusion, and even guilt over not being able to know all there is to know. Left unchecked, our reactive habits leave us feeling stymied and deprived, and promote other self-defeating patterns that rob us of self-confidence and creative solutions just when we need them the most.

The Reactive mind-set requires exacting effort and rational analysis. Using the Reactive mind-set, we spew predictions, expectations, estimates, plans, and measures. In a rapid-fire world, the Reactive mind-set makes us spin out of control, rushing out of time and luck. We wear ourselves out trying to tame and direct—getting nowhere, faster and faster.

Seven blunders of the world that lead to violence: wealth without work, pleasure without conscience, knowledge without character, commerce without morality, science without humanity, worship without sacrifice, politics without principle.

Mahatma Gandhi

Exhausted, we burn out before we ever exert control over anything.

If we adopt the Reactive mind-set under rapid-fire conditions, we always come up short. We never have enough time, energy, know-how, money, or "whatever" to bring about a satisfactory resolution. As faster-harder-smarter demands rob us of the precious rest and leisure that are so essential to sustained, long-term, goal-oriented effort, we are forced to steal from a focus on family to service the interest charge on ever-escalating career debt. We borrow energy from loving and dancing and planting the tomatoes in order to pay the pipers of Keeping Up or Getting Ahead.

Because it is not creative, the Reactive mind-set scans for "the" right answer, "the" correct moral stand, "the" fundamental truth. When we adopt the Reactive mind-set, we seek truths that already exist and confirm beliefs that we already hold. The Reactive mind-set chokes on ambiguities, contradictions, dialectical intersections, and emergent possibilities—all things that fuel and sustain the Creative mind-set.

The Creative mind-set

Opting for the Creative mind-set makes you a Creator. Your creativity is a vast, untapped resource within you that you can put to work immediately in order to transcend faster-harder-smarter techniques and transform problems into opportunities. Every aspect of reality—the chaos, the speed, the barriers, the mistakes, the windfalls—becomes material for your creativity. Through the Creative mind-set you gain access to the inner resources you need most. You tap the resilience you need to turn barriers into checkpoints, you trigger optimism that can help you use mistakes to generate surprising new alternatives, and you use your passion to cut through chaotic conditions so you can decide where to place your attention. Being a Creator offers you power and influence impossible to derive from the Reactor position.

The Creative mind-set is juicy. Wild. Constantly curious for whatever can happen next in the world of rapid-fire possibilities. When we adopt the Creative mind-set we are alert, awake, in touch with the far-ranging implications that ignite and fuel the flames of discovery in a rapid-fire world. We lean into the winds of new, emerging, converging trends. Our decisions flow with the currents toward the future, ready to encourage whatever shifts toward solutions that occur. We thrive on the excitement of new beginnings, of enlightenment, of what's just over the horizon.

When we are in the Creative mind-set, we search out ways to collaborate and cooperate. Within the dart-dash, push-pull of a relentlessly demanding world, we yearn for engagement, for "connecting with" the who-what-when-why of it all. No matter what the emotional consequences of "connecting with" may be—aching, breaking, thrilling—"connecting with" is always the path we will choose because we know intuitively that we are not meant to undertake our journey in solitude. We will pull others into our orbit as

> *Man's mind stretched to a new idea never goes back to its original dimensions.*
> Oliver Wendell Holmes

we discover what they can offer us, as well as what we can offer them. We may emulate others who already possess a quality we need, or who have already achieved something we admire. Because the Creative mind-set is always authentic, it leads us to form rejuvenating relationships with others who understand our greater purpose.

The Creative mind-set enables us to transcend paradoxes. We seek unity and merge truths. The rapid-fire world barrages us with two-pronged contradictions (now/then, mine/yours, gain/loss, fast/slow, hard/soft, full/empty, simple/complex), all of which are true simultaneously. When we are in the Creative mind-set, inhaling multiple, paradoxical contradictions is like breathing pure oxygen. We are able to breathe in pairs of opposites and breathe out clarity and wisdom. In a rapid-fire world, where everything has its opposite, the Creative mind-set allows us to absorb the tension and charge that emerge from opposite polarities and to direct this energy into new awareness and imagination. The Creative mind-set is yin and yang. It understands that opposites cannot exist without each other, and that unity begins with separateness.

The courage to create is the courage to stay open in those very moments when you must make a definitive decision. When we are in the Reactive mind-set, we jump on these opportunities and choose the most efficient answer. But when we are in the Creative mind-set, we mine the power inherent in the decision and use it to shape the outcomes we want. This power is what makes life inspiring and worthwhile. It is in these deeper zones of experience—the ones less visible, less tangible, not easily accessible—that the true forces of success or failure reside. What is in store for us is an amazing adventure.

How Do You Respond to Life Events?

Tumult, Uncertainty, Upheaval

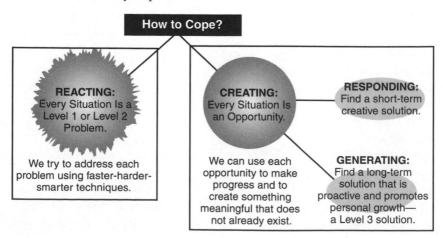

Guidance is all you need to start.
Creativity will do the rest.

Most of us have plenty of daily challenges that tether us to the talents and skills we already know how to use. Coping with daily pressures—short deadlines, unexpected demands, frustrating mistakes, temper flare-ups, missed opportunities, and so on—traps us into working faster, harder, and smarter, using the tools and methods we already have mastered. Rapid-fire challenges have a way of being all-consuming. They give the impression that there is simply no time to learn any new ways of responding. When you see someone using a cell phone to make a business call on a ski lift, or driving with one eye on the road and one on a laptop computer, or leaving the office on Friday with a huge pile of paperwork to review, you can be pretty certain he or she is over-relying on faster-harder-smarter techniques.

Sometimes a reactive response is "good enough," or even essential. But faster-harder-smarter methods can be addictive, and, like any other addiction, they are a cheap, easy substitute for the real thing. Rescuing victory from defeat can be intoxicating when the stress of the situation gives us a kick of endorphins and an adrenaline rush that makes us feel powerful in the short term. High achievers, in particular, get hooked on the feelings of invincibility that characterize a good save. But

> *A man is not idle because he is absorbed in thought. There is a visible labor and there is an invisible labor.*
>
> Victor Hugo

moving from crisis to crisis cannot generate the lasting sense of passion and purpose that responding creatively provides.

Repetition and force are the hallmarks of the reactive mode. Are you constantly debating and convincing, trying to sell an idea that hasn't caught on? Do you feel you have to "win" at all costs? Are you able to resolve differences, or do you have to avoid people or live with strained relationships? The quickest way to determine whether you are using the same old faster-harder-smarter techniques is to check how much you are repeating yourself and how often you resort to strong-arm tactics.

To evaluate how creative and adaptable you are, take a look at the flip side of the six step creative process that is central to this book. These steps are like the evil twins of the creative steps we've already discussed. How much do they apply to you?

Six Steps for Creating	*Six Steps for Reacting*
Step One: Take Your Blinders Off	Have Tunnel Vision
Step Two: Be Outrageously Optimistic	Be Rigorously Realistic
Step Three: Make the Future Happen Inside You	Wait for the Future to Come to You
Step Four: Get Others on Board	Go It Alone
Step Five: Stack the Odds in Your Favor	Fix Problems and Close Gaps
Step Six: Celebrate Every Victory, Large and Small	Focus on Specific Results

It's clear there is no future in the Reactive mind-set.

If you identify strongly with being a Reactor, you may be wondering how much effort it's going to take to jump-start your creativity and begin to shape the future you want. Let me reassure you: Once you switch into a Creative mind-set, everything you do begins to contribute to a new vision for your future. Paradoxically, you'll find strength in becoming more vulnerable, less authoritative, and more collaborative. You'll know your creative process is working when things in your life begin to mesh in serendipitous ways. Moreover, you may still be working hard, but you'll be energized, not drained, by your pursuits.

Go ahead—take the plunge.
There are no hidden rocks.

All of us have the capacity to experience every situation in life, especially intense, stressful, challenging ones, on three levels:

mentally, emotionally, and spiritually. When we adopt the Creative mind-set, we make a commitment to nurturing ourselves on all three levels. If we react automatically and superficially, we miss the power of life's ups and downs, gains and losses, windfalls and disappointments.

> *The heart has its reasons that reason cannot know.*
>
> Blaise Pascal

Most people do not know exactly how to shift from reactivity to creativity, especially when they need it most. Skeptics want proof in advance that this is something worth doing. Other people are interested, but feel confused or hesitant about where to begin. We've all had experiences that require a leap of faith, such as diving off the diving board, jumping off the bungee platform, or even parachuting out of the open door of an airplane. Once you actually take the plunge, you're immediately hooked. *The secret is to dive down into the vortex of complexity, upheaval, and challenge, and to stay in the swirl long enough to fully experience the storm.* Becoming as conscious as possible of all the forces at work transports us into the Creative mind-set. Then we can respond with intentional moves that come from deep, inner reservoirs where our imagination and ingenuity are ready to activate the

> *Nothing can bring you peace but yourself.*
>
> Ralph Waldo Emerson

vast, hidden resources of the forces of the situations we face. With the Creative mind-set, we can be curious enough, resilient enough, and wise enough to live fully, freely, and effectively in a rapid-fire world. Creativity sets us free.

STEP ONE

Take Your Blinders Off

How to See What You Don't See

- Question Reality
- Feel What You Feel

*B*efore deciding what to do, your first steps are to see the big picture (externally) and to be aware of your emotional landscape (internally).

> The greatest revolution in our generation is the discovery that human beings, by changing the inner attitudes of their minds, can change the outer aspects of their lives.
> William James

HOWARD SCHULTZ

Howard Schultz has ample reason to be proud of the phenomenal growth of his company, which has become one of the great retailing accomplishments in recent history. The company's success realizes Schultz's vision of providing customers with exceptionally high-grade, rich tasting products in a relaxed and congenial atmosphere that offers a break from the frenetic pace of everyday living.

What started out as a business selling coffee beans and equipment to a handful of coffee-tasting aficionados has turned into the Starbucks of today, which satisfies the java-craving palates of millions who consume the brew at home and in over 1500 stores across North America and Asia. It was Howard Schultz, not the founders, who saw how hungry society was for a place other than pubs to gather and to share a drink.

Schultz provided bold leadership in creating more of what the world wanted. It all began when he noticed that a small Seattle retailer was ordering more coffee makers than big volume buyers such as Macy's. He flew to Seattle to investigate and was amazed by what he found. "It was the strongest coffee I ever tasted, but by the third sip I was hooked." Schultz recalls that he drank watery, bland airline coffee on his return flight, and by the time he landed he knew he wanted to work for Starbucks.

Schultz's path to becoming CEO of Starbucks was anything but smooth. He had to start his own company, which eventually bought out the Starbucks name and stores to realize his vision of a warm, inviting, neighborhood stopping place where people can refuel their spirits night or day. He writes about his Starbucks adventure in his book, *Put Your Heart Into It: How Starbucks Built a Company One Cup at a Time*, and tells readers, "I'm convinced that most people can achieve their dreams and beyond if they have the determination to keep trying." But he added, "Success is empty if you arrive at the finish line alone…. The more winners you can bring with you—whether they're employees, customers, shareholders, or readers—the more gratifying the victory."

Question Reality

What you need to DO	See the Big Picture
What you need to BE	Curious and Committed

Indiana Jones comes to mind. Now there's a guy who needed to check out reality on every level, seen and unseen. Right away we think of him escaping the obvious threats, like flames, snakes, hurtling boulders, rising water, shootouts, and so on. Jones saved his neck repeatedly by seeing what was happening ahead of him and behind him at the same time. His awareness of the present was *richer* than most of us have. He also was pretty sharp about sensing the presence of danger, whether in the form of hidden spikes or enemies in disguise. By thoroughly immersing himself in every situation, he was able to dive *deeper* into events and to anticipate dangers as they unfolded. But what really enabled him to succeed was his resourcefulness. Fly a plane? Sure. Go under-cover? No problem. In any situation, Jones figured out which of his capabilities he needed to activate, and then of course executed them perfectly. He was *wiser* than most of us about connecting his inner abilities to outer events in order to advance his agenda.

When we question our *outer* reality, we clarify not only what others need and want from us, but also our options—the different roads available to us. When we question our *inner* reality, we discover what we most deeply value—the best of who we are and could be. What's missing? What's the next step? What are our long-term goals? Without this type of inquiry, especially in a rapid-fire world, we are sure to lose sight of everything that is important to us.

Why taking your blinders off is a good idea

In our fast-forward existence it is easy to miss the signals that something wonderful is ripe and ready to happen. You might be someone who is faced with endless days crammed full of demanding routines and constantly shifting battles. Or you may be on a roll, hitting your stride, achieving milestone after important milestone. Even success can blind you from seeing what new possibilities might be in store. If you suffer from either of these forms of "rapid-fire blindness," you are not alone.

Still—in a way—nobody sees a flower— really—it is so small—we haven't the time—and to see takes time, like to have a friend takes time.

Georgia O'Keeffe

Racing around all day isn't necessarily a bad thing. However, there is no doubt that getting caught up in the demands of a rapid-fire existence can be highly distracting. If you spend most of your time putting out fires and reacting to problems, you'll never clear your head long enough to think about your larger goals, let alone achieve them.

When you learn how to question your inner reality, you discover ways of asking yourself about what you most deeply value—about the best of who you are in your own eyes, and the best of who you are in the eyes of people you need and people you love. You also ask yourself about what's missing, but the immediate question is: What is ready to pop? What is it that you could be, but you're not yet being? What could you do more— more often, more deeply, more thoughtfully—to become the best possible you? As you ask and answer questions like these you begin to form a Level 3 agenda for yourself. And remember, it's having a set of clear, robust Level 3 goals that leads to creating the experiences you want—every hour, every day, every year.

Innerdirected inquiry is crucial to achieving more of what you want, especially in a rapid-fire world. Without this type of inward, positive, proactive exploration, you are sure to lose sight of your own potential to be more effective and to fully realize everything that is important to you. In the din of keeping up with what the world needs and wants from you, it is possible for the core of who you really are to wither, and for you to lose track of who you can become. If you don't apply your curiosity and commitment to growing and bettering yourself, your best talents, interests, and virtues will surely die.

We all know what it is like to meet someone who is displaying what I call the "Empty Suit Syndrome." We can see the face, shake hands with the body, hear the voice, witness the behavior— but for all practical purposes, on the inside, we sense that "nobody is home." Living in the rapid-fire world doesn't have to zap us of our core identity. By learning to question ourselves deeply, we can achieve Level 3 goals that help us become vital, energetic, forceful, focused achievers who thrive, not merely survive, no matter how fast and furious the existence.

Observing is almost entirely an acquired skill. It is true that certain individuals are born with an aptitude for concentrated attention, and for the eye-and-hand coordination in the act of recording what is observed. But in most cases the eye (and other organs of sensation) have to be trained.

Herbert Read

Great idea … but where do you start?

One of the best ways to begin living your Level 3 goals is to follow in the footsteps of someone who has been effective at doing just that. A coaching client of mine whom I'll call John is a prime example of a person who decided to challenge himself to grow personally and professionally while pursuing a tough business assignment. When John first came in to see me, he was a brand new CEO who had been hired to grow his company from annual revenues of $30 million to $200 million in the next two years. Early on, John told me he had made up his mind that he would look at his business challenge as a prime opportunity to expand his capabilities as a leader. I showed him how to identify the specific leadership behaviors that were most personally fulfilling and at the same time most relevant to achieving his business results.

Here, I'll tell you the story of what John did to establish his Level 3 agenda. Later, you'll read the details of how John grew in skill as a leader, maintained a creative culture in his company, and inspired others in his organization to learn how to lead—all the while achieving his revenue goals. In each step, I will show you the Best Practices John used to successfully master each of the six steps in achieving a new brand of leadership that fostered extraordinary business results.

I hope you will use John's story to learn how to set compelling long-term goals for yourself that will take your skill, your relationships, and your results to the next, highest level. There is no quicker form of learning than by imitation. Let the way John pursued

If you want to identify me, ask me not where I live, or what I like to eat, or how I comb my hair, but ask me what I am living for, in detail, and ask me what I think is keeping me from living fully for the thing I want to live for.

Thomas Merton

his aims and achievements instruct and inspire you in establishing a Level 3 agenda for yourself. What you are about to read is an account of my own experiences of John just *before* I became his coach.

How John's story began

It was Monday morning. After listening to a voice-mail message from John, I recalled having met him briefly over two years ago. I hadn't seen him since. In his message, he explained that he'd like to get together for some coaching, and he said that he had sent me an e-mail outlining what he wanted to accomplish.

I tried to remember what I knew about John. I had heard from a mutual colleague of ours about a bold career move that John had made: he left his position as vice president of marketing with a Fortune 100 company to become the CEO of a rapidly expanding company with interests around the globe. I also had seen a hint of how successful John had been in an article in *Fast Company* magazine touting the outstanding double-digit growth of his new company.

As I stood in the reception area of our office, I asked my assistant to print a copy of John's e-mail. I glanced at my watch and sighed, thinking it was 11:00 A.M. and already it had been a difficult day. Since six that morning I'd been putting out fires—managing schedule conflicts, planning upcoming seminars, and juggling crises large and small. So although I was happy to hear from John, his request was just one more item for my to-do list.

With the hard copy in hand, I gave John's e-mail a quick read. My eyes landed on key phrases. *I want to get the words and pictures to match ... I want to grow into who I want to be ... I want to be more user-friendly ... I love the challenge of being both bigger and better ... I want it all.*

I reread the last line, *I want it all*, and realized there was much more to this letter than my quick scan had revealed. For a deeper, richer experience of John's message, I had to shift from a reactive mind-set to a creative one. I went back to the beginning and started over. John's way of articulating his dilemmas captivated me. I screened out all the distractions competing for my attention and focused my attention on understanding John's letter.

> Kathryn,
>
> Here's my headline: I want to get the words and pictures to match. Right now, who I want to be and who I am are not the same. I want to grow into a better people-person, and have been heading in that direction, but I want to make sure my path is clear. There is convergence, but I want some confirmation and acceleration!

John's letter drew me in further. I realized he was not asking for help in how to handle the typical challenges of everyday living—the familiar exercises of juggling priorities, making decisions, and coming to terms with setbacks. John did not seem to be stymied by the usual minute-to-minute, hour-by-hour, day-after-day pressures of living. The letter continued:

> Who I am: I have been relatively successful along the way. The money's good, business is good, and my brain functions. However, people who report to me perceive me as being elitist, a bit unapproachable and overly critical. Being perceived as "exclusive" is not working for me or for them. In fact, it's really not who I am underneath it all. But I do not let people get too close too fast, and I don't know how to open up in a compassionate way.

I clearly saw that John was setting his sights way beyond simply burnishing his people skills. He was looking at the horizon, where his leadership, the morale of his staff, and his company's productivity all converged. He was addressing issues that mattered deeply to the people in his organization. John was calling upon himself to be different—to reveal more of who he truly was so he could better serve his company and the people who were building his business.

> Who I want to be: More approachable, and I want to be able to get people to open up because they see that I do care. I want to be able to deliver constructive criticism in a helpful

way. I want to be more user-friendly. And I want my optimism to shine through. But don't get me wrong—I am not going soft, and I certainly don't want to evolve into a jelly roll, or a spineless empty suit, or a politician playing the crowd.

I was amused by the part about becoming a "jelly roll." I could tell that the hard-driving part of John was not entirely comfortable with his idea about becoming more "user-friendly." He wanted to be more approachable, but his executive side was afraid of losing authority. I made a mental note to talk to John about the importance of transcending paradoxes. He needed to be reassured that he could be caring and effective at the same time.

I heard the deeper call that John was responding to. He had a vision of the future. He just didn't know how to get there. Line by line, he named each aspect of what he would require of himself. He showed me he was willing—even eager—to do whatever was necessary to respond to his own inner invitations for personal growth and leadership development. John knew he couldn't do this kind of growing alone. He wanted me to know he was ready for help. He wasn't exactly sure how to respond to the bigger challenges that he was setting for himself, but he knew his more typical faster-harder-smarter approaches would not be enough.

> I am a problem solver and a builder ... an energetic answer-man who likes to cross stuff off the project list. I typically do a lot on my own, more than I should. At my corporation, I am motivated by four things: (1) the art and science of the business, (2) my company's emotional power, (3) the pursuit of excellence, and (4) the challenge of being both bigger and better simultaneously!

I knew that for John to be successful in achieving his new goals, he would have to rely on others as well as on himself. He would have to start asking for answers as well as supplying them. John did not yet know how to build more collaborative relationships or how to make the inquiries and learn from other people. He had only a glimpse that this was even possible. He did realize, though, that by moving in this direction, he was signing himself up for a gigantic effort. To his credit, he seemed optimistic about learning what he didn't yet know how to do. As he ventured forth, I thought he would be resolute enough to overcome the inevitable roadblocks and setbacks along the way. I found myself inspired by his vision of what could happen if he successfully developed the creative, people-oriented side of himself.

> I love to birth and grow things. So who I want to be in the end is the guy who (1) creates order and provides direction, (2) is user-friendly and affirming, and (3) is full of optimism, with lots of hope and imagination. I want to "radiate" in a way that builds trust and confidence in me.

By saying yes to his own growth as a person, and yes to better serving the interests of those he leads, John was entering into uncharted territory where he had never navigated before. In order to make progress, he would have to move out of his zone of comfort. John would find himself a walking paradox, feeling awkward and hesitant as well as smooth and decisive, being anxious one moment and calm and confident the next. In the process of creating a brand new way of existing,

> *Discovery consists of seeing what everybody has seen and thinking what nobody has thought.*
> Albert Szent-Györgyi

he would discover that each answer raises a multitude of new questions.

As I tuned into the Level 3 agenda that John was beginning to set for himself, I found myself impressed by his curiosity and determination. I sensed that John was on the threshold of making big changes, and I realized I wanted to help him in any way possible.

I read John's letter one more time, letting myself become completely absorbed. All the busyness in my day had faded into the background. John's words had my full attention. Then it dawned on me that as I joined him on his journey, I was developing a more creative mind-set myself. I was not reading faster, thinking harder, or planning smarter, as I normally do when I hurry to cram every activity into every second I can find. Instead of fighting a battle against the pressures of time, it seemed I was operating outside of time. Physically, I felt almost weightless—airy—as if the wind could blow right through me. I no longer seemed so heavy, so weighted down by the burdens of the hour.

35

When John wrote *I love to birth and grow things*, I was flooded with feeling. It seemed I had said those words and thought those thoughts myself. John's mind and my mind were synchronized—we were on the same wavelength. I had experienced this feeling before, with other clients whose creative process was unusually collaborative and exciting.

Life is a mirror and will reflect back to the thinker what he thinks into it.

Ernest Holmes

So who do I want to be in the end? I want to radiate. John's desire to radiate kindled a spark in me as I read his words. It was as if what he was most passionate about was catching fire in me.

Then, abruptly, I came back to reality. Can this guy be for real? I thought. What does he *mean* by "I want to radiate"? My skepticism broke the spell. I felt my reactive mind-set kicking in, raising more questions and more doubts. How *did* I know John meant what he said? How did his employees see him, anyway?

The more creative side of me bounced back: Don't analyze, explain, or dissect John's desire to radiate. Wait until you can explore this *with* John. Assume that he means what he says, and that what he says is true. Now I could see this as an exciting opportunity. I recovered my enthusiasm about connecting more closely with John in his effort to become a better leader while he grew his company.

In the end, I found myself 100 percent committed to helping John. I love working with people who are developing their most masterful agendas, so I couldn't wait to see him for our first coaching session. I also looked forward to our work together because my intuition told me that John was prepared to dig deeply. Had his focus remained exclusively on the surface, he would not have had to change. In the eyes of the world, John looked highly competent to meet the challenges of growing his business. No one, not even a seasoned observer, would have spotted the emerging need for him to become more effective in such fundamental ways.

It's in these deeper zones—the ones less visible, less tangible, not easily accessible—that the true forces of success or failure reside. John could have ignored the subtle, yet powerful, messages pointing out the new ways in which he needed to change.

But he didn't. In fact, he did just the opposite. He transformed his unrest into questions that he began to answer for himself: "Who do I want to be in the end? I want to be the guy who creates order and direction, is user-friendly, and is full of optimism."

The fast-track growth of John's company certainly provided plenty of daily challenges that could have kept him completely occupied using the talents and skills he already knew how to use. Expanding market share, accelerating new product development, opening new offices, establishing strategic alliances—pressures like these can often be met by working faster, harder, and smarter with all the tools and methods we already have mastered. And rapid-fire challenges such as these have a way of being all-consuming. They give the impression that there is simply no time to learn any new ways of meeting demands if we intend to keep pace or get ahead.

But in spite of the nature of these business challenges, John didn't allow himself to be seduced away from tackling more essential, emerging calls for new behaviors and insights. He didn't let a successful track record lull him into a false sense of security and satisfaction.

I was heartened by the fact that John was willing to grow in new ways that were foreign to him,

> *The habit of thinking of things in plastic and pictorial terms must have its influence upon the writer's art, when you practice both as I do. First of all, I see! The first—and last—things that I do is to use my eyes.*
>
> Wyndham Lewis

and that he sensed would make him more vulnerable, less authoritative, and more collaborative. He was determined to learn how to demonstrate his care and concern for others, how to show others he wanted to be influenced by them and to connect with their beliefs, experiences, and motives—all for the good of the company and everyone involved. I could see that John wanted to engage his newly emerging imperatives in an open, creative way. As a result, he set himself up for an amazing adventure filled with the rewards and excitement that only a Creative mind-set can foster.

With a good deal of respect for the goals John had set for himself, I called him to arrange our first coaching session. The Best Practices you are about to read are those John and I used to help him identify the specific Level 3 personal, leadership, and organizational goals he wanted to pursue.

BEST PRACTICES

Imagine yourself on a long journey—traveling by car or boat or on foot—crossing a vast expanse of land, water, or mountains. In a journey like this it is just as important to keep track of where you've been as it is to watch where you are going. Every milestone or setback, every stretch of progress or unexpected detour, every breakdown or bit of good fortune you have encountered along the way has taught you something.

What you have learned and the ways you have grown in skills and in perspective you take with you into the future. These lessons belong to you. They have seeped into the very fabric of who you are and what you know about yourself and about life. These lessons are available any time you need them to guide you and to give you confidence in yourself as a learner and as someone who is developing greater and greater reservoirs of knowledge and skill with each experience along the way.

We often think that our affairs, great or small, must be tended continuously and in detail, or our world will disintegrate, and we will lose our places in the universe. That is not true, or if it is true, then our situations were so temporary that they would have collapsed anyway.

Maya Angelou

There is little doubt that experience can be one of our best teachers, and yet too often we fail to harvest the lessons from our experiences. If we don't take the time to reflect and to "connect the dots" between what has happened, how we have responded, and what the eventual consequences were, then we are living life on the surface, merely skimming over the treasures hidden beneath. We know we are speeding past the deeper lessons our experiences have to offer when we find ourselves repeating the same mistakes again and again, or when we catch ourselves reinventing the wheel we've made before, or when we keep rediscovering the same truth about ourselves and our situation that we've discovered many times over. No one wants to live a life learning the same lessons time and time again. To prevent this debilitating "instant replay syndrome" from destroying our sense of progress in life, we must take the time to reflect on our experiences. We need to make sense out of whatever happens, to *take our blinders off* so we can see more fully how we have used our experiences to grow in competence and confidence, if only we would step back and pause long enough to notice.

From time to time, just as John did, you need to step back far enough from the unique person you are and from the unique life you are living so that you can see the big picture. What has been happening? How have you been responding? Who are you becoming in the process? It's amazing how easy it is to be so caught up in our rapid-fire world that how our life has evolved becomes a blur. Making a map of your life, one that charts signature events over time, is one of the best exercises I know of to help question the reality you have experienced, are now experiencing. Mapping the course of your life establishes an edge for you to push off, as you would push off a dock. We all need a place to begin. The chart of your life to come begins with a map of the life you already have lived.

I've personally witnessed the power of Life Mapping to inspire creativity. Every year hundreds of people who participate in leadership development courses at the Cramer Institute use this process to open their eyes to how they have grown both personally and professionally.

BEST PRACTICE #1

YOUR LIFE MAP

Examine the Life Map on pages 41–42. (This one has been filled out for John as an example.) The categories are:

Peak Experiences: high points in your life, periods of great joy or accomplishment

Episodes of Misfortune: low points in your life, periods of great disappointment or bad luck

Turning Points: significant changes in your life's course or in your self-image, periods of transition

Significant Role Models: people whom you greatly admire or who take special care to nurture and promote your welfare

Significant Critics: people who undermine your confidence
and competence by criticizing you, or who hinder your
welfare in any way

Step 1: First you look back

Copy the chart onto a blank sheet of paper. Spend no more
than 60 minutes recording on your chart the key events and people who have shaped your life. Use John's chart to prompt your
memory as you complete this brief survey of your life. I'm certain
you could spend hours filling in your chart, but that would miss
the point. Your aim should be to capture your first thoughts
about the major highlights of your life that stand out to you.
Explore different aspects of your life: education, family, career,
hobbies, friendships, health history, work life, athletics, and any
other areas relevant to you.

Step 2: Look for themes

After you have made a spontaneous, yet thoughtful, search
for the events and people that have played a major role in your
life, review your notes to determine if any patterns appear.
Sometimes it is helpful just to state the obvious. Other times the
connections may be subtle. Spend at least 45 minutes deciphering
the meaning of these mile-
stones and key relation-
ships. This is not terribly
difficult, but most of us are
completely unaccustomed
to questioning reality in
this way. Reviewing your
life may feel awkward at
first, like writing with the
wrong hand or wearing
shoes that are too big, but this self-consciousness should quickly pass.

*Karl von Frisch, who decoded the dance
language of bees, would lie for hours
between cliffs, motionless, watching
living things: "I discovered that
miraculous worlds may reveal themselves
to a patient observer where the casual
passerby sees nothing at all."*

Some people don't like to look back because their lives have
been painful. This is their chance to take that pain and use it for
something positive. John and I noticed that he had significantly
more peak experiences as an adult than he did as a child or adolescent. John attributed this pattern to the fact that he is more
engaged in life as an adult. We noticed that he associated peak
experiences not only with excelling in academics and athletics,

The Life Map

The notes in this Life Map are taken from responses made by John during our first coaching session. I have included John's notes for your review so you have his example to guide you in making your own notes on the most significant people and situations that have shaped your life.

	Childhood 0–10 years	Adolescence 11–20 years	Adulthood 21–40 years	Adulthood 41–60 years	Adulthood 61 and up
Peak Experiences	• Learning to ski • Summer camp in Michigan	• Quarterback varsity football • Getting a 4.0 senior year	• Living in Malaysia • Asking my wife to marry me • Being in delivery room when my children were born	• Being named CEO	
Episodes of Misfortune	• My dog was stolen • Lost my grandfather's watch • Broke my arm	• Death of my grandfather • Death of my best friend Charlie		• Firing my COO	
Turning Points	• Moved to new house	• Switched from premed to corporate law	• Stopped going to church	• Deciding to leave secure job for challenging one	

continued on next page

The Life Map (continued)

	Childhood 0–10 years	Adolescence 11–20 years	Adulthood 21–40 years	Adulthood 41–60 years	Adulthood 61 and up
Significant Role Models	• Best friend Charlie	• My father • My grandfather	• My boss on my first job • My wife	• My wife	
Significant Critics	• The choir master • Third grade history teacher	• Baseball coach • Latin teacher • My sister	• My son	• My son	

42

but also with major relationship milestones and with opportunities to lead others. Interestingly, John viewed his greatest misfortunes to be episodes during which he lost his key relationships (by death and firing). We concluded that he valued his relationships highly and was motivated to establish deep, strong ties with others. This pattern of valuing close relationships also shows up in John's entries in the Significant Role Models and Critics categories. From his Life Map, John observed that although people made a big difference in how he viewed himself and in how fast he learned, most of his life he turned to family members and close friends for support. John felt he was ready to move beyond his closest ties, and to find people in his profession who could serve as role models.

Step 3: Look for growth

Think about how you responded to each situation and person on your chart and ask yourself how each entry made you more effective, creative, or resilient. What did you learn? How did you grow? Allow only enough time for the most spontaneous insights to emerge. Explore how your growth and increased effectiveness, creativity, and resilience may have contributed to the success of other individuals, groups, and organizations. John was quick to note that every time he had a major disappointment or setback he learned to be more self-reliant—perhaps to a fault. He admitted that his wife often encouraged him to reach out to her and to others for support when he needed to solve a problem or come to terms with disappointment. John explained that he felt reluctant to impose on other people (even his wife). We discussed that his hesitancy to reach out to others may mislead others into thinking their help was not valuable. This was, in fact, an error John wanted to correct.

John was amazed as he charted the strength of character and sense of humor he had acquired while dealing with episodes of misfortune. He knew he always tried to be compassionate with others when they made mistakes or fell short of expectations, and now he made the connection to his own experiences with criticism. He felt so ashamed by his encounters with a punishing choir master and Latin teacher that he grew up gun-shy and overly sensitive to criticism. He even felt crushed when criticized by his rebellious son. John vowed never to humiliate others as he had been humiliated.

Step 4: Use the Life Map as, well, a map

Commit yourself to preserving your Life Map notes. One reason is that you will be referring to your Life Map in later exercises. In a larger way, however, your Life Map will sharpen your memory and help you develop a kind of filter through which you can view your life. This deepens your understanding of how effective, creative, and resilient you can be in response to life-shaping forces to come. John and I returned to his Life Map notes frequently through the course of our work together. Each time John set a Level 3 goal, he used his Life Map as a point of reference.

Many of my clients extend this exercise by actually illustrating their Life Maps. Try this yourself. With pictures, you can more creatively display how significant events and people have had an impact on your life, for better or worse. Some of my clients highlight different themes and patterns using different colors. Others use titles, slogans, or phrases to characterize different periods of their lives.

Developmental psychologist Dan P. McAdams, researcher at Loyola University, has devoted his career to the study of how people form their sense of personal identity. McAdams concluded that human beings construct a sense of their own uniqueness by creating what he terms a "heroic study of the self." McAdams's methods are similar to the Life Mapping process that is so helpful to my clients. Readers who want more extensive support in exploring and expressing their life story should see McAdams's popular text, The Stories We Live By.

Some people find that looking at their Life Map is so encouraging, they hang it on a wall in full view. Others add to theirs from time to time as significant events and milestones come to mind in the privacy of their own reflection or in conversation with a close friend or confidant. Consider extending the process of life mapping in these ways and in other ways that suit you best.

BEST PRACTICE *#2*

FRAMING THE BIG PICTURE: THE THREE DOMAINS

All other things being equal, there is nothing better than to be completely absorbed in creating the next, best version of yourself, your relationships, and what you are trying to make happen for the world. The question is: How? How do you arrange your daily, weekly, and yearly agendas such that you are so deeply committed, so engrossed, so enthralled with what you are up to in your life that you can't imagine being or doing anything else? Finding your own answers to this question is what this Best Practice is all about.

Imagine yourself on that long journey one more time. In the first Best Practice, you learned how to take your blinders off and question the reality of your past experiences so you could gain a new perspective on how far you've come, and a new appreciation of how you have grown in the process. Now it's time to build even further on the way you understand and develop your life. The more conscious you become of where you've been, where you are going, and how the two are connected, the more intentional you can be in creating the life you want—a life that you are generating out of the deepest essence of who you are, what you have to offer, and what matters most to you.

This Best Practice shows you how to build a frame around the future that will be most rewarding and meaningful to you. There are two benefits: You will envision the richest possible future for yourself, and you'll make an unswerving commitment to your goals. Research shows that when you pursue a goal for its own sake, because it is valuable to you in its own right, you become more autonomous and less vulnerable to being thrown off course by the generic or situational pressures of our rapid-fire world.

In this exercise you will gather information essential for creating your Level 3 agenda, first from yourself, then from others who know you well. The way you proceed will frame the boundaries of your future and provide an initial sense of direction for creating what you want to happen in your life.

Step 1: Ask yourself what matters most
Before reading further, sit back and think about the three or four things that matter most to you. Reflect on the most meaningful and important aspects of your life. Some people find it helpful to project themselves into the future and ask themselves, "What would I be thinking about in those moments before death? What three or four things would fill my mind?" While this

sounds a little morbid, it makes a lot of sense. Make a mental or written note of the three or four things that matter most to you and then continue reading.

Step 2: What would you attempt to do if you knew you could not fail?

Everything of major importance to human beings can be grouped in either your Personal Domain, Partnership Domain, or Productivity Domain. The *Personal Domain* includes the mental, emotional, physical, and spiritual aspects of the way we function. It encompasses our values and beliefs, our expectations and perspectives, our attitudes and feelings, our sense of hope and confidence, our faith, our skills and capacities, our ability to learn and remember, our bodily health, energy, stamina, and endurance. The *Partnership Domain* pertains to the nature and types of relationships we create in our lives. It includes intimate, collegial, family, and community ties. We relate to people in our roles as leaders, parents, children, neighbors, fellow citizens, bosses, teachers, mentors, direct reports (subordinates), and friends. The *Productivity Domain* describes our purpose and interests in and for the world. In a broad sense it refers to the impact we produce in the world as the result of our contributions and achievements in work, family, and community life.

Take a few minutes to copy the chart on page 47. Please stop reading for a minute, get the paper and pen, and do this. You will need this chart later when you put together your master list of Level 3 goals.

On the chart you will see three columns labeled Personal Domain, Partnership Domain, and Productivity Domain. These will help you to define the broadest horizon for your Level 3 agenda. Let these three domains encompass the full spectrum of your life. (I have found that high achievers tend to forget to focus on personal growth and partnerships in favor of targeting productivity results.)

Everything in your life ends up in your act.

Comedian Aaron Freeman

I have added John's goals to the chart to help you get started, but I hope you will not be unduly influenced by them. Think about the questions above the chart, then note your answers in each column. Try to be both spontaneous and thoughtful. Go with your first response, note it, and then continue to explore more deeply. This is no time for censoring your thoughts or feelings. Express yourself fully, and you will glimpse a future worth living into.

I strongly recommend that after you answer these questions privately, you pose the same questions to other people who want the best for you and who play an important role in your life, whether at work, at home, or in your community. They will help you take your blinders off by offering additional, fresh perspectives. From their vantage points you may be able to see crucial aspects of yourself, your relationships, or your work that are not so obvious to you.

As you consider who could shed valuable light on your longer-term goals, be sure you select people from different walks

Framing the Big Picture

The Three Domains

Ask yourself: What do I want to create? What do I need and want to learn? What is my next level of effectiveness? What am I aiming for? What is ready to happen, with my help? What contributions do I make? What legacies do I want to leave?

Personal Domain	Partnership Domain	Productivity Domain
The perspectives, skills, and capacities most important to my effectiveness	The nature and quality of the relationships I have in my personal and professional life	What I contribute and accomplish in my work, home, and community life
John's Personal Goal	John's Partnership Goal	John's Productivity Goal
To become as effective at asking questions as I am at answering them.	To be collaborative by seeking others' opinions, allowing them to discover and implement solutions.	To maintain a highly creative culture as the company's size triples and annual revenues grow from $30 million to $200 million.

of life. Receiving feedback from a wide variety of people with far-ranging perspectives will generate richer, more stimulating scenarios. Also, when you talk to others who know you well and who want the best for you, make sure they answer the questions *as they apply to you*. Occasionally people misunderstand what is being asked of them. In my experience, however, most people are flattered to be asked and want to be useful.

Remind your helpers that you are interested in finding out what they believe to be your most fruitful areas of growth (1) as a person—your perspectives, capacities, and skills; (2) as you relate to others; and (3) in what you get accomplished on the job, at home, and in your community. Emphasize that you are interested in their feedback regarding which *new* developments and skills would add the most to your effectiveness.

When you are finished gathering the opinions of others, compare your own answers to the answers they gave. Incorporate any new targets for your own development that seem rewarding to you. You will use this initial horizon, rich with possibilities, to craft more specific long-term goals as you work your way through each step of achieving what you want.

After you have filled all three domain columns with both your thoughts and the suggestions of others, pause a moment to notice what a compelling future you have framed for yourself. Step back and appreciate the vast potential you have identified in yourself, in your relationships, and in the areas of productivity that are most important to you. Viewing the big picture—the whole panoramic horizon of what could happen—is inspiring. Give yourself enough reflection time for this inspiration to sink in.

> *Three great mysteries there are in the lives of mortal being: that mystery of birth, at the beginning; the mystery of death, at the end; and greater than either, the mystery of love. Everything that is most precious in life is a form of love. Art is a form of love, if it be noble; labor is a form of love, if it be worthy; and thought is a form of love, if it be inspired.*
>
> Benjamin Cardozo, Judge,
> New York State
> Court of Appeals

Next, think about how your goals within each of the three domains are relevant to and synergistic with each other. Glance across your page of notes from left to right and think about how your aspirations in the Personal Domain are related to what's emerging for you in the domains of Partnerships and Productivity. Then look at the center column and see how beginning with your Partnership Domain seems to further your understanding of the inter-connections between all three of these growth areas. Finally, start with what you have noted in the Productivity Domain and then read from right to left across the other two domains. Take one final look at the possible synergies between your productivity, relationship, and personal long-range options.

Some people like to emphasize the links between growth areas by drawing lines. If you like this method, use different colored pencils or pens to connect items so you can see the pattern more easily. Finally, as one final check for synergies, I recommend that you compare your Life Map notes and discoveries (see pages 41–42) with your Framing the Big Picture notes and discoveries. This part of your reflection process will help you see how your past experiences and patterns feed into how you want to shape your future—inside and out.

Like most people, John was interested in what others would say when he asked them for feedback. Because he tended to be carefully methodical, he wanted to design a system for eliciting the most useful feedback. We devoted one entire coaching session to creating and rehearsing his feedback-interview process. By rehearsing, John believed that he could get more value out of his interviews. He conducted his interviews in the manner shown below. You are welcome to adapt it to your needs. On paper, John created an interview guide for himself that included the following questions, with spaces for recording the comments made during his interview.

Opening statement: I'm in the process of identifying some long-term goals for myself and I'm vitally interested in your opinions and feedback about the direction and focus I should take. I would like to ask you three questions.

Question 1: When you think about what would serve me most in my relationships with other people, what capabilities and skills could I develop to significantly improve those relationships over the course of the next one to three years?

Question 2: When you think about my productivity and what I am responsible for accomplishing, which areas of achievement do you feel are highest in priority? In those high-priority areas, what kind of results would indicate success to you over the course of the next one to three years? Please be as specific as you can about success criteria.

Question 3: When you think about me as a person—my strengths and weaknesses, and what kind of productivity and partnerships I am striving for—what capacities and skills would you suggest I develop in myself over the course of the next one to three years?

John ended up choosing seven people to provide him with perspective on what he should strive for personally, in his key relationships, and in terms of his productivity. He selected one board member from his company, two direct reports, one customer, the vice president of sales, one integration team leader from an organization John's company was acquiring, and one trusted colleague who had worked closely with John for five years prior to John's appointment as CEO.

BEST PRACTICE #3

TAKING AN INVENTORY OF YOUR CREATIVE RESOURCES: THE DO'S AND BE'S

Now that you can see the wide, rich horizon of possibilities just waiting for you to nurture them into existence, it's time to contemplate what creative resources you need to realize the next, best version of you, your relationships and achievements and contributions. The resources most essential to achieving what you want are inner resources. Although external resources like time, money, opportunity, and help from others are important, your very own internal, creative resources are more essential than any other. In fact, how you tap into and apply your vast supply of creative resources will either expand or contract the supply of external resources you have at your disposal in creating the life you want.

Step 1: What you need to do, and what you need to be

Each step of the six step process for achieving what you want is associated with specific tasks (what you need to do) as well as an optimal outlook (what you need to be). Review the list of Do's and Be's on pages 51–52 that reflect your vast inner array of creative resources. Think about which of the Be's and Do's are your strong suits and which aren't. Which ones do you tap into and apply on a regular basis in achieving the life you want? Which ones are dormant and untapped?

Step 2: Evaluate your strengths and weaknesses

Put a check (✔) next to each creative resource that is a strength for you. Mark each underutilized resource with an X. Be as thoughtful about this as you can, because later on you'll be referring back to this exercise.

Step 3: Determine which creative resources you need the most right now

Next, think about your aims and inspirations, what you want to learn and what you want to make happen across and within each of the three main domains: Personal, Partnership, and Productivity. Which creative resources from the list would help you most in shaping and pursuing your longer-term goals? Which resources do you need to tap into and apply in order to be successful in shaping your future? Circle those resources (Be's and Do's) that are most crucial to your growth, the growth of your relationships, and the advancement of your contributions.

Your Inventory of Creative Resources

What You Need to Do:	*What You Need to Be:*
STEP ONE: TAKE YOUR BLINDERS OFF	
See the big picture	Curious and committed
Access your internal landscape	Intuitive and aware
STEP TWO: BE OUTRAGEOUSLY OPTIMISTIC	
Use upheaval to fuel your creativity	Calm and reflective
Become energized	Optimistic and responsive
STEP THREE: MAKE THE FUTURE HAPPEN INSIDE YOU	
Challenge the Status Quo	Imaginative and visionary
Give up your old habits	Observant and innovative
STEP FOUR: GET OTHERS ON BOARD	
Consolidate your relationships	Influential and collaborative
Lead the way	Articulate and persuasive

continued on next page

Your Inventory of Creative Resources (continued)

What You Need to Do:	*What You Need to Be:*
STEP FIVE: STACK THE ODDS IN YOUR FAVOR	
Watch your progress	Resilient and resourceful
Speak the truth	Fearless and authentic
STEP SIX: CELEBRATE EVERY VICTORY, LARGE AND SMALL	
Wake up to your new reality	Passionate and proactive
Realize untapped potential	Inspired and confident

You have just completed a quick assessment and inventory of your most active and most dormant creative resources. Don't be surprised if you end up circling every one of these resources as crucial for shaping the life that you have determined is worth living into. As you read on, each step will illuminate the value of specific resources and will show how you can tap into them and apply them just when you need them the most.

You have just finished systematically gathering lots of information. You thought about your life so far, and framed the Big Picture for the life you would like to lead. Now it's time to contribute more to this picture by looking inward.

Guiding Principles: Question Reality

- Life will appear as you see it. What you pay attention to will expand. Your reality is like a large mosaic, and the tiles can be rearranged in many ways.
- As a child needs a parent, your long-term goals need your full attention and unwavering commitment. Keep them in the forefront of your mind so you can use whatever happens to nurture your progress.
- You cannot lose, once you realize that whatever happens is designed to make you more creative and keep you moving toward your Level 3 goals.

Feel What You Feel

What you need to DO   Access Your Internal Landscape

What you need to BE   Intuitive and Aware

In order to be deeply in touch with what you want, you need to give yourself permission to feel what you feel. Now you will see why acknowledging the full range of your emotions in response to any stressful situation or challenge is well worth the effort. To live a life that is richer, deeper, and wiser, you need to learn how to take in the whole spectrum of your emotions. Rather than letting your first set of feelings take over, you will practice inviting your second and third waves of emotions to emerge. As you are able to let go of your taboos against sensing and feeling, a rich, rewarding experience is in store. I will show you how to tune into the emotional zones of experiences in such amazing ways that you will wonder how you ever lived without paying closer attention to the vibrance in life that only your sensations and feelings can bring.

Yes, feeling what you feel is a learned skill. Actually, it's an unlearned skill. We need to unlearn years of prejudice against strong emotions. We have to unlearn the way we try to be extremely logical whenever a problem pops up. High achievers have to unlearn the way they set their feelings aside in order to race ahead to the finish line. Professional women—all women—have to unlearn the idea that showing their emotions means they are the weaker sex. And all of us have to step out of our faster-harder-smarter mode in order to recognize that our generalized sense of urgency tunes our emotional radio into just one station: anxiety.

But don't worry, this is not about wearing your emotions on your sleeve. Remember how my client John was afraid of turning into a jelly roll? Even he made it safely through this process. You don't have to contemplate your navel or show anyone how sensitive your are. This is not about wallowing in emotions or becoming immobilized by them. It is about diving into the sea of your emotional life so you can more wisely find your way through the rapid-fire pressures and demands that will inevitably come your way as you work toward realizing your Level 3 aspirations.

It's never all one feeling.

Ever heard of a toaster with only one setting, a sunrise with only one color, or a racecar with only one gear? Once you look for it, diversity is everywhere, even in our strongest feelings. "Pure joy" can be tinged with worry—how long can this euphoria last? Anger can be marbled with fear, love mixed with resentment, and disappointment modulated by relief. We tend to focus on the strongest feeling, like the most robust baby bird in the nest that drowns out all the other hatchlings.

Imagine a country well. Perhaps you've seen one. Your well could have a stone wall around it, or a white well house on top. It could stand alone in an grassy yard, or it could be half hidden by a tangle of sweet-smelling honeysuckle, or it could be at the end of a mossy path. There's a bucket sitting on the rough edge of the well, with a rope attached to its handle. When you look down into your well, you might see a reflection gleaming on the surface of the water deep down inside. Or you might not. Let's say you take the bucket and lower it down into the darkness. You hear the splash, then feel the heavy tug on the rope as the bucket quickly fills with water. You haul it up, hand over hand, until you can grab the handle and set the bucket again on the edge of your well, overflowing with sweet, clear, cold water. Maybe there's a cup nearby that you can use to take a drink. Or maybe you make a cup with your hands, trying to catch a drink before all the water runs through your fingers. Or you could just plunge your face into the bucket and cool off your whole head.

My clients usually like this image because it awakens all our senses—what we see, smell, feel, hear, and taste. We smell the honeysuckle, hear the splash, taste the cold water, etc. It's quickly clear from this example that our senses determine our experiences.

I also use the image of the well to help my clients start thinking about their deeper feelings. All of us have a wellspring of emotions inside us, but many of us have learned to be stoic. We believe we're better off not acknowledging how we feel. We think it's not okay to be vulnerable—we will appear weak. It's not okay to get mad—we will look like we lack self-control. It's not okay to show how disappointed we are—we're supposed to be grown-up. Don't show them you're surprised—make them think you expected this. Don't look nervous—you'll appear incompetent. Be efficient and act confident at all times.

What are we so afraid of? Feelings are what add richness and meaning to our life. Why would it ever be a good idea to stuff them?

The home of our dreams is a safe place, a still place. A communal place, to which we contribute; to which we have real ties; a place that feels more stable, perhaps, than ourselves. How American this is—to long, at day's end, for a place where we belong more, invent less; for a heartland with more heart.

Jen Gish from "Coming Into the Country"

Shouts and whispers

What do these sentences have in common?

"Let's take a look at what this means."

"They were deeply touched by your words."

"Did you grasp what he was saying?"

"This situation has a familiar ring to it."

"I have a gut feeling we are off to a good start."

"Something tells me I smell a rat."

"How can we make sense out of all of this?"

Reread this list and figure out what you think these sentences share before reading on.

Most people have trouble seeing what the sentences on this list have in common. Nothing seems obvious. But after rereading the list several times, it dawns on them that each of these sentences has to do with coming to a deeper appreciation or understanding of something. There is, however, another answer that is rarely guessed. Each sentence on the list contains a word or phrase that describes a sensory approach to understanding what has been experienced—take a *look* at, deeply *touched*, *grasp*, familiar *ring*, *gut feeling*, *smell*, make *sense*. Sensory-rich language such as this, so often heard and spoken in everyday conversation, reminds us of the fact that almost everything we know has its earliest roots in our sensory perceptions and in our emotional responses to whatever we have experienced. Sometimes our feelings are unmistakable and come through loud and clear. On other occasions they are subtle—a ripple of unease, a sense of disturbance, a little intimation of happiness. We need to be attuned to both the shouts and whispers, since both provide us with essential information we need in order to create what we want.

As individuals maturing from infancy to adulthood, and as a species evolving from tribal to high tech, human beings are hard-wired to perceive, sense, and feel before we respond in thought, word, or action to the demands and challenges we encounter. This chain reaction from perception to action lays the foundation for our beliefs, values, and aspirations. Perceptions determine what we believe to be true, good, right, and beautiful. They influence what we prefer and expect, what we value and find meaningful, what we know how to do, and what we hope to become. The sum total of our sensations, feelings, thoughts, and responses to any given situation (rapid-fire or not, challenging or not) constitute what we refer to as our *experience* of that situation. Our experiences build on one another, and become our best teachers about how best to survive and thrive.

> *Have patience with all things, but chiefly have patience with yourself. Do not lose courage in considering your own imperfections but instantly set about remedying them—every day beginning the task anew.*
>
> Saint Francis de Sales

We need to remind ourselves about the critical role that sensations and feelings play in forming our experiences because, over the course of time and evolution, we have forgotten about them. In fact, as we get more and more caught up in meeting the demands of a rapid-fire existence, we tend to concentrate on what we are *thinking* about a given situation, and ignore how we are *feeling* about it. In this Information Age, we have learned to trust our intellect more than our sensations and our Emotional Intelligence. To determine the best way of dealing with whatever happens, we try to lead with our head, not our heart. For many high achievers, the more demanding the situation, the less likely they are to feel what they are feeling. They think they will prevail by being very logical. Ironically, they don't access their feelings right when they need them most.

Getting off the train of thought

In the midst of demands from this rapid-fire world of too fast, too much, and too long, we have become masterful at screening out distractions and noticing only those facts that are essential to satisfying our most immediate demands. Taking time out to register our sensations and feelings seems superfluous at best. At worst, we believe this process may slow us down, confuse us, or make us vulnerable. We ignore our feelings, block them out, or suck them up so as not to jeopardize our conviction, determined effort, and sense of progress. In this rapid-fire world of ours we behave as if the fastest path to whatever it is we want is along the logic highway, which is paved with analysis and rational assessment.

Sometimes being extremely logical is comforting. When nothing seems to make sense, we fall back on reason to create structure out of chaos. This approach can work for your Level 1 problems, which are mostly logistical anyway. For your Level 2 challenges, and for your Level 3 agenda, rational analysis is not by itself sufficient. You need access to both reason and your emotions, preferably in equal measure. Many people over intellectualize their experiences, while a minority emote at the expense of being rational. You don't have to change who you are in order to feel what you feel, but try to bring your impressions into balance. Being only in your head is as limiting as being overly emotional.

Don't feel anything? You're not alone.

To feel what you feel requires that you be alert and vigilant, tuning into all the cues and experiencing life at a gut level. To have a full-fledged set of feelings, you must become acutely present to all the sensory details of whatever is happening. Although it is human nature to focus

> *Life is not a problem to be solved but a reality to be experienced.*
>
> Søren Kierkegaard

on a few select, intense sensations, absorbing all the sights, sounds, smells, sensations, and rhythms of an event gives you a far richer reservoir of experience.

Learning to feel what you feel might sound simplistic at first, but like most simple truths, it's easier said than done. Many people find that they have developed defensive roadblocks that make it difficult to get in touch with their deepest feelings. Whether you are male or female doesn't matter. Culturally, men are probably more encouraged to deny their feelings than women, but I've met both extremely sensitive men and extremely tough women!

Here are four common emotional roadblocks.

1. Are you trying to stuff feelings back into your subconscious?

At one time or another everyone makes an effort to squelch their painful feelings about a situation or person and to erase the negative emotions once and for all from memory. Under especially traumatic conditions, temporarily "forgetting" our anger, fear, or horror can buy us the period of recovery we need to heal. But even in cases of emotionally traumatizing events, it is important to realize that hidden feelings, no matter how deeply buried, retain their power and continue to affect us. Left unresolved, negative emotions come back at us like a boomerang, often when we least expect it. This helps explain flying off the handle, being all wound up, having a short fuse, feeling teary, losing patience, or riding an emotional roller coaster. Whenever you experience episodes of free floating emotions like these, it is time to explore what previous disturbances are still lurking inside you, so highly charged with emotion that you are ready to erupt at even the slightest provocation.

> *We do not receive wisdom, we must discover it for ourselves, after a journey through the wilderness, which no one else can make for us, which no one can spare us, for our wisdom is the point of view from which we come at last to regard the world.*
>
> Marcel Proust

2. Are you focusing on a few select, intense feelings?

Sometimes, without realizing it, we exaggerate the pleasant, positive emotions we want to feel and we undervalue the negative, unpleasant emotions that disturb us or that could burst our bubble about someone or something. Being blinded by love is a good example of how this type of emotional block works. "I am in love," so I allow that all-powerful elixir to obliterate my lesser feelings of "I am annoyed" because we never seem to see the movies I want to see or go to the restaurants I enjoy most.

It is easy to see how anyone could get carried away by the thrill of falling in love or even exultation over landing a coveted job. It feels great—why rain on your own parade? But when feelings of annoyance are buried, they can over time build in intensity and eventually turn into stronger feelings of hurt and resentment. The wisest course of action is to honor the full range of your emotions in any emotionally charged circumstance. It is especially important not to let intensely positive or negative feelings exert undue influence at the expense of lesser yet nonetheless important feelings at the opposite end of the spectrum.

3. Are you trying to control and direct your feelings?

With good reason, society creates taboos against acting on certain feelings, in certain ways, at certain times. For example, cultural disapproval of giving in to unbridled anger saves lives and prevents abuse. Social taboos against being a scaredy-cat inspire us to face adversity with courage. Taboos against immediately giving in to our desire for physical pleasure helps us delay the gratification we experience from eating a wonderful meal, drinking delectable wine, skiing our way down a just-groomed hill, or making love with our favorite person. Taboos can be life-giving and life-enhancing. They are invaluable in helping us resolve conflicts peacefully, gather the courage we need to master tough challenges, and develop a healthy relationship with food, alcohol, drugs, recreation, and sexual activity. We would not want to live without those governing forces of civilization that assist us in constructively channeling our individual and collective emotional energy.

On the other hand, every person has developed some sort of unhealthy, deadening taboos that interfere with leading a rich, full life. We may habitually set our emotions aside or discount our feelings because we are too shy, too guilty, or too embarrassed to acknowledge what we are feeling. In essence we have created our own individualized taboo that diminishes our vitality and our effectiveness. Each time we let false pride or false humility govern how we feel about a situation, we have rendered our truest, most authentic feelings off limits. All self-inflicted emotional taboos are aimed at looking good and preserving decorum. The more successful they are, the more we end up disconnected from our emotions.

Trying to control and direct your feelings is like playing a piano that is missing half its keys, or leaving out half the ingredients of a recipe. To stay engaged and to respond appropriately to whatever challenges may come our way, we need access to the full complement of our feelings.

4. Are you moving too fast?

Nothing is more dangerous to leading an emotionally vibrant, intelligent life than trying to keep up with the demands of our rapid-fire world. Speed sucks the feeling right out of our lives. When we rush through daily demands and pressure-filled situations without pausing to register what they mean to us emotionally, we lose perspective. Without the perspective that only emotions can provide, it is impossible to know what's important and what's not, what's exciting and what's not, what's disturbing and what's not. As our sense of urgency numbs us, we become detached from the feelings that are there to help us create the lives that most please and thrill us.

Self-determination studies have told us that we all need to feel that we are competent, that we belong, and that we are autonomous in order to achieve a state of well-being. And yet, we know that an excess of independence and individualism can lead to dissatisfaction and depression. The responsibility for our choices often becomes a burden, leading to insecurity and regret.

Without direct access to your emotions, you will never be as effective as you need to be in mastering tough challenges. Remember, blocking out your emotions is like living life in "black and white" rather than in full Technicolor. Not only do you dull your existence, you deprive yourself of a major source of creativity.

How should you respond to an emotional punch?

Let's assume that you have taken these lessons to heart, and that you have become adept at tuning in to your feelings. Uncovering hidden emotions sometimes makes people feel worse before they feel better. If you have been holding in negative feelings that are now making you feel distressed, or if all your feelings seem to be negative, consider asking a professional for help. More likely, you have simply become more adept at identifying your inner reactions to people and events, and at using this information to respond creatively.

If you are going along with your Level 3 agenda and suddenly find yourself feeling confused and angry, this is a warning sign. Feelings can knock us off course, or they can be a sign that something else has knocked us off course. If you are upset without being certain why, look for the hidden conflict. What kind of feeling is attached to each of your goals? What kind of interference is making it difficult for you to move forward? Is something switching you into a Reactive mind-set ("He's crazy" or "Poor me!") instead of a Creative mind-set ("What can I work with here?" "How could I build on that?"). Paying attention to emotional warning signals can enable you to recover your Level 3 agenda more quickly.

There's no question that having access to the whole panorama of human feelings enables you to be more creative in setting and achieving your goals. But there's also another benefit: You will be able to expand your powers of empathy. Being sympathetic is an agreeable quality in anyone, but being able to emotionally put yourself in another person's place adds to the depth of your experience in each situation. Empathy can help you interpret or even anticipate others' behavior, which allows you to help them even as you stay on track yourself.

Knowing what you feel, and feeling what you know

If I were to ask you to tell me about your bedroom, you would most likely describe the details of its color, size, shape, closets, windows, type and placement of furniture, decor, etc. What you are likely not to mention is your bedroom's ambience and overall "feeling." To describe the "feeling" of your bedroom, you might say that it is cozy, or uplifting, or sleek, or warm. Descriptions like these reveal a deeper, more sensitive impression of what your senses are picking up.

Everything we encounter in life—every object, place, event, person, interaction—has a certain "feeling" to it. We know this is true, but forget to acknowledge it. Taking your blinders off includes both searching for the facts and becoming aware of subtle or hidden emotional messages. The "feeling" given off by something or someone can be just as important as what they are saying or doing. How many times have you had a "hunch" that something was not right? Did you act on this "feeling"? If not, do you wish you had? As we make feelings more of a priority, we strengthen the powers of our intuition at the same time.

Everything, uplifting or disturbing, will guide us.

When I first met Beth, a seasoned account manager, she was basking in the glory of landing the largest single contract in her 20-year career as a public relations executive. Not only was this particular contract with a New York brokerage firm lucrative, but also its future business potential and high visibility allowed Beth to assemble an account team made up of the most talented, experienced people in her agency. This in turn meant that Beth could spend more time building a strong relationship with her premium client and less time locked into hands-on management and firefighting. For Beth this contract was a career milestone that lifted her out of the trenches and boosted her to a higher professional plane. There she could direct and guide the project to completion.

Beth charged her team with writing the copy and drafting the graphics that would be key in communicating the brokerage firm's message to their individual and institutional investors. The deadlines were tight, but her team got up to speed almost immediately. Beth couldn't have been more pleased with how well they were performing. The copy and the graphics they created were the best she'd ever seen. They set the stage for unprecedented success for the team, their agency, and her.

Beth had religiously kept in contact with the project team formed by the brokerage company to oversee her agency's work. Aside from one new person who came on board in the third week, each member of the project team approved the copy and graphics every step of the way, from concept to final draft. If you've ever tried to get a committee to sign off on something, you know how hard it is.

At the brokerage firm's request, Beth flew to New York to preview the final drafts of the copy and graphics. Since several members of the project team were unable to attend, other brokerage firm managers were invited to sit in on the review of Beth's creative package. The presentation lasted the better part of Wednesday and concluded by mid-morning on Thursday.

Beth didn't sleep well Wednesday night. She couldn't shake off a strange sense of unease. Somehow, her presentation was not received as enthusiastically as she had anticipated. Those who were participating in the review seemed polite enough. They nodded their approval during her presentation, but their reactions seemed almost circumspect rather than spontaneous. Beth was confused and deeply concerned.

Thursday, at 10:00 A.M. on the nose, the leader of the project review team ended the meeting, thanked Beth for her effort on behalf of the brokerage firm and told her the project team would call her with the results of their evaluation in a few days. Beth felt cut off, dismissed. She knew the curt, cool send-off signaled a rejection of the work, but no explanation was forthcoming. She left New York feeling blindsided, angry, and bewildered.

The brokerage firm's project leader called Beth on Friday just before lunch. He announced that the team had decided that the copy and graphics Beth presented were not acceptable. "We do not believe you and your team will be able to meet our standards and requirements, so unfortunately we are forced to cancel this contract with your agency."

Beth hung up the phone feeling like a ton of bricks had just fallen on her head. Her heart was racing but she couldn't move a muscle. After what seemed like an hour, but was only several minutes, she stopped staring at the wall and sank back down into her swivel chair. As she leaned back she began the painstaking process of assessing the gravity of the situation.

Beth felt devastated. She started gingerly teasing apart her thoughts and emotions, as if she were feeling for broken bones. First she evaluated whether the loss of this contract would jeopardize the Level 3 goals she was pursuing for herself and her company. She knew immediately that trying to recover this contract had to become her top priority. This assignment offered

Beth the biggest opportunity she'd ever had to develop a list of top-notch clients loyal to her while she made a significant contribution to her agency's profitability and roster of prestigious clients. Her motivation for recovering this contract was not a matter of healing her bruised ego, or even a bold attempt to prove she could get even. She needed the contract, and she deserved it. With her conviction rock solid, she started to think of ways to work through this Level 2 mishap.

Beth began to compose a letter to the president of the brokerage firm. Line by line she turned the crisis into a compelling, revealing story that told the truth about the errors in judgment and injustice that had occurred. This story seemed to flow effortlessly out of her feelings and thoughts into her fingertips and onto the page.

Beth wrote and rewrote the letter five times, but before sending it, she asked me to review it. Together we discussed what had happened and how she wanted to proceed. I reassured Beth that she had already taken an extremely positive first step toward creating the best possible outcome in response to this unexpected crisis. No matter what she decided to do with the letter, writing and rewriting it had helped Beth become more vividly aware of her initial feelings of thrill and excitement brought about by the tremendous business opportunity and creative challenges of this contract. Drafting the letter also highlighted for Beth her feelings of betrayal and disappointment. She was as forthright in her emotional assessment of what had transpired as she was logical about the sequence of events. Because she voiced her negative emotions with as much grace as she did her positive feelings about the account, her letter was balanced and effective.

As we discussed her situation further, I applauded Beth for trusting her intuition that something was not right at the presentation. To better understand the driving forces behind the contract cancellation,

A study examining the personality traits of all U.S. presidents found that the most successful presidents tend to be hardworking and achievement minded, be willing and able to speak up for their interests, and value the emotional side of life. Openness to experience produced the highest correlation between personality and greatness.

Deborah Smith from "What Makes a President Great?"

Beth contacted a friend who worked at the brokerage firm. Her friend worked in a different department, but she did a little detective work and found out that as Beth and her team worked on the project, another public relations agency was brought in by a new vice president of marketing to work on the same project. This disclosure stunned Beth.

As the hidden facts of the situation revealed themselves, they served as a kind of sanity check for Beth about what had actually transpired and why. Beth and her team had been led to believe that they were the only vendors and that their work was exemplary. In the next breath they were chided for producing work of inferior quality—not because of any actual decline in quality, but because a new vendor, more in favor with someone in power, had arrived on the scene.

With all the facts and a newfound confidence, Beth revised her letter one more time. She wrote directly to the president of the brokerage house, deliberately going over the heads of the project team. She demonstrated the quality of her agency's work, and expressed her dismay with the way her agency had been treated by his company.

Within a week the president reinstated Beth's contract.

Putting your emotions to work

When you want to capitalize on intense levels of emotional pressure—for example, those caused by the unexpected downturns or upturns that always occur in the pursuit of important goals—tapping into your Emotional Intelligence will provide you with amazing insights. Use your emotional awareness to inform your behavior and your decisions. To do this, ask yourself these questions:

> "What do my emotional responses tell me about the relative importance of this challenge in achieving my Level 3 long-term goals?"
>
> "How can my emotional responses guide me in determining my wisest course of action going forward?"

You don't have time to waste on things that aren't important. Tuning in to your feelings is one way of separating worthwhile tasks from worthless pursuits. You can link your emotional response to the importance of each event by asking, "Is it worth it?" If a situation sets off a complex cascade of emotions inside you, ask yourself why you feel the way you do.

Stop to think about how thrilling it is to be in confident pursuit of long-term goals that offer you meaning and a strong sense of accomplishment. There is no better feeling than stepping into a whole universe of possibilities at once—with your mind, heart, and spirit working in tandem so you can achieve a worthwhile outcome. Mihaly Csikszentmihaly has dubbed that optimal experience as *flow*. His research reveals that being in flow tends to occur when your skills are fully engaged in overcoming a challenge that stretches you just beyond your previous level of competence. It is this fine balance between the next level of your ability to act and the opportunities available on that next level that give rise to the optimal, thrilling experience of being in the zone.

BEST PRACTICES

What follows are some Best Practices to help you cultivate your Emotional Intelligence as Beth did. These exercises are designed to help you monitor and use your intuition in ways that will help you succeed in mastering tough situations and in achieving your most challenging long-term goals.

BEST PRACTICE #4
How Do You Hide Your Feelings?

Remember the four emotional roadblocks that were discussed earlier? Assume you have 100 points, and distribute them across the four most common defenses listed on the chart on page 67. For example, if you know that you most often tend to block your emotions by "trying to control and direct your feelings," you might assign 40 points to that column and distribute the remaining 60 across the other three.

Becoming more aware of the defensive maneuvers you employ to block out your feelings is a good first step to take in raising your Emotional Intelligence. This new level of awareness will help you catch yourself in the act of setting up barriers, so you can stop blocking and start letting your feelings flow.

Defensive Routines That Block Emotions

	Sample Score	Your Score
1. Trying to stuff feelings back into your subconscious	30	
2. Focusing on a few select, intense feelings	10	
3. Trying to control and direct feelings	40	
4. Moving too fast	20	
Total points:	100	

BEST PRACTICE #5

TAKING YOUR EMOTIONAL TEMPERATURE

The most successful people I've known and studied make it a priority to stay in touch with their feelings. They know that when the pressure is on, keeping track of how they are responding emotionally may make the difference between moving forward or taking two steps backward. While you are coping with your agendas at every level—your Level 1 daily demands, the pressures of your Level 2 situational stressors, and the challenges of achieving your Level 3 long-term goals—it is relatively easy to keep tabs on your emotional temperature.

Taking into account how the intensity of your emotions fluctuates over time will give you a chance to modulate your feelings in response to rapid-fire demands. Charting your emotional temperature over the course of a day, a week, or a month enables you to see how you could reorient your priorities in the direction of more positive emotional experiences. One of the nice things about positive experiences is that they tend to spill over into other areas of life, setting off a benevolent chain reaction. You can teach yourself to keep tabs on your feelings by following these three simple steps:

Step 1: Your emotional thermometer
Your first task is simply to start noticing how you feel throughout the day. Begin by reviewing the events of your day and assigning an emotional rating to each event using an emotional scale like the one that follows:

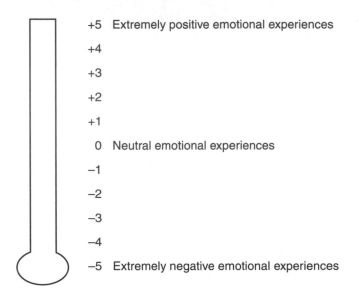

+5 Extremely positive emotional experiences

+4

+3

+2

+1

0 Neutral emotional experiences

−1

−2

−3

−4

−5 Extremely negative emotional experiences

Many people find it easy and efficient to note their emotional temperature in their calendar or daybook next to each appointment or event. Don't feel self-conscious about this, just do it. For example, next to "staff meeting" you write +2, while on a sales call you note –3. Some people go through this exercise mentally on the drive home or before sleep. Once you get into the habit of rating your emotional responses to any given situation, you'll do it all the time.

Step 2: Look for patterns

Notice any patterns to your emotional temperature readings over time. Ask yourself, "On balance, have I had an emotionally positive or negative day/week?" Don't stop there, however. Ask yourself what types of situations seem to trigger extremely positive or negative feelings in you. This insight is invaluable in managing your day-to-day responsibilities and in reaching your Level 3 goals.

Gauging your emotional temperature can in a matter of weeks become automatic. Keeping in close touch with how you feel will help you see your emotional landscape as it wanes and brightens. It allows you to spend more time in the positive zones than in the negative ones. Plus, the closer contact you have with your feelings, the more richly, deeply, and wisely you will move through the barrage of rapid-fire demands that surrounds you.

Step 3: Accentuate the positive

Reflect on how you could create more positive emotional experiences. Ask yourself, "How could I change my expectations of myself, of others, of the situation, to move my emotional responses in a more positive direction? How could I shift my priorities to foster more positive feelings? How could I tap into people who could help me infuse my days with more positive emotions?"

BEST PRACTICE #6

INCREASING YOUR EMOTIONAL INTELLIGENCE: THE CHALLENGE/COMPETENCY ZONES

Remember the illustration that showed the different zones of our experience in relation to our skills? Each zone represents the relationships between the challenges we face and the skills we possess to meet those challenges. Take a moment to review the emotional response that is characteristic of each zone.

Just for a moment, think about how you feel when the challenges that present themselves are too far out of your reach. If you are like most high achievers, when you encounter a challenge that far outstrips your capacity to meet it, you start out

Challenge/Competency Zones

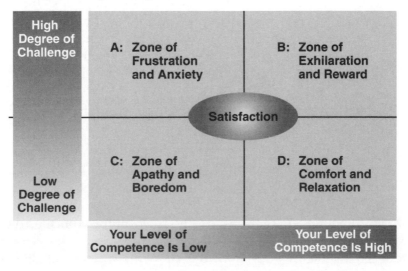

frustrated and end up anxious. In a situation that is the reverse, when the demands of a challenge are low and the skills you possess far exceed those that are required to master the particular challenge, you are likely to wind up feeling bored. In either case, *knowing* how you are feeling about mastering a challenge is a key indicator of whether you'll end up gaining or losing ground in the process. Tuning in to your feelings about a challenge can provide you with invaluable insights about how best to proceed. Feelings keep you grounded, in a deeper relationship with yourself and everything that's going on around you.

As you study the zones, you can see that:

Zone A. *Frustration and Anxiety* are created when the demand of challenges exceeds your skill to respond effectively. In this zone you are on a constant state of alert and alarm that can wear you down and burn you out.

Zone B. *Exhilaration and Reward* occur as the demands of your challenges require higher levels of skill. If the coping skills required exceed your current highest level of skills, you may decide to enter a learning mode, within which you can begin to grow in skillfulness. This stretching and growing leads to a deep sense of personal reward. This is the favorite zone of high achievers.

Zone C. *Apathy and Boredom* describe what happens emotionally when you encounter minimally demanding challenges that require the lowest of skill levels. Low-demand, low-skill situations often trigger periods of inertia that are particularly disturbing to high achievers.

Zone D. *Comfort and Relaxation* are a direct consequence of demands that are low in intensity yet require a high degree of coping skill. These tasks can offer a well-deserved emotional sabbatical following long bouts of frustration and anxiety, or even after a rewarding but intense growth experience.

Step 1: Cast a wide net

Think about what you see on the horizon for your life. What attracts you? What is just out of reach? What is waiting around the next corner for you? Consider the wide array of challenges you could set for yourself. Review the variety of advancements you could target that would take your skills, your accomplishments, and your relationships to the next level. No doubt your potential challenges hold positive emotional value for you—that's why you have selected them as options. Now you have a chance to take your blinders off and to see which of your personal challenges hold the highest charge for you. This will help you focus on achieving new life goals that will create equity in your emotional bank account for years to come.

Step 2: Next, narrow your focus

On a separate piece of paper, copy the Challenge/Competency graph (page 69). Make it big, because you're going to be writing inside the quadrants.

Now turn back to page 47 and review the list of Personal, Productivity, and Partnership goals you identified as top priority options that could take you to the next level of effectiveness, personally and professionally. Use the Challenge/Competency graph to assist you in calculating the emotional value associated with pursuing and achieving each one of your potential priorities. Then write down each goal in the appropriate zone—the one that most closely approximates its challenge-to-competency ratio.

Finally, rank each priority within each zone. If this sounds like a lot of work, please know that this graph is very important! You'll be referring to it later as you create a master list of your Level 3 goals.

As you rank your goals by the relative degree of exhilaration and reward they each promise, make a point of noticing how your goals cluster together. Most should be grouped in Zone B, Exhilaration and Reward, since you have preselected these goals as most meaningful and potentially fulfilling. Usually people are able to better see the synergies between Level 3 goals as they rank them and reflect on how emotionally exciting and thrilling achieving these goals will be. For example, if you reflect on the story of Beth, the account manager, you will recall that she had two Level 3 goals that were intimately related to one another.

> *Only intuition, resting on sympathetic understanding, can lead to insight; the daily effort comes from no deliberate intention or program, but straight from the heart.*
>
> Albert Einstein

Beth aspired to elevating herself out of being in the trenches, doing the design work, so she could devote herself to building stronger client relationships. She also wanted to grow the list of premium clients for her agency. When Beth explored her feelings toward each of these goals, she found that her goal of "climbing out of the trenches" brought with it feelings of relief, freedom, and the thrill of launching a new phase of her career and learning new skills. Her goal of "attracting premium clients for the agency" made her feel a deep sense of pride, plus appreciation for the agency that had given her the chance to develop and grow. Beth was filled with inspiration and enthusiasm when she realized she was now ready to set a leadership goal for herself that also had the potential of reaping huge business benefits for the agency that had provided so many personally meaningful benefits to her.

> *On a gray afternoon, I sit in a silent room and contemplate din. In the street a single car passes—a rapid bass vowel—and then it is quiet again. So what is this uproar, this hubbub, this heaving rumble of zigzag static I keep hearing? Mainly it is the buzz of the inescapably mundane, the little daily voice that insists and insists: right now, not now, too late, too soon, why not, better not, turn it on, turn it off, notice this, notice that, be sure to take care of, remember not to.*
>
> Cynthia Ozick from "Where to Connect the Inner Hum?"

Beth's sense of commitment and confidence soared as she became more keenly aware of her feelings of relief, freedom, and thrill (associated with her career goal), blending with her feelings of pride, appreciation, inspiration, and enthusiasm (associated with her business goal). She was absolutely certain that these two goals were vital to her success, and that achieving them offered a wealth of emotional rewards far greater than she imagined when she initially decided to pursue them. At first these goals seemed logically sound, but now she could sense how emotionally valuable they were, too.

As you rank your Level 3 goals, give yourself a chance to experience more fully the positive emotional charge associated with each. When you delve deeply into the emotional bounty that comes along naturally with achieving your Level 3 goals, you will be—like Beth—more uplifted and inspired than you ever believed you could be.

Guiding Principles: Feel What You Feel

- Moving too quickly to judgment in the face of challenging goals and situational stress cuts us off from the full experience and blinds us.
- If we don't feel all of what there is to feel, we cannot come into conscious contact with all there is to work with.
- Lack of emotion denies us a chance to "radiate," and instead leaves us reacting on automatic pilot to the best and worst of our situation.

JOHN'S STORY, CONTINUED

Initially, John's emotional commitment to his Level 3 goals was extremely high. He felt exhilarated just thinking about them. He was going to learn how to ask penetrating questions, build collaborative relationships, and maintain a highly creative corporate culture, all while growing his business exponentially.

John said that striving to accomplish goals like these is what made him "high on life." His description was right on. Setting our heart on becoming more competent in such fundamental ways *is* intoxicating. We wake up in the morning already pumped and ready to dive into our day, primed with the enthusiasm and lift that come only with the pursuit of meaningful, challenging goals.

It gave me great pleasure to see the positive intensity of John's emotional connection to his Level 3 goals. As he reviewed them with me, he noticed that his love of learning would be reinforced by the pride he would feel while helping all of his managers succeed. He imagined that it would be the thrill of a lifetime if he could successfully maintain his company's highly creative culture during periods of rapid growth. This was a feat he had never before seen accomplished in his industry. John's emotions clearly fueled his determination to succeed on all three fronts.

The emotions John and I discussed next were equally important to his long-term success, but they were the farthest thing from John's mind. I reminded John of the fact that every goal that carries with it great emotional promise also carries with it inevitable bouts of emotional pain. The simple truth is, the more positively charged with exhilaration and reward your Level 3 goals may be, the more likely it is that you will experience episodes of frustration and anxiety in pursuit of them. Just think about what I'm saying for a moment. If you have chosen to establish challenging goals that require skills that are just beyond your current level of competency, then it stands to reason you won't hit the mark immediately. It also follows that you are bound to go through some frustrating

Do not be conformed by this world, but be transformed by the renewing of your minds.

Romans 12

periods of trial and error and bouts of anxiety in moments of defeat.

Like most high achievers, John hardly ever considered the emotional toll pursuing his most challenging, important goals might entail. He focused on the bright side, the thrilling side, the side that turned him on emotionally. John's natural bias for seeing the most pleasurable aspects of his goals (in combination with his emotional blindness to the pain) made it essential that he anticipate the emotionally disturbing moments to come.

I'm not suggesting that anyone dwell on the possibility of disturbing circumstances. To do so could foster worry and even increase the probability or frequency of disturbances. I'm recommending that it is beneficial to remember that painful struggles are part of pursuing any type of challenging goal. A moderate amount of frustration and anxiety are normal in the quest for goal-achievement. In fact, if you don't struggle, your goals may not be challenging enough. If you struggle too much, you probably need to lower your expectations and reduce your target. Striking an emotional blend of 80 percent pleasure and 20 percent pain usually encourages the best success when it comes to achieving the most rewarding Level 3 goals.

Be Outrageously Optimistic

How to See Potential, Not Problems

* Scout for Opportunities
* See the Glass as Half Full ... with a Pitcher of Water on the Way!

*N*ow *it's time to imagine the best possible outcome, goal, or solution, and to become energized by how excellent it is.*

> *A person is the center of a circle whose circumference is determined by their self-imposed limitations.*
>
> Gandhi

EDWIN HERBERT LAND
(1909–1991)

By the time he was 20 years old, Edwin Land, a gifted Harvard undergraduate, had already conceived, produced, and patented the first modern filters to polarize light. Within a few years he formed a company to market those filters for use in sunglasses, glare-free automobile headlights, and stereoscopic photography. Though still very young, he had conceived and brought to fruition more ideas and products than inventors three times his age.

The idea for his most important invention, however, came from his three-year-old daughter. After her father had taken her photograph one day, she asked him why she couldn't see the picture right away. Land thought, Well why not, indeed? He immediately set to work creating a system of one-step photography, which he first demonstrated to the American Optical Society in 1947. Within a year the Polaroid camera, which used the principle of diffusion transfer to reproduce the image recorded by the camera lens directly onto a photosensitive surface, was available on the market. Knowing he still had a ways to go before he could show his daughter her picture right away, he kept improving his product. Finally, in 1963, he marketed Polacolor film, which made instant color photos possible. Over the next ten years, the SX-70 replaced the wet, peel-apart development process with a dry film that developed in light.

Throughout his adult life Land continued to nurture an almost childlike openness to possibility, scouting for opportunities at every turn. Over the years, his ongoing research and experimentation in the field of optics resulted in 500 patents, a record that stands second only to that of Thomas Edison. No wonder, then, that he was ultimately awarded the Medal of Freedom, the highest honor granted to American civilians.

Scout for Opportunities	
What you need to DO	Use Upheaval to Fuel Your Creativity
What you need to BE	Calm and Reflective

The appointment you had such difficulty scheduling gets blown away by a more pressing issue that pops up out of the blue.

Your deadline becomes tighter and tighter, not because of what's happening with you, but because of the pressures closing in on your boss, or your customer, or your spouse.

Your company wants to start up a new branch office on Majorca ... and you're in charge.

The painstaking progress you've made so far gets completely wiped out by someone who breaks a promise.

Your child care plans fall through the day you're supposed to make an important presentation.

Upheaval is a hallmark of living in a rapid-fire world. Every day, just to meet our Level 1 duties, we have to ride the waves of uncertainty and try to stay on course in the wake of tumult. Most days it feels like a full-time job just keeping our heads above water. The ever-shifting, ever-mounting waves of our daily rapid-fire demands seem endless. Making progress toward important goals while we are trying to stay afloat seems almost impossible.

Let's say you're out there bobbing along in an ocean of day-to-day obligations, swimming as hard as you can and getting tired. Suddenly, something unexpected happens. Your Level 2 surprises could be anything. In this scenario, you might be pursued by a shark, or run the risk of smashing against a rocky shore. Surprises at this level can send us back to square one, or change our direction, or even fling us forward when we are least prepared. Without warning, situational pressures can render our best-laid plans obsolete and can take over our day.

You can't fight Level 2 problems and win. You have to learn how to use unanticipated explosions, 90 degree detours, and even windfalls to your best advantage. *Achieving what you want in a rapid-fire world depends largely on your ability to turn situations to your advantage.*

This is about learning how to spot the opportunities hidden in the tumult that comes your way. If you want to thrive, not just survive, in a rapid-fire world, it is imperative that you create a sense of challenge—not danger—out of upheaval and uncertainty. When you focus primarily on realizing positive potential, you automatically ward off danger at the same time.

Replace your instinct to survive with your decision to thrive.

Most of us, when we encounter uncertainty of any sizable magnitude, instinctively switch into a Reactive mind-set. In the face of danger we have an inborn reaction that physiologist Walter Cannon termed our "fight or flight" response. We are hardwired this way for our own protection. Our adrenaline starts to flow, the striate muscles in our arms and legs fill with blood to become more powerful, our breathing becomes more rapid and shallow, our attention narrows, and all of our senses function on full alert. We become hypervigilant, and scan for signs of any more hidden danger coming our way even as our mind races through alternative courses of action. As individuals, and as a species, the "fight or flight" response has enabled us to survive all manner of impending disasters.

Our survival instincts do a great job at keeping us out of harm's way, but rarely do we need to enlist this elaborate biochemically based system of self-defense in our rapid-fire world. In fact, the more threatened we feel when confronted with uncertainty, upheaval, and surprise, the less likely we are to solve our problems in the short run and to achieve our Level 3 goals in the long run.

Cross-cultural studies indicate that people are motivated not only by the pressures of adaptation and survival, but also by the need to reproduce optimal experiences. The need to engage in behaviors that make them feel fully alive, competent, and creative.

When we create a sense of challenge, instead of threat, we inspire ourselves to meet uncertainty with confidence and optimism. This allows us to work with whatever the upheaval has to offer. When we feel challenged by uncertainty, instead of moving away (flight) or trying to prevail (fight), we can engage whatever is happening and scout for the benefits it can provide.

It's true that much of the time the advantages inherent in our daily demands or sudden surprises are not obvious. Because the benefits associated with pressing problems are often obscure, we have to make it our top priority to scout them out. The moment we begin to search for hidden benefits and opportunities, we help ourselves shift from a sense of threat to a sense of challenge—even in the face of major adversity.

You can use stress as a stepping-stone to success by proceeding as if every stressful situation—no matter how intense or uncertain it may be—is an opportunity, however disguised, for you to advance your Level 3 agenda. To use upheaval to fuel your creativity and achieve important goals, you need to examine every breakdown, turn of events, or sudden development for hidden benefits. No one else can do this scouting for you.

Do you see problems or potential?

Suppose someone you know has a serious illness. If he focuses on recovery, he will do everything necessary to regain his health. Then it stands to reason that he is reducing his risk of dying prematurely. Striving to regain health encourages determination and drive. Engaging the Creative mind-set helps to find a whole host of actions aimed at recovery. In bleak contrast, if your friend focuses on trying to prevent his premature death, this will make him feel helpless and depressed, which unnecessarily compromises the possibility of a favorable outcome.

I assure you this isn't just a matter of semantics. Generating a list of gains, preferably enough to outnumber your losses, contributes to optimism, and then the dynamic of attraction takes over. When we face a situation that is flush with benefits, we are compelled to squeeze every drop of opportunity out of it. When we are outrageously optimistic, we find whatever is waiting to be realized in the heart of every challenge. Our optimism grows in direct proportion to the time, attention, and effort we devote to achieving whatever there is to gain.

Most of us would like to find immediate solutions to our most pressing problems. This need to "find the answers fast" usually escalates in proportion to the degree of difficulty we are having in dealing with a stressful situation. We want an instant cure, especially if we've not made any progress for an extended period. But even when we have hit major barriers that are holding us back, it is crucial to search for opportunities that guide us to multiple right answers and best solutions. If we think about it, we know from experience that breaking through barriers requires operating from multiple angles at once to ensure as many beneficial outcomes as possible.

But how do we identify the array of opportunities and benefits waiting to be realized that lie hidden in complex, disturbing situations? One way to get out of the Reactive mind-set and into a Creative mind-set is to step outside the situation altogether and to view it as a bystander or eyewitness might. This is the type of attention that remains somewhat detached, yet highly focused on encouraging positive outcomes from a given situation. Anyone who is an avid sports fan has experienced this passionate detachment. Sitting in the stands, you are in the game and out of the game simultaneously. Parents of adolescents have to master a hands-on yet arm's length perspective as they attend to their children's welfare and accommodate their growing need for independence at the same time.

In order to scout for opportunities and unleash the positive potential in any stressful circumstance, you have to learn how to step outside all of your boxes—the box that defines your current assumptions and beliefs, the box that puts boundaries on your imagination, even the box that holds the sum total of your attitude toward life. By stepping outside of all these boxes, all at once, you are better able to discover what is happening in its entirety, which in turn enables you to glimpse the best of the possibilities that could potentially unfold.

There is no security on this earth, there is only opportunity.
General Douglas MacArthur

When you are completely caught up in a disturbing problem or demanding uncertainty, you don't have a chance to see how you can influence a situation for the better, or to see which solutions are best. It takes courage to slow down and reflect, so you can then speed up and succeed.

Yes, you could walk away. But should you?

I stood looking out of the large picture window that framed Richard's executive office, waiting for him to arrive for an appointment we had made two weeks ago. Richard and I had known each other for years, and he often used me as a sounding board. I was under the impression that the purpose for this meeting was to discuss the leadership potential of one of his subordinates. I soon found out that Richard had a different agenda in mind.

I watched a flock of geese cut across the sky. I remembered that as long as they flew in formation, each bird made it a little easier for the bird flying right behind it. I figured every little bit of energy they could save would make a difference over the long trip to their next, best destination. But what about the goose out in front? Who made the trip easier for him?

Richard's voice interrupted my reverie. "How are you, Kathy?" he said earnestly as he pulled out a chair for me at the conference table in his office.

"Just great," I answered. "How was your trip to Paris?"

Usually when Richard and I are together we have lively conversations, but this time he fell silent. I knew something must be bothering him deeply, so I waited.

He clasped his hands behind his head, leaned back in his chair, and looked out the picture window. Finally he began to speak.

Richard had just spent two weeks in Paris on business. Before he left, he and his boss—the CEO of the company—had several clashes that severely disturbed Richard. For the last six months, the company had experienced unusually tough pressures, and the CEO had gotten progressively more ornery and unpleasant. He was prone to outbursts, blaming Richard, Richard's peers, and any person at any level who was the bearer of bad news. Richard believed the CEO was out of control. He feared he was damaging a whole host of people and their careers, and worried that he was antagonizing those outside the company as well.

I listened intently and occasionally asked a clarifying question. Richard described his disturbing experiences in vivid detail. The CEO appeared to be a bully who vented his own frustrations by blaming and humiliating people less powerful than he. He berated and belittled those who reported to him, but expected others to treat him deferentially. Richard mentioned an article he'd read in the *Harvard Business Review* about the "narcissistic leader"—someone who wields power and authority in order to satisfy his or her egotistical needs, rather than to further the good of others and of the organization—and provided me with numerous examples of how the CEO exhibited all the pathological characteristics of a narcissistic leader. Richard had come to feel that his boss was a pitiful excuse for a CEO who probably could not change even if his life depended on it.

While I was trying to understand the CEO's rampant abusive behavior, I noticed that Richard looked like he was ready to explode. His nostrils flared, his cheeks were flushed, his body language was stiff and taut. Now he was leaning forward, pounding the mahogany table, looking me fiercely in the eye and declaring he would not stand for this outrageous behavior any longer ... not even for one more minute!

Richard was hurt, exasperated, indignant, and furious. A few months ago he was still trying to make the best of the situation, but now he was so angry he was simply thinking in terms of getting even. When I asked him what he wanted to achieve in this scenario, he said he wanted to stop the CEO from inflicting any more harm on people both inside and outside the company. He also wanted to get out of the line of fire. He had considered distancing himself as completely as possible from the CEO, and avoiding the other vice presidents, who drew him into the middle of their battles. He was even considering leaving the company.

This negative, standoffish behavior was completely out of character for Richard. It was clear to me that he was stuck in a Reactive mind-set. His Level 3 agenda had been completely overpowered by the daily stress of having to work with such a volatile boss. The CEO had created such havoc that Richard's days were reduced to waiting for the next eruption. I knew that Richard rarely ran out of patience or energy when it came to stepping in to remedy a bad situation, so I decided to probe what might be causing his decision to retreat.

Richard explained that his boss had been hired three years ago to help the company recover from ten years of mismanagement. Whenever Richard's peers or other leaders in the organization complained about the CEO's "command and control" style, he had always stood up for the CEO, giving him a break because the pressure was on him to turn the company around. Richard helped others to see, time and time again, that the CEO was not being harsh because he lacked confidence in his team—he just was so eager to get the company back on track that his sense of urgency made him seem abrupt.

Unfortunately, Richard now saw that because he had defended the CEO so often, and because the CEO was now unmistakably abusive, his own credibility had been damaged. In addition, by being the CEO's biggest defender, he felt he had naively sacrificed the well-being of his peers and the whole company. He was crushed to think that his defense of the CEO may have contributed to the escalating rage in the organization.

What pushed Richard over the edge, even to the point of resigning, was a tirade the CEO directed at him personally. The CEO berated him for taking on too much responsibility in helping other parts of the company reach their goals and recover from setbacks. Richard was an excellent mentor and motivator, so this accusation was like a punch in the nose. The criticism hit him particularly hard because the CEO had once confided to Richard that he wanted to groom him to become the next CEO. With this succession plan in mind, the CEO had encouraged him to reach out and help his peers cross-functionally, so he could learn the intricacies of each part of the complex organization and see how they best worked together to achieve results. Richard had gladly done just what the CEO had suggested, and now he was being reprimanded for it.

You can't scout for opportunities when you're in a foxhole.

After he unburdened his anger and confusion, Richard's mood evened out a little. Putting the problem on the table and venting his frustrations had a calming effect on him, as it does on most people. Now we needed to step back and examine the CEO's

> Composer Igor Stravinsky argued that music itself forces us to distinguish between hearing and listening in much the same way that modern art makes us look rather than simply see. "It obliges the hearer to become a listener, summons him to activate relations with music."

behavior, the damage he had done, and what he did that made Richard the most angry. Then we could creatively and carefully exchange ideas about how best to respond to the situation.

Richard cheered up a bit and moved into a more Creative mind-set. The situation was still desperate, but he was starting to feel challenged instead of threatened. We slowly and thoroughly began scouting for any opportunities or positive potential that might be buried in the tumult.

As we reviewed what the last few months had been like, Richard was surprised to realize that he had gotten so caught up in his angry response to the CEO's unjust and damaging behavior that he had completely neglected his own Level 3 agenda. His outrage had thrown him off course, and he had neglected to keep doing what was necessary to prepare himself for the role of CEO. Now he could see that retreating and isolating himself would hurt him more than it would hurt his boss. Recognizing that his strategy of hiding out would actually hurt his own prospects of becoming a skilled, competent CEO—maybe at this company, maybe somewhere else—Richard decided to rethink his decision to retreat. But he could not yet come up with a viable alternative.

Richard was in a tough position. A severe Level 2 problem or disruption can easily distract you from your long-term goals, especially if you are in an early state of the six step process for achieving what you want. It is vital to take a time-out and actively search for the opportunity hidden in the situation. This opportunity may require perseverance and resourcefulness on your part, but at least you will be back on track, attending to your Level 3 agenda.

Richard explained to me in detail why bullies were so abhorrent to him. He had grown up in a tough, urban area, and he and his younger brothers had been routinely harassed by a group of teenage bullies who would tease them in school, chase them down the street, rough them up, steal their lunch money, throw their books into the river, write obscenities on their jackets, and generally make their lives miserable. Richard tried to stick up for his little brothers, and as a consequence got beaten up on a regular basis.

In part because of this background, he took a special interest in helping others. Deep in his heart, he had enormous compassion. He loved to protect the less powerful from the high and mighty. He always rooted for the underdog, and he found it personally satisfying to turn an employee who was a poor performer into an outstanding performer. He did not judge others harshly, and believed deeply in each individual's potential to become more effective.

Back when Richard was a plant manager, he helped an employee named Lilly Lee move from an entry-level position to supervisor. Richard helped a lot of employees get ahead, but he was particularly pleased about Lilly's success story. She was a single mother with seven children, and right away Richard admired her determination. He figured if Lilly could effectively raise seven kids as a single working mother, she could surely handle greater responsibilities at work. He saw that Lilly needed both decent wages and self-confidence. He made a point of coaching her, and watched her bloom—no pun intended!—before his eyes.

I was moved by how much Lilly Lee's success clearly meant to Richard. Her story reminded me that he derived as much reward from coaching and mentoring as he did from sharpening his own effectiveness. This led me to wonder if Richard could link his love of coaching with the problem he was having with his boss.

I posed the question: "Richard, could you see that your boss might be as much in need of your coaching as Lilly Lee? Do you think you could help him, instead of running away from him?"

He didn't respond right away, but I knew the question had gotten his attention. It seemed that he considered it but came up empty-handed: "How in the world could I help my boss? He's the one who gets the big bucks, remember?"

We exchanged our ideas and together scouted for any opportunities that might exist in this situation. Eventually we came up with a profoundly different way for Richard to view his CEO. Instead of seeing him as a bully, Richard began to see his boss more like the wounded person he was. The CEO really *was* under intense pressure, as Richard had reminded his colleagues, but it appeared that he had no skills for coping with his stress. Over time he had become gratuitously nasty, but Richard recalled that in the early days, his boss hadn't been so short-tempered and unfair. With this simple but significant reframe,

Richard could begin to feel some compassion for his boss, who was utterly handicapped in his ability to respond effectively in the face of performance pressures.

Mama exhorted her children at every opportunity to "jump at de sun." We might not land on the sun, but at least we would get off the ground.

Zora Neale Hurston

With compassion as a starting point, Richard was able to see an opportunity for him to coach the CEO to live into his potential—a role Richard had always enjoyed with other employees, but one he'd never thought of taking with his boss. First, he had to let go of his belief that a CEO should *not* be abusive and ineffective under pressure. Although Richard had a right—and, I believe, a responsibility—to hold his CEO to a higher standard, focusing on his boss's inadequacies was not the place to begin reparations. If Richard was able to focus on an image of the man he believed his boss could become, he had a better chance of moving his CEO in a positive direction.

Richard was a huge believer in human potential, so he soon discovered that he had it within himself to believe his boss could change. He also felt he would be a good person to help his boss become less reactive and more creative under pressure. He thought he would be able to address the issue with his boss, and figured he could informally give him some constructive criticism. This might have a beneficial effect on his boss, and in turn the whole company. But most important, Richard reconnected with his goal of preparing to become a CEO himself.

Begin scouting for opportunities by mining for diamonds.

The purpose of stepping back to reflect on a situation, assessing it in terms of its actual and potential losses and gains, is to respond creatively and to shape a vision of what you want to happen. The chart on page 87 helps illustrate the difference between viewing a stressful situation as a problem to be fixed—i.e., the current reality is not good enough—or viewing it as full of opportunity and potential, i.e., the current reality is good enough and can be built upon.

Alternative Views of Upheaval

Problem to Be Solved	*Potential to Be Realized*
Focus on the problem	Focus on what is possible
Perform root cause analysis	Envision what might be possible
Derive solution	Discuss what should be possible
Make action plan to correct the problem	Shape what will be possible

The most creative approach will maximize the gains and minimize the losses inherent in the situation. You will need a Creative mind-set to discover opportunities and tap the myriad lessons hidden inside of every debacle, course correction, or lucky strike. The most important thing is to put on the brakes, stop reacting out of anger or fear, and very deliberately shift into neutral. Even if your emotions are running wild and you feel you must immediately take action, don't. First, scout for opportunities and ask yourself how you can use the situation to further your goals. Try to make sure that your response, when you make it, is calculated to help you and the greater good. Then, whatever you do, you will be operating from a position of strength and conviction.

> *Don't be discouraged by a failure. It can be a positive experience. Failure is, in a sense, the highway to success, inasmuch as every discovery of what is false leads us to seek earnestly after what is true, and every fresh experience points out some form of error which we shall afterwards carefully avoid.*
>
> John Keats

Responding creatively to every stressful situation creates a positive ripple effect in a rapid-fire world. Creativity is contagious.

BEST PRACTICES

The following exercises will help you cultivate your capacity and skill in scouting for opportunities to benefit from any pressure that might come your way, be it welcome or unwelcome. Do as

Richard did: Be open-minded and willing to thrive, not just survive, in the face of tough situations that throw you off course and jeopardize your Level 3 goals.

BEST PRACTICE #7

SHARPEN YOUR CREATIVE EDGE: THE ORANGE EXERCISE

This exercise is a favorite among those who attend my seminars. In order for you to get the most out of this practice, I suggest you find yourself an orange and a partner. The whole experience takes no more than ten minutes from start to finish.

Step 1: Contemplate
Examine your orange in detail for about one minute. You may hold it, smell it, look at it, and feel it—but please don't eat it!

Step 2: Describe
Now I would like you to describe in detail as many qualities and attributes of the orange as you can. If you are working with a partner, brainstorm your responses together. Give yourselves three minutes to compile and record your list of qualities and attributes.

Step 3: Brainstorm
Next, I would like you and your partner, if you have one, to generate ideas about the wide range of benefits and opportunities that are provided by this orange. Discuss the array of positive potential inherent in this orange. Make notes on how you, other people, and the world at large could be better off because of this orange. Accumulate your responses for another three minutes.

Step 4: Compare
In this final step, please review and compare your list of your orange's qualities and attributes with your list of the benefits, opportunities, and positive potential inherent in your orange. Note the main differences between these two lists.

When making a list of qualities and attributes, most people describe the color, texture, aroma, shape, and visible flaws of their orange. It doesn't dawn on them to describe the beneficial qualities or positive potential that can be attributed to the orange. Left to our own devices, most of us assess the qualities and attributes of people and situations the same way we assess the orange: We stick to what we first perceive.

This exercise demonstrates that a simple orange possesses a vast array of potentially positive qualities that, if tapped, could benefit many—if only we stop to notice. My seminar participants often note the orange's ability to prevent disease, or the potential the orange holds for flavoring a roasted chicken, or the ability of the orange to seed the landscape with orange trees, or its use in a holiday wreath. Once you begin scouting for them, the potential positive qualities seem endless.

Try this approach with the weather (even a rainy day), a book, a chance encounter with a friend or stranger, or an assignment at work. The more you scout for opportunities, anywhere and everywhere, the more skilled you will be at finding the buried treasure during periods of upheaval. Learning to see opportunity in crisis, positive potential in negative situations, and benefits hidden within whatever happens, is a basic skill for achieving what you want, even when the odds are against you.

BEST PRACTICE #8

SHIFTING FROM THREAT TO CHALLENGE

What would you guess is the most admired characteristic among Americans. Power? Wealth? Physical attractiveness? Fame? Enviable lifestyle? If you guessed any of these, you may be surprised to learn that the trait Americans admire most in others is *the ability to overcome adversity*. We intuitively know that if a person can meet adversity with courage and creativity, then many of the lesser, yet highly valued, characteristics will be forthcoming. So the question becomes: How do we find it within ourselves to beat the odds and overcome adversity?

In 1999, Lance Armstrong, who had already won other prestigious bicycle races, won the Tour de France. What is so remarkable about his victory is that in 1996, at the age of 25, he was diagnosed with advanced testicular cancer and underwent several operations, plus aggressive chemotherapy. Armstrong attacked his disease with the same single-minded fortitude and spirit that characterized his career success. He gathered friends and family around him and dedicated himself to conquering the disease and to returning to the sport he loved, stopping only to get married in 1998 and to welcome his newborn child in 1999. In 2000, Armstrong won the Tour de France again!

Lance Armstrong is the prototype of being outrageously optimistic. He never gave up his hope of beating the odds and surviving, and he never gave up his Level 3 goal of winning the Tour de France—twice! The illness brought Armstrong and his wife closer together, and the weight he lost during chemotherapy actually made it easier for him to prevail in the 2000 Tour de France. Today Armstrong is an international hero, not because of his strength, or his looks, or his personality, but for the determination he modeled when his life and career were turned upside down by a deadly disease.

I wanted you to see what real courage is, instead of getting the idea that courage is a man with a gun in his hand. It's when you know you're licked before you begin but you begin anyway and you see it through no matter what.

Harper Lee from
To Kill a Mockingbird

I have studied thousands of people faced with incredible demands and upheaval who became creative and optimistic to a degree that the rest of us find hard to believe. How did they sustain such positive attitudes? In each case, whether they are aware of the process or not, these individuals use a similar creative approach. The same steps will work for you, whether you face an enormous challenge or just need to find a way over a speed bump in your life.

Step 1: Calculate your potential losses

Calmly fine-tune your assessment of what you have to lose if you do not prevail over the adversity you face. This will help you gain an accurate perspective of the gravity of your situation. Sometimes this assessment shows that the downside risks are less serious than you thought, while other times this assessment will increase the magnitude of the danger. The important thing is that you engage fully with the potential for damage before moving on to more optimistic pursuits.

Lance Armstrong could plainly see that his life was at risk, as was his career, his capacity to father children, and his chance to have a long and loving marriage. He had everything to lose if he was not successful in his fight against cancer. He may have experienced denial—a normal reaction to a diagnosis of cancer—but before long he clearly recognized he was in the fight of his life.

Step 2: Search for potential gains

Now it's time to get optimistic. To overcome adversity, you can't stop at damage assessment—you move on to opportunity assessment. Now you estimate the real or potential gains you could experience as a result of the upheaval you face. You can begin by noting the flip side of your potential disadvantages from Step 1. This process is intimately related to the way you searched for benefits and positive potential in the orange exercise. It is helpful to know at the outset which benefits to shoot for.

Situational pressure, including getting cancer, almost always feels like something happening as the result of forces operating outside our control. Then we feel victimized and powerless. However, we put ourselves back in control when we identify and pursue our Level 3 goals. Lance Armstrong's list of the gains he could realize by outsmarting his disease would have included recovering his health, regaining or even surpassing his former athletic abilities, winning the race of his dreams, having children, enjoying a long marriage, becoming involved in supporting other cancer patients, raising public awareness about the prevention and cure for his disease, sponsoring fund-raising for research and treatment of cancer, and learning the lessons of resilience.

Step 3: Rig your results

Now that you have considered both losses and gains, tally them up. It is not "cheating" to make sure the gains outweigh the losses. In fact, it's a good idea to keep looking for ways you can gain from your particular challenge until the advantages outnumber the disadvantages.

I would like you to reflect for a moment on how the two different lists affect your motivation. Focusing on damage control is a strain. We become burdened by the gravity of the situation and feel its weight on our shoulders. Trying not to die can be motivating, but not very uplifting. Striving for positive goals, on the other hand, helps us get out of bed in the morning. A positive, attractive, compelling benefit gives us the lift we need to persevere in any high stakes situation.

BEST PRACTICE #9

GO FOR THE GOLD: MAKING A MASTER LIST OF YOUR MOST EXCELLENT LEVEL 3 GOALS

Back in Best Practice #2, "Framing the Big Picture," you learned how to conduct an inquiry with others and within yourself to identify an array of Level 3 goals. You examined your personal capacities and skills, your partnerships, and your productivity, and set goals within each of these domains. These goals reflected your aspirations, your interests, what you and others believe you are ready to achieve, and the contributions and legacies you want most to make. Then you looked at how the different goals reinforced and supported each other. Go back and find the three-column chart you filled out (see page 47).

Back in Best Practice #6, "Increasing Your Emotional Intelligence: the Challenge/Competency Zones," you ranked your Level 3 goals on the basis of how exhilarating and rewarding it would be to achieve them. You sorted your goals into different quadrants on a chart to give a much better picture of which goals are most meaningful and compelling to you. Find that chart you filled out, too (see page 69).

Now it is time for you to continue to shape your best possible Level 3 agenda by evaluating each goal in terms of how it will benefit you, other people, and your world. (You will enter this in the "Go for the Gold" master list on page 93.) Assessing the real and potential benefits associated with each of your Level 3 goals is extremely enlightening. Estimating the range of potential benefits that could accrue when you achieve your goals is an important way for you to become outrageously optimistic. The more beneficial your goals are, the more motivated you—and others involved with you—will be to do whatever it takes to accomplish them.

Step 1: Narrow your list of goals
Review the Level 3 goals that you grouped in the Challenge/Competency graph and identify the most exhilarating and rewarding. Write each of these high-priority goals on a separate piece of paper. This will be the beginning of your master list, or your formal Level 3 agenda.

John told me he could actually feel his optimism rise and his hope for the future expand as he transferred his goals onto sep-

Go for the Gold: Your Master List

Type of Goal	Five rewards/benefits that are likely to occur if I achieve my goal	One problem that is likely to occur if I don't achieve my goal
Personal Goal		
Partnership Goal		
Productivity Goal		

arate sheets of paper. He liked the idea of reviewing his goals and letting each one stand or fall on its own merits.

Step 2: Polish the diamonds you mined earlier

For each of these high-priority goals ask yourself the following question: "When I achieve this goal, what benefits (advancements, opportunities, positive rewards, etc.) will this have for me, for other people, and for the situations most immediately affected?" For each goal, write down at least five ways in which the people and situations affected will be better off.

John was already very successful, he liked his job, and he had an optimistic, "can do" personality, so he figured he would breeze through this step. However, as we scouted for the host of benefits that achieving his Level 3 goals might bring, he dug deeper into his beliefs and ambitions—and was amazed to find himself becoming even more optimistic. He discovered that the process of purposefully sorting through goals does much more than reveal obvious benefits. John was able to increase his appreciation for the potential buried deep within his Level 3 goals. When we go beyond our initial rationale and augment our reasons for achieving our hopes and dreams, we foster our creativity to the greatest extent possible. Once you are able to reflect more broadly on the ripple effects of achieving your Level 3 goals, your faith that it will truly be possible to create a positive future naturally grows. This is helpful, because the more challenging your goals are, the more important optimism is in sustaining your motivation when the going gets rough.

Step 3: What's at stake?

Now ask yourself this question: "When I achieve this particular goal, what is the number one problem (conflict, crisis, impasse, dilemma, etc.) that will be resolved for the people and situations most affected?" On the pages you have already begun, write down your answer to this question for each goal. These answers tell you what might be sacrificed or lost if you are not successful in achieving your goal.

In this Best Practice, John systematically increased his optimism for achieving the wide array of benefits associated with his Level 3 goals. He actually augmented his positive, proactive agenda with more reasons to be excited. Lance Armstrong didn't have the luxury of setting a proactive agenda. Cancer set his agenda for him. Even so, he was able to apply his formidable willpower to the business of getting well and living well.

Step 4: Consider choosing one high-priority goal in each domain: personal, partnership, and productivity

Your master list now should show what could be gained (the benefits) and what's at stake (the problems) for each goal. Review each page until you have reached a richer and deeper appreciation for the importance of each goal. This will motivate you to do whatever may be necessary to achieve them.

This Best Practice is designed to solidify in your mind which of your Level 3 goals are the most important. Many people find that their priorities shift after they view their goals through this "benefit lens." Often it becomes clear that certain goals are more likely than others to benefit the people and situations that are of the greatest importance to you.

If you are having trouble deciding, consider how much frustration you would experience in the process of achieving each goal. If a goal is too easy, you'll be bored by it. If it's too difficult, you'll become exasperated. All worthwhile accomplishments are accompanied by a certain amount of frustration, but making your goals too lofty just sets you up for failure.

After reflecting upon your goals, you should be able to narrow them down to just two or three. At least one of these will be a personal goal. It's convenient, but not required, to have a goal for each domain: personal, partnership, and productivity. If this doesn't work for you, don't worry. All of your Level 3 goals will create cascading benefits in different domains.

When you complete your master list of rewards and benefits, containing two or three of your highest priority goals, you will share in the "Go for the Gold" mentality that inspires every Olympian, every explorer, every earnest scout who has charged forth magnetized by a future he or she wouldn't want to live without.

Marshall Haith, Ph.D., a scholar of memory and University of Denver psychologist, has conducted over three decades of research exploring how babies think about the future. He theorizes that infants use their experience to predict future events. "It's exhausting to be a slave to the world and simply react to everything as it happens," he said. "Infants lighten their load, I believe, by staying a step ahead of the flow." Haith discovered that even before children can talk, parents are talking to them about the future at least five to seven times more than they talk about the past. This early exposure to future oriented thinking helps prepare children to think about what is to come.

Siri Carpenter from "Future-Oriented Thinking Is a Staple for Infants and Toddlers"

John's master list included three goals, with their potential rewards and benefits (see page 96). Initially he had too many goals, but he was able to let some go and to fold others together. You can see why his optimism rose so significantly when he wrote everything down!

Go for the Gold: John's Master List

Type of Goal	Five rewards/benefits that are likely to occur if I achieve my goal	One problem that is likely to occur if I don't achieve my goal
Personal Goal To become as effective at asking questions as I am at answering them.	• Learn a skill I need and that I admire in others • Develop my listening skills • Improve my capacity to lead and to influence • Focus less on my own opinions • Depend on others for feedback	"If I don't learn to ask penetrating questions, I will never understand other points of view, and I will miss important input."
Partnership Goal To be collaborative by seeking others' opinions, allowing them to discover and implement solutions.	• Key people will develop confidence and skill • I will have more time to negotiate new deals • Better solutions will be generated • More trust in team approach • More pride in team members	"If I don't learn to collaborate, I will foster undue dependency on my opinions and solutions. As the company grows, I will be stretched way beyond the limits of my effectiveness."
Productivity Goal To maintain a highly creative culture as the company's size triples and annual revenues grow from $30 million to $200 million.	• Increased speed to market of new products • Attract highest caliber work force • Maintain current client base and attract others • Achieve what is rarely done in business • Attract publicity and global recognition	"If our creativity diminishes, our product line and client base will be severely compromised."

Guiding Principles: Scout for Opportunities

- The bedrock of the future depends on how optimistic you are about achieving it.
- Realize there are "guardians at the gate" who want to keep you from achieving your goals. They test your resolve to determine if you are willing to stay the course. They are left over from the survival mentality.
- Ask yourself: What future do I crave with all my heart? What has brought me to my knees? To what am I willing to give 100 percent?
- Mentally revel in how each experience strikes you, and how you want to use it to benefit yourself and those people and situations most important to you.
- When we step back and reflect on a situation, thoroughly assessing its actual and potential losses and gains, we can respond to it creatively and shape a vision of what we want to happen—and become outrageously optimistic about it!

JOHN'S STORY, CONTINUED

With his "Go for the Gold" master list of rewards and benefits in mind, John had conversations with several people who had a keen interest in his success. He asked these key stakeholders to think about how they personally would benefit as a result of his achieving his Level 3 goals—learning to ask effective questions, building collaborative relationships, and maintaining a highly creative company culture.

First John spoke to Amy, who was responsible for acquiring new products. She told him that if she could have the benefit of his input earlier in the acquisition process, she could find out what she needed to know to be almost completely self-sufficient in preparing acquisition proposals. Todd, the company's operations manager, confided that he could accelerate the cost-reduction results in manufacturing if John would teach him what he knew about setting up best-practice exchanges between supervisors. And so it went with each key individual. John was amazed at how much value achieving his goals would add to the job of each person he interviewed. It was as if he doubled and tripled the intrinsic value of his goals after each conversation. The net worth of his goals increased, as did his optimism about his ability to accomplish his top-priority goals. Intuitively, John could sense that as the result of his conversations, each person he talked with became committed to his success. This was an added benefit, giving his optimism another boost.

> *The past is but the beginning of a beginning, and all that is and has been is but the twilight of the dawn.*
>
> H. G. Wells

See the Glass as Half Full ... with a Pitcher of Water on the Way!

What you need to DO   Become Energized

What you need to BE   Optimistic and Responsive

You're in the midst of a world of rapid-fire demands and you want to achieve sizable goals. Solve challenging problems. Overcome unforeseen obstacles. Make progress against formidable odds. And, as if that weren't enough, keep all of the other "balls" juggling in midair. So, you're wondering, how do you make it all happen?

Before you make a move, evaluate your attitude. This is a little like a pilot doing a preflight check of his instruments. Are you feeling energetic? Check. Optimistic about being able to influence the circumstances at hand? Check. Ready to respond to all the opportunities hidden in this situation? Check. Good—you're okay to go.

What if your attitude isn't so enthusiastic? Don't blame yourself. Adopting a spirit of optimism toward turbulent forces runs counter to our strongest survival instincts. What comes more naturally is to try to exert power and control over our circumstances to achieve the results we want. In addition, most of us have been socialized to address our challenges with the same kind of authority we ourselves, as children and adults, have always submitted to: the "command and conquer" brand of authority. Every institution and discipline that has touched our lives—education, medicine, business, religion, government, science—has marked us with an indelible conviction that we should dominate when we are in charge and submit (or rebel) when someone else is our authority.

> *Thoughts are energy. And you can make your world or break your world by thinking.*
>
> Susan L. Taylor

Why should you cultivate an outrageously optimistic view of yourself?

To help you stay your course during upheaval, you have to believe in yourself: your character, your determination, your abilities, and your creative capacities. A full supply of optimism will help you realize your most challenging goals. I don't mean an artificial, have-a-nice-day, phony veneer. I mean optimism that is grounded in your accomplishments and skills—optimism you have earned, and to which you are entitled.

Martin Seligman, noted researcher on optimism, suggests that we are prone to be optimistic when we can clearly see aspects of ourselves as good and relatively permanent. The clinical research of psychoanalyst Susan Vaughn reveals that we can modulate our moods and shift from negative to positive views with the help of realistic, yet positive, input from other people in combination with our own honest self-appraisal.

I believe that we all have the capacity to cultivate "self-optimism"—a strong, optimistic belief in ourselves—and that we can develop habits of mind and heart that focus our thoughts on the good, abiding aspects of ourselves. One of the fastest ways of learning self-optimism (especially in the face of difficult challenges) is to listen to a description of our strengths and abilities as reflected by trustworthy people who know us well, who care deeply for our well-being, and who are able to put what they appreciate and treasure about us into words.

We all know when someone's view of us has the ring of truth to it. And we sense when feedback is shallow or misses the mark.

Numerous studies of patients with life-threatening diseases suggest that those who remain optimistic show symptoms later and survive longer than patients who confront reality more objectively. An optimistic patient is more likely to practice habits that enhance health and to enlist social support.

The positive reflection of ourselves, through someone else's eyes, can help us rely on our own best inner qualities when faced with any tough challenge. Turning inward in this way builds the courage and confidence we need to move forward. A dose of self-optimism is often the prescription for promoting the best possible results.

Leave your worries at the doorstep.

Colleen sat beside me. We were both exhausted from a day of preparing for a global conference at which we had been asked to give a joint presentation. Almost nothing had worked in our favor. We were supposed to be practicing our speech, but the CEO showed up unexpectedly and commandeered our rehearsal slot, leaving us to retreat to the lobby bar of the hotel.

Colleen gulped her ten dollar glass of chardonnay. I was struck by how worried she looked.

"I can't believe Bill pulled rank on us like that," Colleen complained. Her comment seemed innocuous enough until she stared at me and continued, "I hate the hierarchy thing. Bill acts like he can cut anyone short anytime just because he's in charge. Most people follow him around like servants. It's disgusting."

A small voice inside of me told me not to respond right away. I felt Colleen's dark eyes stare at me with full attention. They didn't drill into me, yet they didn't waver, either. They didn't judge me, yet they were distracted. I looked away, and noticed six or seven colleagues streaming through the doors of the hotel. I remembered they would be in the audience during our presentation in the morning.

"I really wanted this to go well, but we can't even run through the slides, so my timing is probably going to be off," Colleen said darkly. Then she blurted, "I guess I should warn you that I am a pessimist in any crisis. I see my glass as half empty and any minute I'll be chipping my tooth on the rim."

I winced. It dawned on me that Colleen was angry because she was afraid—afraid of failing.

Colleen swished the wine in the bottom of her glass and continued, "My husband, Jeff, never folds under pressure. Even in a crisis he sees his glass as half full—with a waiter in the wings and a pitcher of water on the way!"

We both laughed. The waitress brought us our bill. Colleen reminded me of Barbara, one of my oldest friends. Barbara and I faced life's challenges together from kindergarten. Somehow, even at that young age, our approaches were deeply similar. Our drive, our determination never to miss out, to be fully alive in every circumstance, bonded us together. We developed something of a reputation at the Catholic convent school we attended. Whether it was talking our way out of naptime, negotiating one more lap around the skating rink, or nominating ourselves to be angels in the Christmas play, Barbara and I always went for the gold.

I refocused on Colleen, and realized my mind had wandered. By then, she was glaring at me. I smiled and zeroed in on her again. I sensed myself searching for the "who" I was looking at, for the person behind the Irish freckled face, behind those wild black eyes. As my memories carried me behind her surface, I recalled Colleen the mother, who fought the red tape of the Chinese government to adopt her infant daughter, now a thriving three-year-old. I remembered that Colleen was the newest vice president of a global company she had joined as a sales rep only five years ago. I dwelt on her intelligence, wit, and ambition. Colleen's pessimism had no place inside this particular rendition of her.

Abruptly she asked, "Do you think we'll be able to pull it off?"

Colleen seemed to have switched gears. I sensed hope in her voice, and instinctively seized the opportunity to capitalize on her new stance. I heard myself responding, "Yes, we will. Of course we will. You have firsthand knowledge of what the audience wants to know, and I have lots of experience in facilitating panel discussions. Together, we're an incredible team. But Colleen, you also have to remember a few things about yourself. Like how articulate you are with a microphone in your hand. How your spontaneous humor engages people. How your track record in this company commands attention. If you trust *who you are* and *what you know*, that will make up for any minor glitches in our delivery. Then we will both succeed beyond our imaginations."

Colleen sighed. I knew her heart believed what I was saying. It was as if she had forgotten, and I was reminding her, of the good, solid aspects of herself—the skills that would mesh with mine to help us perform well in spite of the missed rehearsal. It struck me that my words were Colleen's very own "pitcher of water on the way." Then I wondered if my ability to be her "water" in this moment was somehow facilitated by my recollections of how Barbara and I behaved together.

Yes—that was it. It was no accident that Barbara had surfaced in my mind when she did. She and I were a dynamic duo, just as Colleen and I would be. Barbara and I had what psychologists have coined "big optimism"—an abiding belief that almost everything will turn out for the best if we find ways of capitalizing on whatever happens, good or bad. Big optimism has a trickle-down effect, and sets the stage for the "little optimism" that sparks our hopeful approaches in day-to-day situations.

> *A pessimist sees the difficulty in every opportunity; an optimist sees the opportunity in every difficulty.*
> Sir Winston Churchill

Like most people facing a challenge, Colleen wanted to perform well, so she worked hard outlining her part of the program, preparing slides, and planning a thorough rehearsal. When our chance to rehearse fell apart, so did her confidence. In fact, at the beginning of our conversation, Colleen was so pessimistic about our presentation that she refused to contemplate any possibility of a positive outcome. In effect, she suffered from "optimism blindness."

When my mind started to wander to my friend Barbara, Colleen had gotten annoyed with me, which broke her train of thought. She stopped ruminating over pending disasters, and her mind shifted to a more neutral zone. It was as if she'd lost a negative thinking partner when I began daydreaming. My shift in attention actually broke Colleen's negative downward spiral and prevented her from mentally doing any more damage to our presentation. At the time, neither she nor I was aware of how my shift in attention had jolted Colleen loose from her pessimism. When I recalled Colleen's inner assets—her humor, spontaneity, passion, presence, and polish—I found the chance not only to be her partner, but also her coach. I recognized what any good coach would have seen—Colleen's capacity to excel under pressure.

Colleen knew herself to be a skillful speaker who could sway the audience with her humor and passion. That's why my portrayal of her, to her, hit home. It was precisely because I was reminding Colleen about her several positive aspects that my coaching worked.

It's important here to notice the unconsciously powerful way that, as a listener and coach, I was able to help Colleen snap out of her pessimistic view. By thinking on a new channel, together we were able to muster the energy and ideas necessary to fortify Colleen with her own best sense of herself and what she was capable of contributing.

Initially, Colleen counted on being able to rehearse our program as our best preparation for giving a great performance. Like most people, she had been taught that diligent effort pays off. When our rehearsal fell through, however, she forgot about the inner resources we would both bring to bear.

My interaction with Colleen shows that there is an approach arguably more fundamental to success than practice and rehearsal: cultivating self-optimism. Self-optimism is hopeful self-reliance. When we are self-optimistic, we often are able to achieve positive outcomes. It's also possible to be self-optimistic when our circumstances are awful. Self-optimism helps us develop a set of positive inner expectations based on the belief that we have what it takes to deal with any and all challenges.

Negativity is contagious—but so is optimism!

Because I was working so closely with Colleen, I was in danger of getting caught up in her frustration, worry, and pessimistic outlook. Part of me wanted to be sympathetic. After all, this *was* an unlucky break for Colleen. I felt sorry for her. Who did this guy think he was, anyway? Didn't he know there were other people in the world who also had work to do? What a jerk!

Like a raging flu in February, Colleen's negativity easily could have infected me. Fortunately, I soon realized that if I really wanted to be a supportive colleague, I'd have to be creative in the way I handled this setback. I had to find a way to fend off Colleen's dark mood before it took hold of me, too. So I deliberately thought about Colleen, the person. I concentrated on her admirable qualities and her track record of achievement. I thought about her competence, strong will, and abiding sense of humor. My new focus put me in a completely different frame of mind. It was as if my psychological immune system warded off Colleen's mental "flu."

By now I was in a completely different frame of mind. I was involved, but not caught up in Colleen's negativity. I was supportive, but did not automatically sympathize with everything she was saying. My aware but detached point of view felt familiar, and I realized it reminded me of when I got in trouble when I was little. As my mother, father, or teacher lectured me for breaking the rules or indulging in bad behavior, I had to pay attention to them without letting the situation get the best of me. If I engaged with the negativity, I would dissolve into tears, so I did a mind-shift that enabled me to stay strong. If you have ever pretended you were listening while secretly daydreaming, you know how to shift into a neutral or even a positive zone in a negative situation. It isn't easy to function on a more positive plane when someone is upset. It takes concentration, but in the long run it is well worth the effort.

First, do no harm.

You've heard this expression before. It guides all physicians as they seek the cause of illness and then nurture our recovery. The principle is the same here: Don't make things worse than they need to be.

Each of us has inside what I call an Internal Optimist and an Internal Pessimist. The Internal Optimist recognizes everything that is true, but chooses to focus on the bright side. The Internal Pessimist looks at the same reality and focuses on the negative. Given a choice—and we do have one—why would we let the pessimist out of its cage?

Our Internal Optimist knows that reality may not be perfect, but can be "good enough." Our Internal Pessimist feels perfection is possible. This struggle between the real and the ideal helps us see the whole landscape. Let each internal voice have its truth. To some extent, the Internal Pessimist and the Internal Optimist are both right. What's important is that there is a person deep inside of us who is registering the optimistic messages from our Internal Optimist *and* the pessimistic remarks from our Internal Pessimist. The very essence of who we are is shaped by either the positive or negative force of the messages we send ourselves.

Many of my clients say to me, "I'm my own worst critic!" We feel obligated to listen to our Internal Pessimist, probably because we have been subjected to criticism from authority figures all our lives. Guess what? Our Internal Pessimist isn't any more powerful or correct than our Internal Optimist.

Pause for just a moment and contemplate this: You are more than your Internal Optimist or your Internal Pessimist. There is a core part of you who listens to and is affected by the commentary

of your Internal Optimist and Pessimist. Thinking about yourself in this way may seem odd at first. But as you do, you will
come to realize that you have a responsibility to care for and
develop this essential core of who you are. It is within this core,
the deepest part of you, that your reservoir of creative resources
resides. With positive, encouraging feedback, this reservoir
grows rich in clear vision, ingenuity, optimism, and resilience.
With negative, discouraging feedback, your reservoir of creative
resources runs dry.

Most people don't even realize that they're damaging the
very essence of who they are when they're self-critical. I encourage you to keep in mind that self-optimism enhances the very
essence of who you are and expands the creative resources you
have at your disposal in dealing in the toughest of rapid-fire conditions. Try to reconnect with who you are—that person who
deserves respect and who thrives on encouragement. Why
deprive the truest part of yourself the kind of encouragement
you would offer anyone else you care about? Commit yourself to
your own enrichment and ultimate effectiveness by learning to
cheer yourself, not to criticize yourself.

BEST PRACTICES

Learning how to put an end to self-sabotaging pessimism and
"optimism blindness" is crucial to keeping our creative edge. Like
Colleen, some of us are plagued by pessimistic thoughts about
ourselves in stressful situations. Others are only mildly distracted. There is no question we all are prone to suffer the vagaries of
"optimism blindness" when we face challenges that threaten to
overwhelm us because they may turn out for the worse and we
don't know how to prevent impending breakdowns. In the early
stages of achieving what we want, we need to be especially vigilant because we are more vulnerable to pessimism and more likely to become discouraged about achieving our Level 3 goals.

Most of us can immediately and vividly recall our most
embarrassing moments. They are etched on our psyches forever,
in part because we keep re-living them long after they have
blown over. It takes a while to recover our equilibrium after we've
blown something, whether we wore two different socks to work,

forgot about an important meeting, or burned through $60 million in startup money for a failed dot-com.

Here is the time and place to remind yourself of your strong points, your capabilities, and the things you have done right. Most of us don't take the time to really think about our successes and how we achieved them, yet finding links to our greatest accomplishments is the key to overcoming obstacles in the future.

BEST PRACTICE #10
How Well Do You Cope?

I want you to conduct a self-assessment to calculate how you excel under pressure. Engaging in this Best Practice will bolster your mood, your self-confidence, and your self-optimism as well. The only focus for this self-test is to estimate your greatest gifts that earn you an A when it comes to handling tough situations. If Colleen had been able to remember her best methods of coping with situational pressure (e.g., her humor, her drive, her ability to think spontaneously of alternative solutions, etc.), she could have reminded herself that she had all the inner resources she needed to compensate for her failed rehearsal. However, while in the midst of crisis, Colleen needed a mental list to help her recall those methods of coping.

If we don't remind ourselves which situational coping strategies make us most effective, then under pressure we will struggle to know how best to respond. Over the next few weeks, notice when you do something right. Following the steps below in your calmer, more reflective times will give you the options you need in the heat of the moment, when coping effectively is essential.

Step 1: Pick a triumph, any triumph

This victory can be taken from any aspect of your life. Refer back to the events you charted on your Life Map (see pages 41–42) as turning points, peak experiences, and episodes of misfortune, and recall the coping strategies that were highly effective in those situations. Or recall any

> *Great spirits have always found violent opposition from mediocrities. The latter cannot understand it when a man does not thoughtlessly submit to hereditary prejudices but honestly and courageously uses his intelligence.*
>
> Albert Einstein

tough, pressure-filled situation that you have handled exceptionally well. Make a list of the values, beliefs, thoughts, attitudes, and actions that you used in that situation to foster such desirable outcomes.

Step 2: Can you transfer these skills or qualities to another situation?

Consider which of the values, beliefs, thoughts, attitudes, and actions would benefit you in dealing more effectively with your current demands and challenges.

Step 3: A new solution creates a new situation

Mentally apply your proven coping strategies to your current situation. Visualize the positive outcomes that could possibly occur as a result of operating with different, more effective values, beliefs, thoughts, attitudes, and actions.

BEST PRACTICE #11

HOW TO SILENCE YOUR INTERNAL PESSIMIST AND TURN UP THE VOLUME ON YOUR INTERNAL OPTIMIST

If another person is not available to coach you into a more optimistic frame of mind, you can focus on the thoughts, images, and intuitions that confirm your own abilities to deal with the situation at hand. If you are able to highlight the opportunities that make dealing with the situation meaningful and rewarding to you, your optimism will grow and sustain your best efforts.

Step 1. Tune into WYOU

Using the positive energy of your Creative mind, focus your curiosity on the inner conversation you have with yourself when something happens to jeopardize the outcomes you are working toward. We all have ongoing internal commentary. As you listen to the messages you are sending yourself, notice the proportion of commentary that sounds critical, and notice the proportion that seems to have a coaching quality. Use the chart that follows as a guide.

The purpose of Step 1 is to get a perspective on how you treat yourself. Are you almost always kind to yourself? Almost always nasty? Are you generally pessimistic or optimistic about

Voice of Internal Pessimist	Voice of Internal Optimist
CRITICAL COMMENTARY THAT FOSTERS PESSIMISM	COACHING COMMENTARY THAT FOSTERS OPTIMISM
• Viewing yourself as a competitor who either wins or loses by exerting control	• Viewing yourself as a creator who always wins by capitalizing on whatever happens
• Monitoring yourself in judgmental and corrective ways	• Monitoring yourself in appreciative and constructive ways
• Intending to be victorious at all costs	• Intending to be resilient at all costs
• Evaluating tough situations as threats to be overcome	• Evaluating tough situations as challenges to be met

your abilities? Does the world seem to punish you, or do you feel you can conquer the world? How much energy does it take for you to feel enthusiastic and optimistic? Is it a struggle?

Step 1 helps us recognize what we are thinking and saying to ourselves *automatically*, so we can decide if this commentary is helpful. Our automatic thoughts and verbalizations are frequently *not* our best, most creative responses. This is because they are deeply rooted in past experiences. Our habitual remarks are formed in situations when we have received negative feedback about our ability to be successful. Over time, we internalize the critical judgments made by external authority figures (parents, teachers, bosses, etc.) who were in the habit of pointing out our mistakes, weaknesses, failures, and errors, even in a well-intentioned effort to help us improve. These internalized negative self-images are just below the surface, just waiting to be triggered by the next stressful situation. Step 1 offers a "creative break" in the action, which is especially beneficial in the heat of the moment when pessimistic thinking may automatically overwhelm a more optimistic view.

Step 2: Thoughts create feelings

You may not realize that language has the power to escalate your anxiety and overall stress level. Words are powerful, so we need to turn up the volume on our Internal Optimist and tell the Internal Pessimist to put a sock in it. When faced with work overload, deadlines, and lack of cooperation from others, critical commentary can fan the flames of your pessimism. On the other hand, you can intentionally coach yourself into an optimistic mind-set that helps douse the fire and frees you up to generate great ideas and take positive action.

Has your Internal Pessimist ever said anything like this to you:

> "I'll never finish, and somebody's going to pay for this mess."
>
> "I am always behind the eight ball—what's my problem?"
>
> "You'd have to be a magician to get all this done!"

Pessimistic statements such as these promote feelings of helplessness that in turn trigger resentment, frustration, anger, fear, and feeling overwhelmed. The comments of our Internal Pessimist foster feelings that lead to self-doubt and low motivation.

Contrast the remarks of the Internal Pessimist with the commentary of your Internal Optimist:

> "Let's see if I can renegotiate the deadline."
>
> "Working intensely makes time fly."
>
> "Giving this my best effort is my reward."
>
> "I'll learn from this tough situation and prevent the same mistakes from happening in the future."

Even when the situation is admittedly tough, with coaching messages we can encourage rather than discourage ourselves. The Internal Optimist mentality will engage our enthusiasm and give us a sense of being in charge of how to respond to any challenge. The self-confidence and determination that follow tilt the odds in our favor so we can maximize our effectiveness in meeting the demands at hand.

Most people never register the personal contributions they make to

For you, there is only one road that can lead to God and this is fidelity, to remain constantly true to yourself, to what you feel is highest in you. The road will open before you as you go.

Teilhard de Chardin

their own sense of emotional upset or emotional well-being. Being determinedly optimistic can influence your own attitude and that of the people around you. It's possible to enjoy pulling out all the stops to meet a deadline. It is even possible, although more challenging, to remain deeply joyful about being alive even while being devastated by a tragic turn of events.

Critical commentary pierces us through with anxiety, anger, and hopelessness. Optimistic commentary, on the other hand, helps us switch into a Creative mind-set.

Guiding Principles: See the Glass as Half Full ... with a Pitcher of Water on the Way!

- Obviously it's important to have goals, but it is equally important to be flexible as circumstances change.
- By trying to micromanage a specific set of outcomes when facing a challenge, we limit the range of our influence.
- Self-optimism helps us respond more effectively and creatively, no matter what the demands. This expands the range of our influence and can yield surprisingly positive outcomes.
- With the exception of ourselves, another person—someone who really knows our strengths and shortcomings, who cares deeply for our welfare, and who is able to articulate how we are best suited to respond to the variety of demands a challenge presents—is our best resource for generating self-optimism.

JOHN'S STORY, CONTINUED

I remember the most productive long-distance coaching session I ever had with John. It happened on a rainy Wednesday afternoon. John placed an urgent phone call to me from Kennedy Airport just ten minutes before boarding a 737 back to St. Louis. "How do you dance with Attila the Hun?" he asked in a strained voice, without even saying hello. I recognized John's voice immediately and could hear his intense frustration tinged with humor, so I decided to play with the humorous edge by replying, "Who

would have ever guessed that you would be the one to discover Attila the Hun alive and well in Manhattan?"

John jumped in. "Attila's first name is Mike. He can be
seen daily committing verbal acts of carnage from his
42nd floor executive suite overlooking Madison Avenue, or
from his ground floor library in Saddle Creek, New
Jersey." We both laughed. I could tell from our brief banter
back and forth that John felt thrown off his game by his
encounter with "Attila the likes of Mike." I could sense, too,
that John wasn't quite sure exactly how to recover. He
talked fast and I listened intently.

In his summary description, John explained, "Mike is a
classic adult bully. He attacks anyone who has what he
wants. He wrestles the goods away from you, insults you
to your face, and then steps on your reputation as he
makes his exit. He has been having conversations with
some of my clients, and is trashing me behind my back.
How in the world do you expect me to 'relate' to an SOB
like this guy? No trust, no tango."

I knew we were very short on time. I wanted to offer
John my support and at least some semblance of an idea
about what his next move might be. My mind flashed on a
story I had just heard about an interaction between Tich
Nat Han—an exiled Vietnamese Buddhist priest—and the
United States Congress. In 1964, Tich Nat Han traveled to
Washington, D.C., to solicit support in the U.S. Senate and
House of Representatives for a cease-fire that would bring
an end to the Vietnam War. My mind kept zooming in on a
particular interchange in his testimony. Senator Goldwater
opened his inquiry by asking Tich Nat Han, "Are you from
the North or from the South?" Reportedly, Tich Nat Han
answered, "Neither. I'm from the Center."

I told John that story and repeated Tich Nat Han's
response to Goldwater's question twice. "Neither. I'm from
the Center. Neither. I'm from the Center."

"Great story, but what does it have to do with me and
Mike the hatchet man?" John said as he cut off what I was
about to say next.

I replied, "On your flight home, consider how you might
shift from negative to neutral, or the center, when it comes
to your overall view of Mike. You don't have to be 'for' or

'against' Mike to 'relate' to him. With an adversarial person like Mike—a guy who loves to fight and looks for the next enemy to conquer—you're better off not taking the bait. Step into the mind-set of a Tich Nat Han or a court-appointed arbitrator. Right this minute you feel like his enemy—someone who has been blindsided and who is one down. You want to retaliate. That's a perfectly understandable reaction. Mike did hammer you, and you are operating with all of your reactive circuits turned on high. However, as you are well aware, there is another way of responding that will lead to many more creative options for 'relating' to Mike. Sit back for a few minutes after take-off, reflect, and move more toward a neutral position when it comes to Mike. Ask yourself how you can minimize the damage he wants to cause, and how you could use Mike's destructive tactics to your benefit. Who needs to know about Mike's unscrupulous business practices—tactics that blow up people's resources and destroy perfectly good business relationships? How could you increase your credibility as a businessman and business partner by bringing the carnage Mike causes to the attention of other interested parties who have a lot to lose if Mike gets in their way?"

John had to run for his plane, but all the way home on his flight, he imagined how he could use this disturbing series of interactions with Mike to his best advantage. By following this train of thought, John felt an immediate shift in his view of Mike—broader, more realistic. He became more optimistic, even eager, to see what good he could make happen as a result of dealing with Mike's destructive moves. He was enjoying the challenge.

The next day, when John and I met at my office, we were both amazed at how differently he felt about Mike and about his prospects for achieving damage control. He had been thinking about turning the trouble Mike had caused to his own advantage.

John's view of Mike had turned from disdain to pity. John transformed his fear of what Mike might do to harm his business relationships into an urgent need to take action. He had spent the morning contacting each of his colleagues who needed to be warned about Mike's latest coup. John had called a meeting of his direct reports to solicit their ideas for regaining the ground they may have lost with clients. He had a quick exchange with his legal counsel to scope out possible lawsuits.

All in all, John felt much less hooked by the way Mike operated in the world. In fact, he now was playing by the rules of his own game, not Mike's, for the first time ever—plus he had mastered another skill essential to achieving more of what he wanted: the skill of shifting from negative to neutral in a tough adversarial situation.

What had changed overnight was John's attitude. When he boarded his flight home, he wanted revenge. By the next day, he had thought of ways to use Mike's meddling to actually strengthen his relationships with certain clients. Mike hadn't changed at all, and probably never would, but John was able to generate self-optimism about his ability to handle Mike, and that made all the difference.

You know the story of the three brick masons. When the first man was asked what he was building, he answered gruffly, without even raising his eyes from his work, "I'm laying bricks." The second man replied, "I'm building a wall." But the third man said enthusiastically and with obvious pride, "I'm building a cathedral."

Margaret M. Stevens, from *Chop Wood, Carry Water*

STEP THREE

Make the Future Happen Inside You

How to Walk Your Talk

- Think Big, Think New
- Be the Change You Want to See

Next you need to bridge the best of what is and has been with the best of what can be, and give up any counterproductive habits that might sabotage your future.

> The best way to predict the future is to create it.
>
> Peter Drucker

115

ALBERT EINSTEIN

Einstein attended the Kanton Schule, whose founder, Johann Pestalozzi, believed that visual understanding must precede all other forms of education. In his younger years, Einstein was thoroughly schooled in mind's eye visualization: seeing and feeling a physical situation, tangibly manipulating the elements, and then observing (in his imagination) the consequences of his "thought experiments."

Later in his life Einstein explained to psychologist Max Wertheimer that he only vaguely understood the nature of his visual thinking and where it would take him. He said his "feeling of direction was very hard to express."

In one groundbreaking visualization, Einstein pretended to be a photon moving at the speed of light. Mentally he stepped inside the photon to imagine what he could see and feel from inside. Then he became a second photon and tried to imagine what he would experience of the first one.

Einstein once confided to his colleague Jacque Hommard that his mental strengths did not lie in the process of language or even, for that matter, mathematics. "The psychological entities which seem to serve as elements in thought," he noted, "are certain signs and more or less clear images which can be voluntarily reproduced or combined."

Think Big, Think New

What you need to DO   Challenge the Status Quo

What you need to BE   Imaginative and Visionary

We are able to invent the future that is most meaningful to us by painting the big picture with the colors of our unique perspective and desires. Once envisioned, and rehearsed within our mind and heart, the future we desire begins to seep into everyday life with magnetic force. We discover the seeds of our vision in all we think, say, and do.

When we are imaginative and visionary, we can think big enough and new enough to conjure up multiple positive scenarios. We need to let go of preordained notions of how things *should* or *must* turn out in favor of allowing many best alternatives to emerge. In place of attempting to control the future by planning it and predicting it, we can be open to the streams of consciousness that flood our awareness until it is overflowing with possibilities. Then our ingenuity will channel the direction of these scenarios. Like digging gullies to channel rainwater in the desert, we dig deeply into the soil of our being, so who we are and what we want most to create will shape the future, and the future will course through the deepest parts of our being. Through reflection and conversation, we form a brilliant, detailed view of the best possible future—the one that we will give 100 percent to bringing forth. Out of the thousand different scenarios possible, this is the future that means the most to us. We've lived it once in our imagination, and now we are ready to live it again for real.

Status Quo: Defender of the familiar, enemy of change

We all learned early and often that the Status Quo has a preference for keeping life the way it is. At its best, the Status Quo keeps things from changing too radically, too fast. At its worst, it makes us stagnate, shrivel up, and die. To be fully alive, we need fresh ideas, energy, and enthusiasm. We need (and deserve) to have hopes, dreams, and ideas that seem crazy. When we begin to imagine what we really want, we fling aside the drapes and throw open the windows of the stifling, sealed room of the Status Quo, allowing light and air to animate our vision of the future.

A vision without a task
Is but a dream,
A task without a vision is drudgery,
A vision and a task
Is the hope of the world.

From a church in Sussex,
England, c. 1730

But the Status Quo won't give up easily. If we are honest with ourselves, we have to admit that often, especially in a rapid-fire world, we derive a certain amount of comfort from knowing that things will have a tendency to remain the way they are as long as the Status Quo is operating. Like gravity, the Status Quo puts us solidly on the ground, to operate in a world we know, so we don't follow wild ideas and foolish notions into uncharted, dangerous worlds. No matter how much we might complain, most of us prefer the known to the unknown—even if the world we know is not serving our best interests.

Here you will learn how to challenge the Status Quo of your own existence so you are better able to achieve the next, best version of yourself, your partnerships, and your productivity. You'll learn how to challenge your internal Status Quo so you don't stagnate and stop creating the life you want. In the process, you will also learn how to let go of the natural human tendency to keep seeing yourself and your world in the same way. You will learn how to unleash the powers of your creative imagination so you can trade in your outdated images of the way your life is and has been for new images of the way your life could be—if only you create it that way.

It turns out that the images we hold, deep within our minds and hearts, are among the most powerful forces we possess in shaping the future we want. If we harbor images of ourselves and our world that protect the Status Quo, we and the world we live in will tend to stay the same. We will stay in the Reactive mind-set, changing only through trial and error or when our very survival depends on it. In this mind-set, change is unpleasant because it forces us to make difficult adjustments. Because we are not creating the life we want, we are forced to make painfully tough adjustments to the blows life deals us. To make matters worse, the blows tend to come more and more frequently in a rapid-fire world, until we feel we're attending the school of hard knocks.

In contrast, if we shift to imagining our future out of a Creative mind-set, the fibers of our everyday existence will absorb those positive images we create like a dry sponge absorbs water. Soon we begin to filter everyday challenges through the positive images of what the future holds. Once positive images of the best possible future flow freely inside our imagination, we will use whatever happens to us and we will do whatever it takes to make that future come true. Being flooded with positive images of what the best possible future might hold defies the Status Quo and motivates us to grow, to change, and to strive for the future we most desire.

Realizing the fullest potential of what the future offers could be easy or difficult, quick or prolonged, simple or complex—it doesn't matter which. When we are filled with positive images, all that matters to us is bringing what we know to be possible into existence. Unfortunately, many of us have forgotten, or never understood in the first place, the power of positive images in shaping the best possible outcomes of our lives.

The chart below summarizes how the Reactive mind-set and Creative mind-set each foster significantly different images of the future. Use this chart to help you deepen your understanding of how the Reactive mind-set cultivates the Status Quo, while the Creative mind-set nurtures growth, development, increased effectiveness, and positive change.

How Do You Imagine the Future?

Reactive mind-set The future is ...	Creative mind-set The future is ...
• Shaped by past performance	• Shaped by future potential
• Activated by external rewards	• Activated by internal desires
• Governed by our reaction to minimize threat, danger, risk	• Governed by our intentional choice to seize opportunities

continued on next page

How Do You Imagine the Future? (continued)

Reactive mind-set The future is ...	Creative mind-set The future is ...
• Focused on stability and maintaining the Status Quo	• Focused on growth and achieving new levels of effectiveness

Ultimately, the shape your future takes is up to you and the way you use your powers of imagination and vision. With positive images and positive visions, you will act in the direction of achieving the next, best version of yourself personally, in your partnerships, in your productivity, and in the world in which we live. I believe each of us will choose positive images over negative images every time. So our challenge is to eliminate negative images and promote positive images that can lead the way to the kind of lives we really want to be living.

Happiness doesn't depend upon who you are or what you have; it depends solely upon what you think.

Dale Carnegie

The power of images makes us weak—or strong

The images we hold in our minds are powerful beyond belief. They can carry us back in time to a romantic summer night, a first kiss, a love come true. They can fill us with anticipation, enticing us to savor one more scoop of homemade ice cream. The images we hold can bring us to our knees with fear or grief or deep regret. *More than the most eloquent logic or reason, more than the purest values or beliefs, images have the power to motivate us and provoke us to take action.*

Years ago I was involved in a training program for preschool teachers. The focus of the program was teaching them how to help young children develop, and we illustrated certain principles with case histories of real children in real situations. A three-and-a-half-year-old little girl named Lynnda was a prime example of a small child who was able to overcome her debilitating fears with the help of a nursery school teacher. The teacher helped Lynnda generate a positive image that gave her the confidence she needed to take a step forward in achieving important goals.

Lynnda's parents were upper middle class, well educated, and in their early forties. They were devoted to Lynnda and vowed to provide for her in every way possible. After searching thoroughly for the best preschool, they enrolled Lynnda in a special nursery program designed to help children develop their mental, emotional, and social skills. Lynnda was somewhat shy, so the program seemed like a good match for her.

Even though her mother remained with her in the classroom, the first few days of nursery school were difficult for Lynnda. She sat silently next to her mother until it was time to go home. Only occasionally did she respond to the friendly encouragement from her teachers and the other children to join in with the group's activities.

On the fifth day, it was agreed that Lynnda's mother would not stay inside the classroom. The girl cried inconsolably as she watched her mother walk out of sight. When the children and teachers coaxed Lynnda to come and play, she cried even harder. Nothing they offered calmed her.

One of her teachers took her hand, sat down next to her and said, "Show me how you and your mommy play at home." Lynnda looked at the teacher, who repeated gently, "Lynnda, can you show me how you and your mommy play when you're at home?"

Lynnda led her teacher over to a box full of brightly colored blocks, looked up and said, "Let's play picnic!"

The teacher was able to calm Lynnda because she realized that if the little girl could conjure up a positive image of her mother playing with her, that internal image would be enough to reassure Lynnda that she had not really lost her mother at all. Her mother in fact was only one, positive image away.

The teacher was wise to choose an activity like playing, because Lynnda was too young to be consoled by language alone, and, since this was only her fifth day of preschool, she had few positive prior experiences to draw upon. If Lynnda had been older, the teacher might have taken a different approach. As we mature, our powers of imagination grow with us, so that by the time we are adults we have the capacity to conjure up highly complex images that can shape our future, guide our actions, and affect the outcomes of our lives. All we have to do is learn how to activate our imagination so it facilitates (rather than retards) our progress toward important goals.

We are what we think. All that we are arises with our thoughts. With our thoughts, we make the world.
Siddhārtha Gautama (the Buddha)

Positive images play an important role in healing and even in sports. Why not in life?

Doctors have long known that giving a patient an inert substance such as a sugar pill can, remarkably, make a patient better. This phenomenon is known as the placebo effect. The patient expects to get better, and does—without any true medical intervention. One patient, in a dramatic case that has been documented in the medical literature, received a saline injection and cured himself of numerous cancerous tumors in a matter of days. Against all odds, he completely regained his health.

The power of the human mind also can make us worse. When the patient above stopped believing in the efficacy of his anticancer injections, the tumors grew back and he died! Another patient with severe allergies to flowers had a full-fledged allergic reaction to a bouquet of *plastic* roses. And in some ancient cultures, where it is believed that certain spells are fatal, otherwise healthy people on the receiving end of a hex will simply lie down and die.

If these examples don't make you want to work on your positive attitude, consider the following. When I was the director of a Stress Center, part of my job was working in a cardiac rehabilitation program. It was indisputably clear that patients who worried about the outcome of their surgery fared worse than patients who believed strongly in the surgery and felt certain of a positive outcome. In this case, their positive attitude augmented the success of a medically viable treatment.

Who else looks for positive outcomes? Athletes, for one. If you've ever watched Olympic high diving, you've seen each diver poised at the end of the diving board, mentally performing his or her gold medal dive before actually making the jump. This is what you will do with your Level 3 agenda.

There is a classic experiment that illustrates how positive mental images can improve physical performance. In this experiment, basketball players are assigned at random to one of three different practice groups. The players assigned to the first group are instructed to spend an extra 30 minutes per day practicing their free throws. Players in the second group are told to relax, to forget about basketball, and to engage in some other 30-minute activity after each practice session. Players in the third group are asked to spend 30 minutes of practice time visualizing themselves shooting and making free-throw baskets.

This experiment has been replicated many times and the findings are consistent. On average, the group that practices their shots improves their free-throw scores by an average of 23 percent. The group that relaxes and engages in an alternative activity does not improve their free-throw scores during an official game. But the players who visualize themselves shooting and making their free throws improve their actual free-throw scores in a game by 23 percent (the same average rate as the practice group!).

Closer investigation of these results reveals that the neuromuscular pathways involved in shooting baskets from a free-throw line are activated in players who conjure up positive images of making successful free throws. This suggests that once you know how to make a free throw, visualizing that action creates the same chain reaction in your mind and body as actual practice. In effect, this experiment is telling us that our neuromuscular pathways may not be able to tell the difference between *imagining* and *performing*. This experiment and others like it lend strong support to the notion that positive images lead to positive actions that lead to positive outcomes.

These three types of positive imaging—the placebo effect, a positive attitude before surgery, and athletic visualization—help to create the best possible outcomes in the world for each individual. Your vision of the future will work in the same way. Once you have a clear and powerful vision, you will create experiences that match it, and through your positive actions your vision will become real. Don't get bogged down in verbalizing and explaining your vision; it is meant to be an action plan. And make sure your vision is more vibrant and compelling than your past or present, so it will keep pulling you ahead into the future you imagine.

Expectations tend to create themselves in the real world, so monitor what you expect of others—and what they expect of you.

Negative images, expectations, and treatment can make even gifted individuals underachievers. But positive images, expectations, and treatment can elevate the achievements of others, even those with severe intellectual, emotional, and behavioral limitations. What astounds me even more is the fact that some researchers report being able to induce the Pygmalion effect in less than 15 minutes! This evidence should wake us up to the contagious power of negative or positive images we hold of others, and that others hold of us.

As you work toward implementing your vision of the future, you are not alone. Bring along those who believe in you, persuade others to believe in you, and get away from people who don't think the best of you. Keep visualizing your Level 3 agenda until it lives inside you and colors everything you do. Make your vision so real that you can almost taste it, and others will be drawn in, nearly as captivated by it as you are. Positive images spur positive actions that promote positive outcomes.

When what you see is brand new, what you get is brand new.

Jake and I met when he was given a leadership assignment that would make or break his career with a best-in-class engineering firm. Fourteen months earlier, Jake had transferred back to his hometown of Chicago to take a position as the corporate director of training and development. His first assignment was to centralize training and development. This was a significant task, and if Jake succeeded in accomplishing it, his position in the company would be assured.

Shortly after he accepted his new job, his boss left, and Jake lost his power base. Every effort Jake made to centralize training and development fell short. People liked the Status Quo, they didn't find the idea of centralized training very compelling, and Jake didn't have the authority to tell them they had to do it. In the end, he reconciled himself to the fact that his training colleagues at the company's eight plant sites and six sales offices would remain autonomous. Jake himself decided to focus only on the needs of the corporate office. He felt defeated and upset with himself for not being able to bring the members of the separate training divisions together as a unified team.

Almost a year passed before Jake's boss was replaced. By that time Jake had settled into a routine existence on the job. Every day, he kept to himself and focused on the training needs of those who worked in the corporate office. He rarely contacted or heard from his counterparts elsewhere.

As soon as the new corporate vice president of human resources had enough of the lay of the land, he set an agenda for the department. Once the agenda was set, Jake's new boss revived his initial assignment. He asked Jake to lead a team of his peers to plan and implement a more centralized service for training and development. This time, however, Jake's boss sent out a memo sharing his expectation of 100 percent compliance. Then he asked me to help Jake be successful in his new leadership role, and to consult with the team on how to best set up the system.

I wasn't sure how Jake would feel about his "new" assignment, given the number of false starts he already had made. To my surprise, and to Jake's credit, he quickly decided that with his new mandate and the full participation of his colleagues, this time his efforts would be effective. From the moment I met him, Jake imagined that centralized training and development could offer higher quality services, at a significantly lower cost, for every level and location of the company.

In our first planning session, I commented to Jake that his enthusiasm and positive vision were rare in a person who had failed in several previous attempts to achieve a challenging goal. Making a comeback from adversity or failure is very hard work. Jake explained to me that he had undertaken his previous efforts alone, without the support and confidence of his boss, and without the help of a consultant and a team. Jake reasoned, and rightly so, that his boss and I expected him to succeed. We both knew of his failed attempts and believed in him in spite of those failures. Jake used our positive expectations of him as an effective leader to give him the boost he needed to try again.

Jake and I decided that the first step he would take with his team of colleagues would be to share his positive images of what the future would hold if the training and development could be successfully centralized. To gain their confidence and support, Jake also would ask his colleagues to offer their most positive vision of what centralization could mean to the company, to all of the employees, and to every colleague on his planning team.

Jake had a conversation with each person individually to exchange positive visions, and he brought the team together to create a shared vision. By the time the team collectively exchanged their positive images of the best possible future for training and development, a whole set of new possibilities emerged. The vision they built collectively was richer and more compelling than any one of the visions they held individually before the team meeting.

It is important to track what happened here. First, Jake allowed his own internal positive image of the best future for training and development to grow in response to the support he felt from me and from his boss. Second, he bolstered the internal positive vision of what could be possible within the mind and heart of each member of the team through the one-on-one conversations with each person. Third, Jake convened the team and asked them to create a positive vision of the future that was compelling for everyone on the team. In three steps, the positive images of the future grew in magnitude, first within Jake, then within each individual involved, and then within the team collectively.

These shared positive images and vision of the future sparked thoughtful, carefully executed effort from all concerned. In a matter of days the implementation plan to centralize training that had fizzled in the past was well on its way to completion. There was no one prouder, nor more relieved, than Jake. As for me, I felt honored to be able to witness and participate in such a prime example of how positive images can help us achieve our goals by galvanizing others to envision what is possible and to undertake the actions needed to realize that best of all possible futures.

Your past can be a bridge between your present and the future.

Rarely do we take the time to realize that the seeds of our future are hidden inside of how we have responded to what has happened to us in our past. In fact, we can get a glimpse of the future we want to achieve by examining how we have responded to the most recent challenges we faced. If we don't understand how we have already grown, and if we can't appreciate how we have already accomplished important milestones that have prepared us to be successful in reaching our newest set of goals, we are left believing that the future is completely separate and distant from the way we have lived our lives up until now.

The future doesn't have to seem like a separate and distant phase of our existence. We can search our past and most recent experiences for evidence of continuity. When you begin to glimpse how your Level 3 goals have emerged slowly but surely out of the life you are living and have lived, you will believe in their goodness and rightness more than you ever have before.

As you analyze the progress you have made toward your Level 3 goals to date, you will build the foundation for discovering your progress in real time, as it is happening. When you are able to recognize your progress firsthand, as it unfolds, this enhances your progress more than you can imagine. You can see yourself grow, and others grow, before your very eyes. You can detect the early signs that progress is being made, and then act to augment that progress.

> *It is by logic that we prove, but by intuition that we discover … Logic teaches us that on such and such a road we are sure of not meeting an obstacle; it does not tell us which is the road that leads to the desired end. For this it is necessary to see the end from afar. And the faculty that teaches us to see is intuition.*
>
> Henri Poincaré

The most important lesson to remember here is that all personal growth and success begins with a positive image to light the way. Once you can hold a vivid image of your future destination in your mind and heart, you can see that future as it most surely exists—in the past, in the present, and even more fully in days to come.

BEST PRACTICES

I have chosen the next set of Best Practices to help you cultivate the art of creating and sustaining positive images. When you combine your positive images, you will be thinking big and thinking new to form a comprehensive vision of the best possible future.

As you read and practice these exercises, you will activate one of your most powerful creative resources: the inner resource we call *imagination*. By using your imagination, you can begin to make the future happen inside of yourself. And, as we've discussed in detail, the future you see from the inside is the future you will bring to fruition on the outside.

To "walk your talk" means being congruent in what you say and do. In the negative ("She doesn't walk her talk") the phrase is a criticism. We mistrust people whose words and actions don't match. The exercises you are about to practice are designed to encourage positive images that will inspire positive actions, positive actions that will trigger positive conversations, and positive conversations that will foster positive outcomes. As you adopt these Best Practices you will be able to "walk your talk" ... right into the future you most desire. You will relish the experience of having what you think, say, and do work in unison to help you achieve the goals most important to you.

BEST PRACTICE #12

As You Think, So Shall You Act

Treat this Best Practice as a warm-up exercise. It is designed to open your mind, to rearrange some of your beliefs about how your images can work to influence your actions, and to sharpen your imaging skills. Initially, when I learned about the exercise, I was highly skeptical. In the beginning I thought it was some sort of "cheap parlor trick." Then, when I actually did the exercise, I understood its value. Suspend your preconceived notions, follow the instructions, and see what happens.

You'll need a piece of household string approximately 24 inches long and a single, metal washer to complete this exercise. Read the directions for each step all the way through before you begin the practice.

Step 1. Attach the washer to one end of the string by pulling the string through the hole in the washer and tying a knot in the string to secure it.

Step 2. Hold the top of the string between your thumb and forefinger. Extend your arm about 12 inches from your body, chest high, letting the washer dangle in front of you. Wait for the washer to stop moving.

Step 3. Once the washer is still, look at it and begin to think about it rotating clockwise. Don't move a muscle. Imagine the washer turning in a clockwise direction until it starts rotating. Despite the fact that you aren't moving, the washer will begin to rotate.

Step 4. After several clockwise rotations, imagine that the washer is still. Keep imagining that the washer is still until it stops rotating clockwise. (Again, do not move your body, arm, or fingers in any way.)

Step 5. When the washer is still, reverse your thinking and imagine that the washer is rotating counterclockwise. Keep imagining a counterclockwise rotation until the washer begins turning.

Stop reading now, and practice the exercise before you read any further.

Most people are amazed that they are able to influence the direction the washer rotates without moving their body, arm, or fingers. When I ask people to explain how the phenomenon actually works, they are usually at a complete loss. I can almost see them thinking, Could what I am imagining actually influence which way the washer rotates? The correct answer is yes *and* no.

Here's what happens to create this phenomenon. As you keep the washer on the end of the string stationary and hold your body, arm, and finger still, you limit the responses of your body to ones that are almost undetectable. However, your thumb and forefinger have a pulse running through them. This pulse is actually a specific rhythm that corresponds to your image of the washer rotating clockwise. This pulse shifts to a different, specific rhythm as you imagine a counterclockwise rotation, and still another unique rhythm as you imagine the washer on the string hanging motionless.

The primary reason I am suggesting you practice this exercise is so you will fully appreciate the fact that what you think is directly tied to the actions you take. When you imagine something is "so," your body will respond in subtle and dramatic ways to act on that thought. Then, the actions your body takes reinforce the thought you hold. The same kind of feedback loop works when I believe someone is threatening me. My physiology responds accordingly and prepares me for fight or flight. My bodily responses increase my fear or anger, and I see the person as a bigger threat.

In effect, this exercise demonstrates a rudimentary form of biofeedback. In laboratory experiments, human beings have demonstrated an incredible ability to lower blood pressure, increase alpha waves in the brain, and increase the vascular blood supply simply by watching a signal on a monitor that shows what is actually happening in their cardiovascular and neuromuscular systems.

As the old adage says, "Seeing is believing." Your experience with the rotating washer and our knowledge of biofeedback might also reinforce the more controversial idea that "believing is seeing." I am certain that both propositions are true. As you imagine that the future you want most is indeed possible, you will begin to see that future emerge inside of you and all around you. And as you see the confirming evidence that your best possible future is coming true, you will believe in that possibility even more strongly.

BEST PRACTICE #13

FINDING YOUR FUTURE IN YOUR PAST

If "seeing is believing" and "believing is seeing," then this Best Practice is one great way to accomplish

Focus, then, means awareness, discernment, order, clarity, insight—they are like attributes of love. The act of focusing itself has beauty and meaning; it is the act that continues into meditation, into poetry. Indeed as soon as the least of us stands still, that is the moment when something extraordinary is seen to be going on in the world.

Eudora Welty

both. This practice will show you how to see your Level 3 goals from a wider perspective than you've ever seen them before. It will help you build newfound confidence and *belief* in your goals so you are better able to see those goals come true in the days and weeks to come.

Step 1: Looking back

Reflect on the Life Map you created for yourself as you learned how to question reality (see pages 41–42). Remember that your Life Map provides you with the highlights of significant events that you have experienced. How you responded to those life-shaping events has determined their impact on your growth and development—for better or worse. In this Best Practice, review your Life Map with the following questions in mind. Your answers will help you see how you have made progress in each important domain of your life.

Question 1: What personal skills and capacities have I already developed in response to my life-shaping experiences?
John believes he developed a reverence for life and an ability to assess the relative importance of emerging issues as a result of experiencing the sudden death of his best friend, Charlie.

Question 2: In what ways have I strengthened my partnerships and deepened my capacity to relate to others in response to my life-shaping experiences?
John noticed that through witnessing the birth of his children and experiencing unwavering support from his wife he has been able to trust other people more than he did as an adolescent and young adult. He also attributes his confidence in himself as a true "people

person" to his growing interest in doing what he can do to help his wife and children realize their unique talents and potential.

Question 3: How have my life-shaping experiences enhanced my productivity?
For the strides he has made in productivity, John gives the most credit to his willingness to emulate role models. He learned from others how best to add value to his business and to the community he lives in. In John's assessment of himself, he discovered that he cultivated mentors who were excellent strategic thinkers, great business minds, successful risk takers, and industry trend setters—in that order.

Step 2: Looking for links
Next, examine the Level 3 goals that you set for yourself (see page 93) and ask yourself the questions below. As you see the connection between how you have already grown and developed, and how you intend to grow and develop, your belief in your Level 3 goals will become much stronger. These connections will prove to you that you are primed to achieve the best possible future you have set your sights on achieving.

Question 1: How will the personal skills and capacities I have already developed prepare me or directly help me to achieve my Level 3 personal *goals?*

Question 2: How will the partnership skills and capacities I have already developed prepare me or directly help me to achieve my Level 3 partnership *goals?*

Question 3: How will the productivity skills and capacities I have already developed prepare me or directly help me to achieve my Level 3 productivity *goals?*

In this step, John considered each of these questions before be responded to any one of them. I recommend you do the same. Let yourself reflect and wonder about the whole set of questions for a while before answering any one of them.

Ultimately John saw that his insatiable curiosity, his ability to learn quickly, his propensity to find and emulate great mentors, his devotion to helping his family grow and develop, and his high need for challenging goals and to be first at achieving something, would all promote his progress toward his current Level 3 goals (learning to ask questions effectively, being collaborative in high-stakes decision-making, and promoting a highly creative company culture during periods of rapid growth).

Even more important, John could see how the progression of his own growth laid the foundation for achieving his Level 3 goals. For example, he noticed that in the Productivity Domain he started out by learning from mentors who were excellent strategists and operational experts. Now he was ready to find mentors who could show him how to foster creativity and be as effective with people as he had become with setting and executing strategy. It appeared to John to be a logical progression. In the Partnership Domain, he realized that his focus on relating effectively to his family was just what he needed before he reached out to establish more collaborative relationships on the job, and in turn worked to establish a strong faith in the wisdom of creating a future with others.

Step 3: Looking for evidence

With your strong belief in the continuity, relevance, and wisdom of your Level 3 goals, it is time for you to see how you might be realizing those goals already—without having noticed that you are. Please review your "Go for the Gold" master list of the rewards and benefits you have imagined will come true if you are successful in achieving your Level 3 goals (see page 93). Use your master list as a guide in discovering examples of how you may already be making progress in your personal, partnership, and productivity domains. Realize as you continue with this exercise that your "Go for the Gold" master list represents, in detail, your positive image of your best possible future. Keeping this master list of positive images in the forefront of your mind will create a vision that acts like a beacon to shed light on how you are already advancing toward the future you imagine.

Ask yourself the next set of questions to explore the variety of ways your vision may be already manifesting itself in your everyday life. Think back over the last day and week—the near past. Be sure you keep your master list of rewards and benefits in front of you at all times. Remember, this list is filled with the positive images that have the power to illuminate the many ways you are already achieving the future you want most.

Question 1: When have I acted in accordance with my Level 3 goals, and which rewards and benefits have I recently experienced as a result?

Question 2: When have others acted in accordance with my Level 3 goals, and which rewards and benefits have others experienced as a result?

Question 3: When have situations turned out in alignment with my Level 3 goals, and which rewards and benefits have been manifested as a result?

As John reflected on his recent past, he identified several experiences that proved he was indeed gaining ground when it came to achieving his Level 3 agenda.

- He recalled an instance when he referred a complaint he had received from a major client to the customer service team for resolution. John asked the team to let him know how they intended to solve the problem. He reassured the team that he would support whatever resolution they offered.
- One of John's direct reports sent an e-mail describing his new level of confidence in the new product development initiative.
- *The Wall Street Journal* referenced John's company as one of the best in their industry for on-time delivery of quality products.

When it comes to achieving the Level 3 goals that are most important to you, this Best Practice helps you form positive images of the history of your growth and achievement over time. These positive images of milestones of progress have the power to encourage you to move forward.

> *The happiness of a man in this life does not consist in the absence but in the mastery of his passions.*
> Alfred Lord Tennyson

This Best Practice also illuminates your most recent and current progress in realizing your positive images of the best possible future you can imagine. Doing this gives you a twofold advantage. It increases your confidence that you are and will be successful in achieving your Level 3 goals—after all, you are beginning to achieve elements of those goals right now. It also provides you with a more refined and comprehensive set of positive images that form a positive vision that pulls you toward the future with magnetic force.

Finally, when you engage in this Best Practice, you counteract your ingrained, detrimental habit of scouring the past for mistakes, failures, and barriers. This kind of pessimism lessens the likelihood of your achieving your Level 3 agenda. It supports your

> *The more faithfully you listen to the voice within you, the better you will hear what is sounding outside.*
> Dag Hammarskjold, from
> *Markings*

reactive, self-protective tendencies to watch out for what's not working and what's holding you back. Negative images and negative actions prevent you from creating a new and better future. That's the Status Quo at work!

Guiding Principles: Think Big, Think New

- You can't create the future without intimately knowing it, down to the last detail.
- A deep sense of what the future holds for us, for others, and for our world propels thoughts, words, and actions in the present.
- If we carry the past forward, it should be the best parts of the past, those that have prepared us and made us ready to create the future.
- A vision of the best possible future emerges as you weave your thoughts, emotions, ideas, fantasies, hopes, desires, and values into many different and compelling positive images.
- Whatever you become 100 percent committed to achieving, you will hang in there for it when the struggle is long.
- Remember this: Positive images lead to positive actions that foster positive outcomes.

JOHN'S STORY, CONTINUED

John was immediately attracted to the idea of encouraging himself and other people who were committed to the success of his company to think big and think new. Together John and I invented an ingenious visionary process called Creativity Quest to inspire new, more positive images of how creativity could be fostered while the company experienced rapid growth. The visionary process we invented followed this sequence of steps:

Step 1. John invited 12 people who had a stake in fostering the creativity of his company to take part in the Creativity Quest process. He included customers, suppliers, business development leaders, and sales and marketing managers.

Step 2. From 8:30 A.M. until 9:30 P.M., the Tuesday before Thanksgiving, John and his Creativity Quest team came together to think big, think new. In the culminating activity, each member of the team was given a piece of paper on which to record the positive image that he or she held of the best, most creative future for the company. There were some images on the back of each piece of paper, but the participants didn't know what the marks meant.

Step 3. John and I requested that each person write a statement that described what creativity would look like in response to a particular stressful situation that was likely to occur during rapid growth. For example, one person wrote, "Failure to satisfy a customer complaint would be viewed as an opportunity for a cross-functional team to win back customer confidence, and to prevent that problem from occurring in the future."

Step 4. Each participant turned his or her page over and wrote down a short personal statement that reflected one positive image of the future.

Step 5. All the pieces of paper were assembled on the wall to represent the vision of what a highly creative company culture would look like to all stakeholders. As the participants posted each one of their positive images of company creativity, a comprehensive vision of the best possible future was formed. And together, the mysterious marks on the 12 pieces formed a human face.

The mosaic made an amazing last impression on the way John internalized the best possible future for his leadership and his company's culture. It was a vision that the group as a whole could share, believe in, and sponsor. It was a vision that guided John and all the company leaders to work toward in unison.

Be the Change You Want to See

What you need to DO	Give Up Your Old Habits
What you need to BE	Observant and Innovative

Your vision is now alive inside of you. So far you've done a lot of thinking and reflecting. You've set your priorities, thoroughly examined the context of your life, and carefully shaped a future that you are completely excited about. Thinking big and new helped you to see that who you are and how you operate in the world can be dramatically different—more effective, more productive, and more life-giving to you and to your relationships that matter most. Like the root system of a magnificent oak tree, your vision of the best possible future will nourish your very existence from now on.

Even though they are very excited about their new Level 3 agenda, I find that many of my clients freeze up at this juncture, not knowing exactly how to step over the threshold into their new future. Others, like a large, lovable, and somewhat oblivious dog, rush headlong into trying to implement their vision right away. In the beginning, *all you need to do is act the way you plan to act in the future.* Little experiences that fit into your master plan will present themselves, and as you handle them in a new way, you will gradually make your vision real.

> *All living things respond to their environment. Your vision of the future is equally flexible.*

Before we delve any further into achieving what you want, let me make a point you'll want to remember going forward. As counterintuitive and paradoxical as this may seem, the more vital your vision, the more it is bound to change. You'll realize this as soon as you start living into your vision. The sheer number of demands, the barrage of pressures, and the volatile dynamics of a rapid-fire world, will offer you many opportunities to expand

and more fully define your vision. If you seize the opportunities, your vision will be filled with details and elements you never could have imagined before living into it.

The changeable quality of your ever-emerging and always expanding vision depends upon how vigilant you are, how deeply the vision is rooted inside of you, and how intensely you are engaged in a stimulating, rich life. Your present will flow through your vision, just as your vision will express itself in your present. This exchange between your vision and what your circumstances have to offer will create your best possible future. The vision you formed in calmer, saner days gone by was not nearly so emergent and dynamic. Now you're riding a tiger.

The greatest force in the human body is the natural drive of the body to heal itself—but that force is not independent of the belief system, which can translate expectations into psychological change. Nothing is more wondrous about the fifteen billion neurons in the human brain than their ability to convert thoughts, hopes, ideas, and attitudes into chemical substances. Everything begins, therefore, with belief. What we believe is the most powerful option of all.

Norman Cousins

When your vision is changing, this is a healthy sign that you are fully engaged in your world, and that your vision is malleable enough and resilient enough to grow as your experience and opportunities grow. Most of my clients find that, although the essence and intent of their goals remain the same, the specific ways in which those goals manifest themselves are often a surprise. Those surprises are what continue to shape and reshape the vision.

One of my clients who now operates out of her company's London office discovered by accident a new way to encourage high levels of enthusiasm in her software consulting firm. One day a client and his team came to Rita's offices for a planning session because they were in the midst of moving their offices. The clients were so intrigued with the consulting firm's open, living-room style work space, brightly colored furnishings, and conference areas equipped with kitchenettes and gourmet-quality food that they didn't want to leave. They stayed for three hours longer than scheduled and were unusually absorbed and involved in the meeting.

That day, the client's team was particularly energetic and alert. They posed such challenging questions and offered such novel solutions that Rita's consulting team was able to complete a comprehensive conversion plan in one meeting—something that had never happened so quickly and creatively before. In this accidental visit, both the client and the consulting team raised their creativity quotient, and as a consequence they defined a superior way to install the new software.

After several more experiments with inviting clients to planning meetings at the consulting firm's office, the practice was adopted by the firm worldwide. Rita and the London team got the credit for being observant enough to link the unusually high level of creativity with conducting planning sessions in the creative office environment of the firm. If she

> *Men make history, and not the other way around. In periods where there is no leadership, society stands still. Progress occurs when courageous, skillful leaders seize the opportunity to change things for the better.*
>
> Harry S Truman

and her team had failed to make this connection, they would never have instituted that client visit practice.

Carefully watching yourself, other people, and changing circumstances is critical to innovation and, in the long run, to "being the change you want to see." Now you will learn how to reap the benefits of being observant and how to modify your vision as your circumstances change, whether for better or for worse. When you see what is happening on its own accord, you can use those natural dynamics to advance your Level 3 agenda. Giving up your familiar habits and preconceived ideas can feel like tightrope walking without a net, but in fact your ingenuity and your commitment to your vision are always there to support you.

Keep an eye on your mistakes. They could hold secrets that can change the world.

We assume when we use a Post-It note or a spark plug, take penicillin or put on a rubber raincoat, that these things were purposely invented. In fact, they are all the products of serendipity. In each case, someone was trying to accomplish something else but had the ingenuity to capitalize on unforeseen events.

One afternoon in the late 1950s, Wilson Greatbatch made a mistake—a mistake that would change the beating of many human hearts significantly. While building an oscillator to record heart sounds, he accidentally installed a resistor with the wrong resistance into the unit. When it began to give off a steady electrical pulse, he realized that this small device could be used to regulate the human heartbeat. Heretofore, human hearts had been regulated by large machines the size of television sets. After spending the next two years refining his handmade instrument, he patented it as the world's first small implantable pacemaker. But he knew his work was hardly finished, as the little device had to be powered in some way. He continued to work over the next several years until he produced a corrosion-free lithium battery to power the pacemakers, which over the last forty years have kept millions of hearts beating regularly and saved millions of lives.

> *Tell me, what is it you plan to do with your one wild and precious life?*
> Mary Oliver

Velcro found its genesis in a walk with a dog. One fine afternoon in 1948, amateur Swiss mountaineer George de Mestral went out with his dog for a long hike in the mountains. When they returned some hours later, de Mestral noticed that his dog and his trousers were covered with burrs, the tiny seed sacs that cling to an animal's fur and thus travel to new planting grounds. He sat down and examined one under a microscope, where he noted all the little hooks that enable the burr to cling ferociously to its ride out of town. While combing the stubborn little burrs out of his dog's fur, de Mestral hatched the idea for Velcro. Though he met with derision and encountered many setbacks, de Mestral ultimately formed Velcro Industries, which within a short time was selling over 60 million yards of product a year. Today, what began as a burr on a dog has become a multimillion dollar industry in a better-fastened world.

> *Something we were withholding*
> *Made us weak—*
> *Until we learned*
> *It was ourselves we were withholding*
> *From this land of living—*
> *And thenceforth*
> *Found salvation*
> *In surrender.*
> Robert Frost

By tuning in deeply enough to the course of our experiences, we can exploit the positive potential inherent in serendipitous happenings. We can use what we see to shape and advance our vision of what is possible. The dynamics we observe will teach us how to make that future come true. In short, we have to surrender as well as lead.

Unanticipated or unusual, emergent dynamics are stepping-stones to success. Observing subtle (or even obscure) opportunities is an art well worth cultivating. Capitalizing on rare, serendipitous, but potentially useful processes makes the difference between feeling creative (rather than reactive) in the course of achieving whatever you may want most to achieve.

Imitate others shamelessly and often.

"Do not copy answers from someone else's paper." "Never plagiarize." "Be sure your thinking is original." "Don't let your work be a poor imitation." Growing up in the world of faster-harder-smarter means learning early that to imitate or copy the thinking, opinions, or ideas of someone else is "cheating" and bordering on sinful. I learned this in school and then at work. The direction was to always strive for greater and greater levels of mastery in domains such as abstract thinking, problem solving, analytical thinking, creative expression (writing, painting, playing music, speech making), leadership, team building, athletic prowess, and the like. I was led to believe that my advancement in these areas depended almost exclusively upon *my* commitment, *my* diligence, and *my* study. It took me years to figure out that I could enrich my repertoire of skill and deepen my reserves of creative resources if I learned my lessons from people who already embodied the kind of changes I wanted to make.

You can use your powers of observation to study people as well as circumstances. Best of all, you can simplify and enrich the process of achieving your Level 3 goals by observing and imitating people who already possess the change you want to see in yourself.

There is nobody better than my business partner, Judy Dubin, in being flexible enough, curious enough, eager and humble enough to change her mind on a dime whenever a situation warrants that kind of shift. Judy demonstrates this rare flexibility day in and day out, circumstance after circumstance. I've watched her closely in many types of conversations. When someone disagrees with a suggestion she's made, Judy asks questions until she is certain she understands the other person's point of view. She probes enthusiastically for how a different opinion might hold merit and be superior to her own idea. She explores someone else's opinion as she might a buried treasure.

When you are on the receiving end of her questions, it feels as if Judy is on *your* side and that she hopes your idea wins out on its own merit. If Judy does come to see that a suggestion made by someone else is better than her own, she is overtaken with joy. She treats her discovery like a gift. She's been known to gasp with sheer amazement as she thanks her thinking partners in the way you would thank someone who just handed you your favorite birthday present. In this department, Judy is my teacher and role model. I cherish every chance I get to observe her in action, so much so that one day it dawned on me that I want to be just like Judy whenever my opinion or suggestion is countered by a better idea. I realized that I wanted to learn more from her than how to develop an open mind. At a deeper, more essential level, what I really wanted to learn was how to experience the thrill and excitement that Judy seems to feel every time she finds a thought that she likes better than the one she came up with herself.

In my own exploration of this matter, I was struck by the contrast between how changing your mind feels to Judy and how it feels to me. When I converse with someone who has a great idea that never occurred to me, I tend to feel frustrated with myself for not thinking of it first. To be completely honest, I'd have to say that often I feel less competent than I believe I should be and want to be. As a result, I experience twinges of humiliation. Judy says she feels lucky to be with a person who can help her see something she's never seen before. For her, exchanging ideas is a learning fest—the better the suggestion she receives, the better she likes the exchange. It's as if she feels she has won the prize.

Which experience would you rather have? My frustration laced with humiliation? Or Judy's exhilaration? It's no contest. You (and any other sane person) would choose Judy's exhilara-

Change is a form of hope.
Linda Ellerbee

tion. Yet her experience is rare and mine is common—especially among high achievers. So how do you and I learn to change our minds generously with enthusiasm and great joy?

The answer I came up with for myself, was to imitate Judy. I literally have forced myself to say and do what I believe Judy would say and do when I'm in a conversation and I like someone else's idea more than my own. First, I smile with appreciation (so I don't start frowning out of frustration). Then I say something with great enthusiasm, such as, "What a fantastic idea. How did you ever think of that?" By this time the other person has caught my energy and is usually very excited about having contributed such a valuable idea. With that kind of energetic excitement in response to my enthusiasm, we're off and running to generate more ideas.

Let me assure you that every word of what I've just told you is true. When I "pretend I am Judy," or try to be as skillful and as thrilled as she is, I know exactly what to think, say, and do. I've watched her hundreds of times and so I can imitate her well. All I need to do is remind myself that I want to create the experience that Judy would surely be able to create.

Why not think of someone you know well who has the spontaneous capacity to have a change of mind and of heart when another person offers an opinion worth adopting? Try doing with that person what I do with my partner Judy: watch carefully. Observe what he or she says and does. Ask questions about what kind of positive rewards he or she experiences as a result of adopting a new point of view. If you don't have your own role model in this arena, borrow what I've described about Judy to guide you, and try it in the world. Finding role models to imitate will help you learn how to acquire any Level 3 skills and capacity you may be seeking.

BEST PRACTICES

To be the change you want to see, you must realize the positive potential of your best, possible future while living and working with the pressure-filled realities of the rapid-fire world. I want to share two Best Practices with you that will help you achieve positive aspects of your Level 3 agenda almost immediately. These exercises are among the most powerful I know to help you cross the threshold from thinking about your vision to living it.

If you have built castles in the air, your work need not be lost; that is where they should be. Now put the foundations under them.

Henry David Thoreau

You don't need to rely strictly on your own creative imagination, vision, and actions to fully realize the potential power of your Level 3 goals. Instead, borrow creative energy from other people. When it comes to achieving what you want in a rapid-fire world, imitating those who already have realized in themselves the kind of resources you need is a terrific catalyst for your own growth and development.

People most quickly acquire and effectively put into practice new knowledge, attitudes, and skills by imitating others who already are proficient in what they want to learn. With this in mind, finding good role models to imitate becomes one of your primary tasks. Look for proficient role models in the circles you travel in most frequently—your work, your family, your friends, and others in the community you may meet more casually. Look for people who are proficient in what you want to learn, who hold positions of responsibility, who are readily visible to you, and who have a proven track record and broad experience in the arenas you are interested in developing. But please don't confine your search to people who fit only these criteria.

I once had a piece of furniture delivered by one of the most charming and cheerful men I've ever met. His job was low paying, repetitive, and backbreaking, yet he practically sparkled with enthusiasm, and immediately engaged me in a conversa-

If you can't change your fate, change your attitude.

Amy Tan

tion on a sports team I didn't know I cared about. After he left, I found I was still in a good mood. His optimism was like magic, and I try to imitate it whenever I fee that *my* job is difficult.

You can find role models in almost every encounter—while checking out of a grocery store, or coaching children to play a sport, or listening to the radio, or watching television, or while reading a magazine, newspaper, or book. All you have to do is remind yourself what skills and competencies you want to acquire, and then scour every situation you are in, every experience you have, for people who are proficient.

BEST PRACTICE #14

THREE EASY STEPS TO LEARNING BY IMITATION

Step 1: What do you need?

Identify the situational skills and capacities you would like to learn through the process of imitation. Then think of people you know well and see often who demonstrate those skills and capacities and can serve as role models.

Step 2: Interview and observe your role models

Ask them questions about how they acquired the skill and capacity you're seeking. Tell them you admire them and intend to imitate them. They will feel highly complimented. You may even want to enlist their informal coaching and feedback support. They could let you know when they observe you demonstrating the skills and capacities they already possess.

Observe your role models in action whenever you get a chance. Pay close attention to how they express their emotions. Notice their body language, tone of voice, and facial expressions. Note the way others respond to their behavior. Remember, 93 percent of communication is *non*-verbal, so observe what your role models *do*, not just what they *say*.

Step 3: Practice makes perfect

Before any situation that might call for you to utilize your new skill or capacity, remind yourself of what you've seen and learned from your role models. Imitate them eagerly and often in dealing with the situation at hand so you can become the change you want to see.

As you will remember, a critical competency for John in achieving his Level 3 agenda was learning how to ask penetrating questions. For six consecutive weeks, everywhere he went, John looked for people whose questions provoked the best conversations. He also listened to journalists asking questions with an ear for which journalists were most proficient and which ones had a style that would suit him best.

After completing his six week search, John realized that he had already picked up an incredible number of skills. He told me he had learned how to pace himself and to pause long enough for a person to think about the best response. He said he learned how to frame a question so people would know why he was asking it. And he became more skillful at asking questions that encouraged people to disclose their feelings and motives and what mattered deeply to them about a situation.

BEST PRACTICE #15

TRADING IN YOUR OLD WAYS FOR NEW WAYS:
YOUR ASSUMPTIONS, ATTITUDES, AND OBSERVATIONS

Giving up your old ways is easier said than done. Learning how to take a strong position, listen before you speak, and be flexible enough to change your mind are as difficult in their way as stopping smoking or starting to exercise. Old mind-sets and comfort zones die hard, and we know it. When change is warranted and desired, most of us crave the magic potion or instant conversion. We know too well that deep, lasting change is hard to come by. Habits have a way of seducing us back into our comfort zones, demoralizing us, and limiting our chances of moving toward our Level 3 goals.

So how do we trade in old ways for new ways? In my coaching practice, I have had the honor of witnessing people who have made profound changes in their ways of thinking, feeling, influencing others, achieving results, building relationships, and believing in themselves. I believe people who are most successful concentrate their attention on changing internally on three levels:

1. *Change your assumptions.* Some of your assumptions are holding you back. Make new assumptions about what you believe to be true and possible about yourself, other people, the dynamics of your situation, and the way the world works.

2. *Change your attitude.* Create a new, more positive point of view about how you and others are uniquely prepared to achieve the Level 3 results you want.

3. *Change your observations.* Revise your outlook so you are gathering evidence and experience that support your new assumptions and your new positive point of view.

This Best Practice shows you how to achieve each level of internal change so you can start being the change you want to see. I have designed these with the pioneering work of the Taos Institute and David Cooperrider at Case Western Reserve in mind. Cooperrider and his colleagues have supported individuals, teams, and organizations in making positive transformations by gaining a deep appreciation for the positive potential for change inherent in every person, group, and situation—if only we have the eyes to observe that potential.

Simone Weil, the French novelist, says, "Absolute attention is prayer." If one looks long enough at almost anything— looks with absolute attention at a flower, a stone, the bark of a tree, grass, snow, a cloud—something like revelation takes place. Something is "given" and perhaps that something is always a reality outside of the self. We are aware of God only when we cease to be aware of ourselves, not in the negative sense of denying the self, but in the sense of losing self in admiration and joy.

Mary Sarton

Step 1: Change your assumptions

Most new goals need a new set of assumptions to support them. Think about your Level 3 agenda across all three domains: personal, partnership, and productivity. You need to generate some fundamental assumptions about what forces are at play that will help you achieve your goals. Because your goals represent new (innovative) levels of effectiveness in the three domains, the assumptions you make about yourself, other people, your situation, and the way the world works may have to shift in order to be aligned with your goals. Your objective in this part of the exercise is to intentionally and carefully state the new assumptions that can help support you in achieving your Level 3 agenda.

Look at the chart on page 149 and review how John articulated his new assumptions, which were fundamental to his Level 3 agenda. Use John's stated assumptions as a guide for how to go about stating your own.

Step 2: Change your attitude

Now it's time to state in bold, affirmative terms your new attitude toward developing new skills and capacities. It is time to let

Personal Domain	**Partnership Domain**	**Productivity Domain**
The perspectives, skills, and capacities most important to my effectiveness	The nature and quality of the relationships I have in my personal and professional life	What I contribute and accomplish in my work, home, and community life
John's Old Assumption	*John's Old Assumption*	*John's Old Assumption*
Leaders tell other people what to do. That's what they're paid for.	I will figure out the answers to my problems alone.	It's impossible for every level and department of a corporation to be creative.
John's New Assumption	*John's New Assumption*	*John's New Assumption*
At their best, leaders seek to learn by asking thought-provoking questions, and they seek to guide by providing sound answers. Gaining commitment and setting the best course of action depends upon a delicate balance of each.	People like to be consulted for their opinions and help. People also like to take responsibility for solving problems and achieving results.	A highly creative culture is key to attracting, developing, and retaining an excellent workforce and customer base no matter what the size of the company may be.

your new assumptions color your perceptions of yourself, your situation, and other people. This way your attitudes will trigger ideas and actions aimed at achieving your Level 3 goals.

As with your assumptions, stating your positive attitudes toward yourself, others, and your situation in clear, concise, memorable, and affirmative terms is essential to making progress. Again, the new attitudes John developed can guide you in sponsoring the new attitudes that best suit you and your Level 3 goals.

John's Old Attitude	John's Old Attitude	John's Old Attitude
I can't learn much from people below me on the corporate ladder.	If it's really important, I'll take care of it myself.	Certain aspects of this business just aren't creative.

John's New Attitude	John's New Attitude	John's New Attitude
I already know how to pose thought-provoking questions, and I am wildly curious to hear the responses.	I can't wait to see people I work with take charge of tough assignments.	I am proud that people in this organization will do whatever it takes to preserve and enhance creativity.

Step 3: Change your observations

With your new assumptions and your new attitudes, you are set to observe every situation you encounter. Look through the lenses of your new assumptions and attitudes to gather any evidence that confirms these newly formed assumptions and attitudes. Yes, you've read me correctly: I want you to bias your observations in favor of the assumptions and attitudes that you have generated to support achieving your Level 3 goals. If you don't, your observations will automatically be geared toward your old, outdated assumptions and attitudes. What we observe is always colored by our assumptions and attitudes. We allow certain information in and filter other information out. So it is your job to intentionally observe whatever happens through the lenses of your

Of the next 10 people who you meet, 8.5 will bear a faith in their unlimited opportunity. The ability to become a ballerina, physicist, holder of patents, teacher of poetry, real estate mogul, pro basketball player, senator, ambassador, president, or even a TV-show host. Pretty much whoever you want to be. A third of everyone in line at the supermarket will be dreaming of fame, and the great majority of those will consider such dreams realizable…. We're not afraid of losing all we have. But we're terrified of losing a chance to have it all.

Richard Powers from
"American Dreaming"

new assumptions and attitudes. This is how you begin to shape the future in the direction you want it to take.

Personal Domain	*Partnership Domain*	*Productivity Domain*
The perspectives, skills, and capacities most important to my effectiveness	The nature and quality of the relationships I have in my personal and professional life	What I contribute and accomplish in my work, home, and community life
Your Old Assumption	*Your Old Assumption*	*Your Old Assumption*
Your New Assumption	*Your New Assumption*	*Your New Assumption*
Your Old Attitude	*Your Old Attitude*	*Your Old Attitude*
Your New Attitude	*Your New Attitude*	*Your New Attitude*

John began to view staff meetings with his direct reports through the lens of his newly adopted assumption that people are eager to be consulted for their opinions. Then he noticed himself asking for opinions, and his staff offering their ideas far more often than ever before. In this process, John discovered that he could learn more about each staff member's depth of understanding than he ever did when he was the person rendering most of the opinions. He told me that he was so amazed by the quality of the suggestions and recommendations he heard, it was as if he was getting to know his staff for the first time!

Clearly, John's new attitude of enthusiasm about seeing other people tackle and solve tough problems was reinforced by what happened in his staff meetings. John realized that his new assumptions and attitudes were in effect self-fulfilling prophecies. In this matter, I believe he was entirely correct. What you see is what you get.

Guiding Principles: Be the Change You Want to See

- Imitation is the fastest form of learning.
- If you are vigilant, you can observe novel, powerful ways of achieving your Level 3 goals hidden inside of mistakes, accidental encounters, happenstance, surprises, natural phenomenon, and almost any other dynamic that catches your eye.
- People you respect and want to emulate usually will be eager to share with you who they are and how they became competent in the areas you most admire.
- Once you internalize the admirable qualities and skills of your role model, those attributes will quickly take on the uniqueness of you. One day you will bear only a faint resemblance to those you once imitated so precisely.
- Act as if the future is now.

JOHN'S STORY, CONTINUED

John scoured business magazines and new business books and networked globally to find leaders who had successfully developed a collaborative approach to building a business that demanded high levels of creativity. He read everything he could get his hands on about the approaches that worked best. We decided that he would set up face-to-face meetings or telephone interviews with leaders who seemed particularly effective in collaborating and fostering a creative culture, so he could learn more about how they were able to accomplish those results.

After John's initial search, he narrowed his list of those he wanted to interview in depth to a handful of leaders who had distinguished themselves in the area of collaboration and creativity. One of those leaders stood out because he was able to pass on to John a method of observing people that changed the way John viewed people for the rest of his life.

Benjamin Zander is conductor of Boston's Symphony Orchestra. Zander has written about what he has learned as a leader of highly achievement-oriented, creative concert musicians. John read the book, *The Art of Possibility*, coauthored by Zander and his wife, attended a keynote address given by Zander at a global leadership conference, and spoke directly with Zander at a reception following his speech.

The observational approach offered by Zander that has completely transformed how John perceives other people is: "Give everyone who works with you an A." Zander explained to John that he developed this approach when he taught students at the New England Conservatory of Music. This is completely unlike most other teachers, who seldom dispense A's, and certainly avoid giving a student an A too early in the year, to make sure he or she will keep working hard. Every student at the New England Conservatory is worried about how his or her achievements will stack up against the achievements of other highly competent students. This anxiety triggers bouts of worrisome thinking that interferes with learning and performing.

As Zander noticed this high anxiety interference, he decided to give all his students an A at the beginning of the year. The only condition he imposed was that students write him a letter, dated the following May, describing what they each had done to earn an A in his course.

Zander told his students to concentrate on describing the musician they would become. He asked each of them to fall in love with that person. Zander explained to John that all at once the students realized that he only accepted A students (who happened to be unique from one another). This level playing field promoted the best possible culture for collaboration, creativity, and achievement.

John improvised the Zander process by suggesting to his direct reports that they each write him a letter at the beginning of the year that described the leader they would become over the next 12 months. Instituting this process allowed John's direct reports to set their Level 3 leadership goals, to establish a vision of their best, possible future, and, most important to see themselves and the other members of John's executive team as highly competent, yet unique in their leadership skills. The collaboration among John and his staff was higher than he could have ever predicted or imagined. This process encouraged him to believe that he led a team comprised of only exceptional leaders (just as Zander taught only A students).

As John began to view each person on his team as exceptional leaders, they indeed began to lead in exceptional ways. He was so proud of their achievements that he couldn't stop talking about their successes. The more he told success stories about his team, the more they exchanged their leadership secrets with each other, and the more excellent leadership John observed.

Get Others on Board

How to Speak and Act from Your Heart

---

* Build Strong Alliances
* Communicate to Motivate

*A*lone *we cannot accomplish anything worthwhile.*
Now you involve in your plan those you love and
those you need.

> *Each of us has a spark of life inside us, and our highest*
> *endeavor ought to be to set off that spark in one another.*
> Kenny Ausubel

BARBARA MCLINTOCK

Barbara McLintock, who earned a Nobel Prize in genetics, talked about developing strong feelings, even empathy, for the organisms she studied. In recalling her relationship with corn plants as she studied their chromosomes, she said, "I found that the more I worked with them, the bigger and bigger they got and when I was really working with them I wasn't outside, I was down there. I was part of the system. I even was able to see the internal parts of the chromosomes—actually everything was there. It surprised me because I actually felt as if I were right down there and these were my friends.... As you look at these things they become part of you and you forget yourself. The main thing is that you forget yourself."

Build Strong Alliances

What you need to DO	Consolidate Your Relationships
What you need to BE	Influential and Collaborative

According to one popular saying, there is no "I" in "TEAM."

Who are we kidding?

It's true that the most successful teams put the needs of the group ahead of any individual needs. But the best teams, whether in the boardroom or on the football field, are also made up of talented players who turn in extraordinary performances. This dynamic push/pull between group success and personal accomplishment means that all teams, and team players, must constantly do a balancing act. When the balance is right, both the team and the individual accomplish more than they ever thought possible.

Alone we cannot accomplish anything worthwhile, so as you pursue your Level 3 goals, you need to get others on board. At the same time, it is your personal vision for the future that will excite and motivate others and persuade them to join you. You, too, have to do a balancing act.

How do you get others to help you meet your individual goals?

The answer is alliances.

Strong alliances pave the way for progress.

All of us can live a more rewarding, fulfilling life, and can make improvements in and for the world, if we each take responsibility for doing so. However, because we live and operate in systems that are becoming more and more interdependent and mutually reinforcing, what one of us accomplishes can have an impact on countless others. When you light the first match, before long there is a bonfire, crackling with the ideas and enthusiasm of other people.

Achieving what you want in a rapid-fire world always begins with you and your unique positive images of what the future holds. Without your Level 3 goals, the Status Quo would win out. You would experience only minimal progress and limited growth, and your vast reservoirs of potential would remain untapped. Instead, you have created your vision of the best possible future, shaped by your personal sense of curiosity and commitment, your intuition and awareness, and your very own capacity for reflection, optimism, and imagination. Now the time has come to enlist others in the pursuit of your Level 3 goals.

In my experience, people who are naturally outgoing and extroverted are happy to go out into the world and recruit allies, while those who are by nature more reserved find it more difficult to get started. There's no way to get around our paradoxical human need for both solitude and for community. It is impossible to get by having one without the other—especially when we're contending with rapid-fire challenges that require both individual and collective achievement to shape a positive future.

We cannot live only for ourselves. A thousand fibers connect us with our fellow humans.

Herman Melville

If we stay to ourselves, seek too much solitude, or become overly self-reliant, we deprive ourselves of the rich, supportive network of connections that are so essential in turning the tide of the future in our favor. On the other hand, if we depend too much on the opinions, guidance, and approval of other individuals or groups, we can lose our sense of direction, and with it our momentum and desire. None of us wants to commit either error.

Building strong alliances solves our dilemma. An alliance, in the sense I am using the term, is a relationship of mutual influence and collaboration between you and those gifted individuals who are more energetic, more knowledgeable, and more influential than the average person. In the best alliances, we have a strong sense of being able to "go it alone" when it counts, plus a deep sense of companionship. If we need it, help is at hand.

Whether you realize it or not, you have already laid the foundation for building strong alliances. From the very start of learning this six step process for achieving what you want, you have sought others' advice and opinions about the clarity, direction, and worth of your Level 3 goals. You have asked colleagues to consider how your goals might benefit them directly and indirectly. You have searched for mentors to imitate and coaches to guide you. In a very real sense you have been cultivating your alliances all along the way. Now you're going to focus your attention on strengthening those alliances and building new ones that will be the most beneficial in helping you achieve your Level 3 goals.

There are four types of friends in need.

To achieve your vision of the best possible future, you need allies. There are four specific types of alliances that are particularly helpful in achieving Level 3 goals. You may only need a few allies, or you may need several. I strongly recommend that you secure at least one ally from each category because they are so helpful, but in some cases you may not need all four types, or certain allies may play more than one role. Although all of your allies should understand your vision for the future, is not necessary for each one to be involved in every aspect of your Level 3 agenda. As an added bonus, these alliances will also help you respond creatively to whatever happens with your Level 2 agenda, whether circumstances are holding you back or catapulting you forward.

Champions. Your Champions will advance your cause because they have adopted your vision as if it were their own. Champions are able to lead others to work toward the success of your vision as enthusiastically and as diligently as you do. Champions help you leverage your leadership. They stay close to you and your followers to offer encouragement and guidance every step of the way.

Endorsers. Cultivating alliances with Endorsers brings legitimacy to your cause. Endorsers are people who have the power to open doors. They will vouch for you and your vision with others who do not yet know and identify with you. Endorsers provide a positive, halo effect that brings you support by association.

Supporters. Your Supporters will spread the word about the direction of your goals and your achievements via the rumor mill, the grapevine, and other robust, informal communication systems. Supporters infiltrate the small but highly influential circles in your world (e.g., the cliques, the teams, the identity groups that form by virtue of education, ethnicity, gender, and the like). A small, committed band of Supporters is invaluable because they will translate your message into the vernacular of each group they belong to.

Companions. Your Companions provide you with a peer group. Although they are in pursuit of their own separate and unique Level 3 agendas, they know you personally and share your desire to achieve important, life-shaping goals. They know how tough it is to do what you're doing. Your Companion group is your safe harbor, your port in good times and in bad.

Don't be shy. No matter how self-sufficient you are, you need allies.

I imagine that some of you reading this book are wondering if Champions and Endorsers and Supporters and Companions are all necessary. You may feel uncomfortable asking for help. Or, if you have a narrow, relatively self-contained Level 3 agenda that pertains mostly to your own growth and development, you may be questioning the value of building strong alliances at all.

Recruiting Champions, people who are visionary leaders themselves, leverages your leadership. Identifying Endorsers, who are well-respected and well-connected, provides you with legitimacy in circles whose influence you need, but within which you are not well known. Attracting Supporters who have informal influence gives you grassroots sponsorship. And, collaborating with Companions, who are in the process of creating their own vision of the best possible future, offers you a community of advocates who identify with your ups and downs because they experience similar challenges in their own pursuit of Level 3 goals.

Never doubt that a small band of committed citizens can change the world. Indeed, it is the only thing that ever has.
Margaret Mead

Let me assure you, cultivating strong alliances is crucial to your success no matter how personal your Level 3 agenda may be. You designed your Level 3 agenda to create the best possible future, not only for yourself, but also for the greater good. You are by definition setting out to change the world! I find that many of my clients tend to forget or underestimate the magnitude of the change associated with achieving their Level 3 goals. Even if your agenda is to strengthen your own skills and capacities, this will affect how you relate to others, and your ability to be productive and to make contributions that matter. Like my client John, you could be targeting changes that range from within yourself to within a large global organization. The relative size and scope of your vision for the future does not alter the need for strong alliances.

Unlike your need for allies, the optimum number of Champions, Endorsers, Supporters, and Companions you need will vary, depending on your goals. Let's say you have a Level 3 agenda that is largely personal. You want to learn how to trust your intuition (a personal goal); you plan to acquire more skills for resolving conflict (a partnership goal); and you wish to increase your sales proficiency and your annual sales revenue (a productivity goal). You may form an alliance with only one Champion, one Endorser, one Sponsor, and one Companion. But each one will make an invaluable contribution to your efforts.

When faster-harder-smarter is not enough, it's time to collaborate.

I find that most of us have steadily increased the demands we make of ourselves without increasing the help we get. We end up a lot like my client Langston. Before I met him, Langston was the kind of person who set annual goals for himself every New Year's Eve, without fail. He qualified as a high achiever in almost every domain of his life—athletics, business, his family life, community service, membership in community service associations, and so on. His annual goals were always stretch goals, and he spent every ounce of his will and determination achieving them. Langston was a true, high-achieving entrepreneur. As I explored the deadlines and regimens Langston had created for himself in order to fulfill his achievement plans, it felt to me like he was a prisoner in a penitentiary of his own making. His schedule was so strict and confining that Langston moved more like a man doing time than a person following his vision of the best, possible future.

During our initial coaching session, Langston and I discussed the nature and range of his Level 3 agenda. I discussed the rationale for thinking about his growth and development from the perspective of the three domains: personal, partnership, and productivity. Langston told me that he had all three domains covered. He developed the following set of goals:

Personal Domain	Partnership Domain	Productivity Domain
• Maintaining a balanced approach to life and achieving my goals as an entrepreneur, a husband, a father, a community service leader, and an athlete • Improve my tennis serve and backhand return	• To strengthen the intimacy within my marriage by devoting more time to my wife and her interests • To encourage my son to be a good student and a good soccer player, and to support him in his efforts	• To expand my gourmet food, wine, and catering business from one location to three locations within 12 months • To lead a fund-raising drive to support low-income housing in a nearby neighborhood • To advance one level in my competitive tennis

We had an in-depth conversation about his goals within each domain. The fact that Langston was a solo player—entrepreneur—influenced his outlook about needing allies. What he didn't realize was that every year, he left alliances out of his plans to achieve his Level 3 goals. He had sentenced himself to solitary confinement. It never occurred to him to build constituencies devoted to helping him succeed because, after all, these were *his* goals—who else would have the interest or time to join the effort?

At first the idea of asking others for guidance seemed foreign to Langston. He said he would feel guilty imposing on people. I reminded him that other people feel valued and respected when they are called upon to help someone they love, admire, or believe in, and reassured him that developing alliances would lighten the load he had put on himself by trying to single-handedly become a more successful entrepreneur, more competitive tennis player, reliable father-coach for his son's soccer team, husband who dined out once a week with the wife he adored—and on and on. Langston admitted that for the past three years, achieving his annual goals had been a hollow victory. He sensed life was passing him by, and that he was blowing past special moments that he could have spent growing closer to the people he loved and respected most if he hadn't been in such a hurry to get to his next assignment.

Langston and I discussed the four roles that allies could play in his pursuit of Level 3 goals. The more we talked about this, the more he realized that alliances could grow naturally out of his existing relationships. Langston was relieved to see that building alliances did not mean going to strangers for help, and that it did not require burdening others with obligations above and beyond what could be reasonably expected of them. Instead, he could talk to people he already knew, tell them what he was trying to accomplish, and ask for their assistance in ways that would not inconvenience them but would be very helpful to him.

- Langston decided he would recruit his wife as a Champion who could express her admiration and respect for him to their children when his work obligations made him late, again, for dinner.

- He would ask two men, his tennis coach and the president of the Fathers Club at his son's school, to be his Endorsers. His tennis pro could tell his doubles partner how much time Langston was spending trying to improve his serve, and the Fathers Club president could raise the confidence level of the soccer team by telling them how proud Langston was to be their coach.

- When we discussed who could be an appropriate Supporter, Langston decided he would ask his wife to support his marriage goals. He wanted to be a loving confidant and partner, so he would ask his wife what he was doing to enhance or detract from the level of intimacy in their marriage.

- Finally, Langston made a deal with his new business partner that they would meet with each other regularly to discuss their progress and setbacks in achieving the goals they had set for the expansion. His partner was a ready-made Companion.

We say you cannot divert the river from the river bed. We say that everything is moving, and we are a part of this motion. That the soil is moving. That the water is moving. We say that the Earth draws water to her from the clouds. We say the rainfall parts on each side of the mountain, like the parting of our hair, and that the shape of the mountain tells where the water has passed. We say this water washed the soil from the hillsides, that the rivers carry sediment, that rain when it splashes carries small particles, that the soil itself flows with water in streams underground. We say that water is taken up into roots of plants, into stems, that it is washed down hills into rivers, that these rivers flow to sea, that from the sea, in the sunlight, this water rises to the sky, that this water is carried in the clouds, and comes back as rain, comes back as fog, back as dew, back as wetness in the air.

We say everything comes back.

Susan Griffin

Once Langston culti-vated his allies, his whole demeanor changed. Instead of his usual driven, relentless pursuit of his goals, he assumed a lighter, freer approach. By giving the people he loved and needed a role in his development, Langston moved closer to his goals with greater ease and con-fidence. As an added bonus, once his family members and colleagues better understood his pri-orities and how they could help, they felt more valu-able and important to him.

You aren't a chicken, so throw out the pecking order.

The story of the Orpheus Chamber Orchestra is one of my favorite examples of how estab-lishing strong alliances can change the way the world works. This group redefined its basic way of operating so that the orchestra could achieve unprecedented levels of excellence in perfor-mance, leadership, and job satisfaction. Their story shows that for groups of people to be richer, deeper, wiser—and therefore more creative—alternatives to the hierarchical world of organiza-tions must be invented.

Classically trained musicians, who spend years honing their individual technical prowess and interpretive skills in conserva-tories, often find themselves ill-equipped to play in a large orchestra where they must submit to the authority of a baton-waving conductor. In a study he conducted in the early 1990s,

Richard Hackman, a Harvard psychologist, found that job satisfaction among players in 78 orchestras in four countries was so low that symphony members reported the same levels of negative job satisfaction as federal prison guards! On the other hand, other research has shown that conductors tend to live longer than the rest of us.

The inspiration for the Orpheus Chamber Orchestra came from founder and champion Julian Fifer. When he was at Juilliard, Fifer experienced an inspiring, exciting intimacy and camaraderie among his peers. He became such a champion of the Juilliard brand of teamwork that he wanted to recreate that experience on a larger scale. Fifer set his Level 3 sights on establishing an orchestral organization within which communication and cooperation could flourish—without a conductor!

As Fifer began to work toward his vision of the best possible future for the orchestra, he essentially turned all the musicians into a network of Champions. Rehearsals became free-for-alls in which all 27 members of the group participated in every decision about every detail of nuance, phrasing, and dynamics. When it quickly became clear that trying to make all decisions unanimous was unworkable, the whole orchestra was divided into several core groups whose members would change regularly. Each group would rehearse a piece and formulate one interpretation of it, then present it to the larger group.

One amazing innovation for the ensemble came in the area of sharing leadership. In conductor-led orchestras, the role of the concertmaster is similar to that of a team captain. In Orpheus, the role has become more like a player-coach, and is rotated. The concertmaster is responsible for running rehearsals, moderating debates, and negotiating solutions. Not only do the core groups and concertmasters change from concert to concert, they also change from piece to piece. This inclusive process allows each player to experience intense leadership training.

With the vision of a collaborative, high-spirited culture in mind, Julian Fifer and the orchestra members have established a financially robust, award-winning chamber ensemble. Orpheus has won world acclaim for artistic excellence while also providing professional satisfaction for its members.

Trust the power of your vision.

Your agenda, whatever it is, will catch on in the world because it is authentic and compelling. The same principles apply whether your agenda is largely personal or largely corporate, whether you recruit four allies or forty, and whether your sphere of influence is across the neighborhood or around the globe.

These days companies, too, need a vision of their future. Our rapid-fire world has changed the rules of succeeding in business in dramatic ways. Today, companies need a global as well as a local presence. They need to expand their markets, not just penetrate them more deeply. They need to think strategically with their customers, not just sell them products or services. They need to invent new products and improve systems at lightning speed in order to remain competitive. Name brand corporations that are used to sitting back and letting the money roll in are finding that they need to watch their backs. Their competitors are focused, savvy, and quick—and, thanks to the Internet, their customers have access to an unprecedented amount of information about options that are better and cheaper.

Most companies know that surviving in a rapid-fire world necessitates a more collaborative and globally connected workforce. The leaders in these companies know intuitively that the success of their business depends upon how well people think together, solve problems together, create innovations together, and support and value each other. In short, they must be unified by a common goal—a vision for the company's future that has meaning for everyone at every level. There can be no more barriers to communication.

Friendship makes prosperity more shining and lessens adversity by dividing it and sharing it.

Marcus Tullius Cicero

Exchanging information, ideas, best practices, recognition, appreciation, good news, trends, opportunities, and watch-outs across all functions and locations is imperative. To share the vision and spread the news, strong alliances are vital.

There are no tried-and-true blueprints to follow in developing highly collaborative relationships. So what's a company to do? Obviously, trial and error is an option. But what approaches seem more promising than others? How can a whole company become globally coherent soon enough so it is able to thrive in a rapid-fire world—and does not implode in the act of transforming itself?

Change can reach up through an organization like fire, or permeate down through a company like rain.

One success story with which I was personally associated involved a three-person, cross-functional team that formed itself into an alliance of Champions. A cosmetics company had offices around the globe, but management was not making the most of the company's worldwide presence. Instead of having a constructive synergy among the different operations, the company just seemed fragmented, as if its shrapnel had landed around the globe.

Three vice presidents with worldwide responsibilities decided to form themselves into a Travel Team. Chris was responsible for operations, Gary led research and development, and Pam was in charge of organizational development. Their goal was to create a global mind-set in the workforce to complement the effective locally focused mind-sets that were already operating. Part of their challenge was to encourage people who were highly invested in the success of one part of the company to adopt a whole company perspective.

In general, people who are invested in one specific area must become mindful of the interests of their larger contexts if the whole is to benefit alongside the part. Like the push/pull dynamic between individual and group achievement, there is often a tug-of-war between local and global interests. Balancing both ensures that the interests of the whole and the part are always considered in tandem. Sometimes sacrifices are made in favor of the part, and sometimes for the whole. However, when people in all parts of the system value both the global and local needs and are willing to discuss how to best meet both, the system thrives.

Most of us live and work in a variety of systems, and feel the tension between satisfying the needs of the part or those of the whole. Even in family life the trade-offs can be tricky. For example, the freedom teenagers need to experiment with other styles of thinking and acting in order to develop a strong sense of who they are often clashes with the interests of the rest of the family—

parents and younger children. The best way to negotiate these kinds of trade-offs is to talk, listen, explain, and explain again, which is exactly what the Travel Team did.

After they established their Level 3 goal of creating higher levels of collaboration and reciprocity within the company, the Travel Team made their master plan. Chris, Gary, and Pam knew they could not simply send around a memo mandating a change in corporate culture. They believed it would be far more effective to win people's minds and hearts in a more personal way. As a first priority, they decided to "be the change they wanted to see" so they could serve as role models. To this end, they set a joint travel schedule that landed them at company locations in Europe, Asia, South America, and the United States for a thorough review of local priorities and issues. They also decided to visit each location at least three times per year. In effect, they were a global team of Champions who made house calls.

In their first round of visits, they identified a small group of individuals at each location whom Gary referred to as "stemwinders." These individuals could galvanize people at their locale to think big and think new as easily as they could wind up their watches. These stem-winders became the local cross-functional Supporters of creating a global mind-set. They met together regularly and formed strong alliances among themselves. Chris, Gary, and Pam helped these teams to get up and running, made sure everyone understood their purpose, and helped each team implement certain Best Practices that would surface creative ideas. Then they got out of the way.

Once every quarter, a total of 10 teams of Supporters, from locations around the world, convened together with the Travel Team to jointly make trade-off decisions that maximized local and global effectiveness. This part of the master plan was aimed at forming strong leadership alliances among locations. Because the teams had been encouraged to be creative from the beginning, there was tremendous enthusiasm as they blended their ideas about actions they could take to foster worldwide collaboration across all functions on a day-to-day, week-to-week basis.

Chris, Gary, and Pam were amazed at how quickly people were able to get on board. The teams were happy to address the complex issues involved with thinking globally and locally simultaneously. In a survey I conducted, members of the support teams told me that this assignment gave them a chance to expand their horizons and to be challenged in novel ways. Because of their natural tendencies toward high achievement, they viewed being called upon to sponsor this next, best version of their company an honor, as well as a chance to make a big difference.

Among other things, the international teams of Supporters decided to hold weekly teleconferences, and to implement Internet-based customer information systems. They established project teams to transfer technical skills, and created global teams for product development. What made these initiatives so successful in the long run was the commitment everyone had to the decisions of the group. This high level of commitment was the result of the thorough, deep, rich, and creative collaborative conversations.

One added feature of the master plan worth mentioning were the alliances with Endorsers that Pam made possible. She sent out a request for assistance to her colleagues in the world of organizational development, asking them to put her in touch with companies that had been successful in globalizing specific functions, such as sales and marketing, purchasing and information systems. Because her colleagues ran interference for her, Pam was able to connect people inside of her company to their counterparts in the other enterprises, to learn from them directly. Pam estimated that this investigation of best-in-class companies saved her company six to twelve months of time and wasted effort. Without the referrals of her Endorsers, this learning exchange never could have been possible.

Although their Supporters and Endorsers were charged up and ready to collaborate, the Travel Team found that collaboration wasn't always easy. It required determination and a new set of skills to think, decide, and act both globally and locally. It took having conversations while dining together, rather than sitting across a desk from one another, to come to appreciate and respect their differences.

BEST PRACTICES

Learning how to collaborate with one another is a major need for almost all of us, especially high achievers who owe much of their success to their own efforts. We've all been taught how to compete better than we've been taught how to cooperate. At the heart of collaboration is cooperation. I am eager to share with you some Best Practices that can help you and your allies overcome the urge to compete so the alliances you form will be as strong and as productive as possible.

BEST PRACTICE #16

VISION STORIES WE LOVE TO BE LED BY: THE HERO'S JOURNEY

Much has been written to reveal the hidden motif of the myths and legends that have lived for centuries in the lore of every world culture. Scholar Joseph Campbell studied the unique structure of *The Hero's Journey* as it is revealed through inspirational stories from around the world. The same structure will provide you with a story line you can use to fashion a particularly compelling way of communicating to your allies your Level 3 agenda and your vision of the best possible future. The story line is made up of the following components:

a. The Call. A hero in the making is called to set forth on an amazing adventure that will benefit the hero and the world. This component is analogous to taking your blinders off so you can see the best of what could be next. John explained his Call like this: "I believe that our company has the opportunity of a life time to prove that our creativity can keep pace with our rapid growth."

b. Threshold Crossing. Crossing the threshold from the way things are to the way things could be is not easy for the hero. Stepping into the adventure is made more difficult by threshold guardians who tempt the hero to stay home, to give up the quest. In the process of achieving what you want, your threshold guardians are your own doubts, fears, anxieties, and pessimistic notions or blind spots that must be overcome so you can *be outrageously optimistic*. John knew there were skeptics who said his plan to make the company more creative could never be done because in his industry it had never been done. He knew he would also encounter guardians who would defend the Status Quo because keeping things the same is always the easiest route. John had doubts himself every now and then, but in general he and his allies were excited to be true pioneers.

c. Embarking In spite of the warnings to remain at home and to maintain the Status Quo, the hero sets forth on the journey, armed with courage, hope, and a strong commitment to what the future holds. Your resolve is strengthened when you *make the future happen inside of you* so your vision lives in all you think, say, and do. John's mind was made up. He knew intuitively that his company had to become creative or die. He developed a simple mantra to explain his vision: "I hope you will join me in believing in this possibility and in making creativity plus growth a reality over the next 18 months."

d. Boons and Blessings. As the hero makes progress toward the goal, many boons and blessings are granted along the way. Angels, mascots, and supporters of all kinds assist the hero. This mirrors the way you will *get others on board* who identify with you, believe in your cause, and toil with you side by side to help you reach your goals. John recognized that the key to his success was collaboration. To help eliminate competition and turf wars, he pledged that he would listen to and support the ideas and efforts of others, and he asked that they do the same with each other and with each new member of the company worldwide.

e. Enemies and Obstacles. The hero meets with mishaps, mayhem, and mischief that is the handiwork of naysayers, detractors, and mortal enemies throughout the entire journey. At some fateful moment the hero's life is often put in jeopardy. For you there will be a variety of circumstances and people who will get in your way and stall your progress. You will find that, just like the hero, you must *stack the odds in your favor* by overcoming obstacles and confronting the conflicts that come your way. John's obstacles were apathy, competition, and time. He helped eliminate apathy by generating excitement for his vision at all levels of the company. He helped eliminate competition by deliberately getting everyone on board and honoring everyone's ideas. In addition, he told his allies, "Our common enemy is time. To accomplish our growth we must speed up; to bolster our creativity we must slow down enough to think and act in tandem. Let us move forward being willing and able to do both. Let's slow down our conversations so we can speed up by acting together."

f. The Return Home. Finally the hero is saved by his or her own ingenuity and the intervention of some divine, universal force for good that is bound to prevail in any adventure that is pursued for the welfare of all. The hero wins the bounty and is drawn home to share the prize with those who he or she loves and honors most. You, too, will be victorious and successful. You will learn in this process of achieving what you want how to keep alert and vigilant, how to leverage your success with and for others, and how to celebrate the next, best version of yourself, your partnerships, and your productivity. John wasn't interested in glory, but he was very interested in the success of his company. He believed that when all was said and done, he and his allies would be able to take great pride in the fact that they never chose to increase the company's market share or profitability at the expense of creativity. John believed that the creativity of his company's services, products, and culture were the keys to rapid growth—and that by the time he was finished, the whole industry would be following his lead.

It's your turn to write your vision story using *The Hero's Journey* template. Let your imagination guide you as you anticipate your success, complete with all the ups and downs of a truly inspiring, worthwhile adventure. Commit the story to memory in such a way that it will motivate you and others every time you tell it. You'll be surprised how this exercise prepares you to articulate your vision in persuasive, meaningful ways to those you seek out as your constituents.

BEST PRACTICE #17

REMEMBERING NOT TO FORGET

Most of us have had the experience of driving to work (or the bank, or the grocery store), parking the car, stepping out, and suddenly realizing that we have no clue how in the world we got there. As if by magic, or some weird form of time/space collapse, we have arrived at our destination without any memory of having traveled there. Of course, if we mentally retrace our route, we can slowly piece together a vague sense that we surely and safely must have driven there.

This type of temporary amnesia is common in a rapid-fire world. We move through our days at such warp speed that living life becomes a blur and we can't even keep track of ourselves. These temporary lapses of attention (and therefore memory) provide a brief respite from the pressures of having to work faster, harder, and smarter. After all, we do know how to drive, and we also know the best route to our destination, so we don't have to be any *smarter*. And since the act of driving is relatively simple and requires little effort, we don't have to work any *harder*. The car itself takes care of *faster*. So when it comes to zoning out on the drive to work, no problem. In fact, the rest and relaxation of an uncomplicated drive somewhere—a trip without traffic jams, near misses, or road rage—may even be good for us.

In the faster-harder-smarter world, driving is not the only experience we may forget to remember. Other, more complex efforts we have put forth to solve problems and to make progress toward our goals may slip away unnoticed if we don't remind ourselves to remember. Remembering what we've done on our own behalf, and on behalf of our Level 3 goals, is one way to become our own best ally. Furthermore, reminding our other allies—our Champions, Endorsers, Supporters, and Companions—how they have contributed to our success is key to strengthening those alliances, too.

So, what is the best way to be sure to remember what was done to move forward? The answer lies in asking a question. Not just any question, but the single most reinforcing question anyone could ever ask. That question is: "How did you do that?"

Step 1: Pop the question

When someone (yourself or another person) makes progress, contributes to your success, overcomes obstacles, or helps clear a path forward in any way, you ask, "How did you do that?" John was impressed when one of the companies he had just acquired reduced their manufacturing cycle time by 30 percent. Suspecting that some creative thinking was behind this huge shift in scheduling, he contacted Maureen, the company's manager of process engineering, and asked her, "How did you do that?" By using some new technology and running several teams simultaneously, instead of one after the other, Maureen had been able to compress the amount of time needed to get a new product to market. Her innovation was elegant in its simplicity, yet no one had ever tried it before.

Suspecting that he might have an ally here, John asked Maureen if she would be willing to share her ideas with her counterparts around the world. He discussed his globalization plans with her at some length, and she became an enthusiastic Supporter of his long-term plans.

About a month later, John heard from Maureen. She needed some guidance. She had won over her whole team of engineers, who were now enthusiastic about sharing their ideas globally. How did John want her to proceed?

John was happy to make plans, but first he again asked her, "How did you do that?"

Step 2: Connect the dots

The person you ask has to stop and think about how to answer this question, just as you had to stop and think about your drive to work. In the process of thinking about how to answer, your ally is able to "connect the dots" between which actions were taken to accomplish which milestones of progress. By retracing his or her route, your ally will create a road map that can be shared with others. Maureen thought for a minute, then said, "Well, first I recognized the success of my engineering team. I scheduled a plantwide meeting just for that purpose. At that special meeting, we asked the engineers to explain how they had cut cycle time. After their presentation, we held a little awards ceremony. I videotaped this recognition meeting, and afterward asked the engineers if they would be willing to share the video with their counterparts in other plants. They not only agreed, but volunteered to answer questions after their colleagues had viewed it—either by teleconference or in person.

Step 3: Celebrate your progress and share the wisdom

Give your ally—or yourself!—a pat on the back for a job well done. Everyone likes to be acknowledged, and your allies need to know how they have contributed to your vision. This will help strengthen your alliance as you continue to work on making your vision a reality. It also doesn't hurt to remind people that your Level 3 goals are designed to create a better future for everyone.

John was impressed. Certainly he had been to recognition meetings before, but they tended to be long-winded affairs that recognized upper management. Maureen's meeting had reinforced the importance of creativity at every level of the company, which was exactly what John was trying to accomplish globally. The videotape was the perfect way to show what he had in mind without lecturing employees about the need to be creative.

Everyone won. The engineers got credit for a job well done, not only at their company, but globally. Maureen won, because her efforts were recognized at the top. John wrote a personal note to Maureen thanking her for her ingenuity, and made a point of visiting her—his new Supporter!—the next time he was in her part of the world. The corporation—every employee, really—won because the engineers shared their new approach worldwide, which contributed to overall efficiency and responsiveness. And John won, too, as he not only made progress on his Level 3 agenda, but also was able to show in a concrete way what he meant by becoming more creative at every level.

Guiding Principles: Build Strong Alliances

- A select handful of gifted, high-energy, high-influence people is all you need to change your world.
- Being vulnerable and self-revealing is more persuasive than being invincible and self-contained.
- Others must experience the rewards of collaboration over competition before they will strive to be collaborative.
- The act of collaboration is an act of shared discovery and shared creativity that leads to coherent action.
- No matter what happens in the end, your pursuit of Level 3 goals constitutes a "hero's journey." And, as such, your efforts are inspiring, and you follow in the footsteps of heroes throughout history who have moved the world forward in significant ways.

JOHN'S STORY, CONTINUED

Several months ago, on the first Friday of March, I watched a group of sixteen people sip coffee on the back deck of The Cramer Institute. Each member of the group was enrolled in a leadership development course I was teaching called "Leading in a Rapid-Fire World." John was standing on the right corner of the deck conversing with the three other people who had been assigned his "learning team." I had divided everyone in the class into four learning teams with four people in each. Within their team, everybody shared their Level 3 agenda, and then they coached each other on how to make progress on their respective goals. In this way, the teams were actually Companion alliances.

John's Companions were:

- Art, a vice president of information systems for a national chain of banks
- Celeste, the CEO of a community-based rural hospital
- Carolyn, vice president of business development for a global public relations firm

Later that afternoon, John told me that he was amazed at the level of support he experienced from the whole class of participants, and especially from those in his learning team. He and I discussed how he could build stronger alliances—right from the start—with the leadership in the companies he was acquiring. In the course of this part of the conversation, John described a method of interviewing that Art has passed along to him. Art's approach was to establish a deeper-than-ordinary connection in an interview by asking thought-provoking, open-ended questions that revealed a person's true beliefs and feelings. In particular, one question John liked was, "What is it that you don't know, that if you could know it, would make a significant positive impact on your ability to get results?"

The moment I heard this question, I realized that it worked on a number of levels simultaneously. When Art, the information systems professional, asked this question, he was looking for answers that pointed to new sources of data or new ways of integrating existing information so he could provide his clients inside of the bank with knowledge that promoted better results. From John's perspective, he could ask the same question and find out how leaders in his newly acquired companies viewed their strategic priorities, their competitive advantage, and their secret weapons of success.

John seemed completely taken with the prospect of listening to what other leaders might say in response to this question. He felt it was provocative enough to solicit an uncensored, unrehearsed answer from someone who might otherwise be out to impress him with how great his achievements were.

John read my mind when he said, "What I really need to know from the leaders in our new acquisitions are the subtle secrets about growth opportunities. What they tend to want to tell me about are the accomplishments that are already visible." We discussed the fact that it must be difficult for leaders to admit what they don't know, but John and I agreed that the question would prompt them to be more self-revealing from the start of the relationship. Ironically, it is the authentic, vulnerable exchanges that build the strongest alliances.

> *We are caught in an inescapable network of mutuality, tied in a single garment of destiny.*
>
> Martin Luther King, Jr.

Communicate to Motivate

What you need to DO	Lead the Way
What you need to BE	Articulate and Persuasive

In many ways, America was built on competition, rugged individualism, and survival of the fittest. We have a cultural tradition that includes solitary heroes like the Lone Ranger, movies like *Home Alone*, and various quirky geniuses and tycoons who did it their way and became famous and successful. We tell and retell the stories of orphans and runaways, adventurers and seekers. You'll need this kind of perseverance and self-reliance to achieve your Level 3 goals, *but* you'll also need to build a constituency. As we've already seen, you will handpick your allies (Champions, Supporters, Endorsers, and Companions). Above and beyond this core group will be other people you are eager to work with, and probably a few people you just have to work with because they have a place somewhere in the big picture.

The Declaration of Interdependence

We have been shaped into independent learners and performers, ready at any moment to defend our position, debate to win, and take the credit for our own ideas or actions. We have been led to believe that we are ultimately operating alone, and therefore we strive as individuals, contribute as individuals, and judge ourselves to be more or less successful on an individual basis. Like the law students who steal books from their college library so no one else can read them, we fear the competence of others who might outshine us.

> *The community stagnates without the impulse of the individual. The impulse dies away without the sympathy of the community.*
>
> William James

Overreliance on an independent mind-set prevents us personally and collectively from reaping the rewards of creative collaboration. The kind of innovation we need in order to reach our Level 3 goals is just not feasible when we think and work in isolation. Two heads are indeed better than one, and just one other person can help you change the world. But three heads are better still.

My emphasis here is on encouraging you to communicate freely and persuasively with others. Enlisting the support of other people dramatically increases your effectiveness. You've already attracted their attention by "walking your talk," and you've thought about who you'd like to have as your Champions, Endorsers, Supporters, and Companions. The next step is to invite others to come on board and get involved in helping you achieve your Level 3 goals. As you invite people to join you, and as you "connect the dots" and appreciate their genius, you'll see your own creativity soar. It always does when we attract the attention of like-minded, like-hearted people.

As you enter this phase of achieving what you want, I have some great news for you. Your vision of the best possible future is going to make your Level 3 agenda irresistible to others. You are going to find yourself extremely articulate about what you stand for and what you want most to achieve for yourself, for others, and for the world. Almost automatically, thoughts will come to you that are heartfelt expressions of who you are and what you want to accomplish. People who listen to you will be struck by the deep integrity and sincerity with which you speak. They will want to ask questions, to hear more, to extend the best advice and effort they have to offer.

As you speak more about your vision of the best possible future, what you might call a kind of "vision community" will begin to build itself around you. This community is indispensable to achieving your goals. In pursuit of your Level 3 agenda, the only way you truly will be successful is by receiving feedback, encouragement, questions, guidance, wisdom, emotional support, faith, and abiding goodwill from those you love and those you need.

In contrast, if you adopt faster-harder-smarter approaches, you will operate as if you are an autonomous, free agent, not deeply connected or committed to anyone. The Reactive mindset conceals the network of interdependent interests that bind you to other people and to your world at large. And when you ignore or deny how truly connected you are, you lose big. You lose momentum, you lose help, you lose opportunity. Like a rat in a maze, you know there's a way out somewhere, but you run your legs off moving from one blind alley to the next, a trial and error process that may or may not be successful. When you run alone, you run long, you run tired, you run scared.

But rapid-fire life doesn't have to be a rat race. Your creativity and your positive vision of what is possible can be contagious. You can intentionally join forces with others who believe what you believe, with people who share your hopes and aspirations, with those who are deep and rich and wise in the direction you are going and in the ways your life is unfolding.

As I will show you, there is magic in letting others influence you and allowing them to edit the specific ways you might achieve the future you want. When you are open-minded and willing to be influenced in your quest for the best possible outcome, you never lose ground. In your authentic exchanges with the people you value, a sense of community is born. And any time a community is bound together by an inspiring vision, the invisible interests that connect people to each other are realized more fully and creatively.

For a community to be whole and healthy, it must be based on people's love and concern for each other.

Millard Fuller

Before, you were listening to others. Now it's time to let others listen to you, too.

For the first three steps in this process of achieving what you want in a rapid-fire world, you applied your personal creativity and effort to revising your priorities, you crystallized your Level 3 goals into a vision of the best possible future you could possibly imagine, and you began to live your life in a new way. You cultivated your optimism and powers of observation, and each step helped you to comprehend how you and your world can change for the better. As you completed the Best Practices and gathered information, you spoke to many different people, asking them questions and incorporating their insights into your vision. In Step One: "Take Your Blinders Off," your first steps were to see the big picture (externally) and become aware of your emotional landscape (internally). In Step Two: "Be Outrageously Optimistic," you imagined the best possible outcome/goal/solution and became energized by how excellent it is. In Step Three: "Make the Future Happen Inside You," you bridged the best of what is and has been with the best of what can be, and gave up any counterproductive ideas or habits that might sabotage your new goals.

Just think about how well your Level 3 agenda and your vision of the best possible future already have served you. You have used them to form a lens through which you can see and seize the opportunities for advancement that are hidden inside of every situational crisis, setback, or leap forward (your Level 2 demands). You have come to rely on your vision to govern what you think, say, and do, so you reduce the negative toll that living in a rapid-fire world can have on your mind, body, emotions, and spirit. Because you are now clear about and committed to what you want most to achieve, you are able to juggle the pressures of a rapid-fire existence so that you attend only to those demands that bear most directly on your Level 3 agenda.

Now you are poised to be more effective as an individual, in your relationships, and in your capacity to make things happen. At this juncture in the process, Step Four, you are to be the one who leads the way. This step requires that you make a shift from using your own initiative to inviting others, to taking initiative on your behalf. It's about reaching out and attracting others to your cause. Your primary focus in this next step, and in every step to come, is to include others in your pursuits. Let others reap the rewards of your vision and experience firsthand the benefits your goals have to offer. The other people who join you will be rewarded as they are able to make your cause their cause.

Some things, like your vision for the future, are meant to be shared.

In his best-seller, *The Tipping Point*, Malcolm Gladwell says that if certain conditions are met, "ideas and products and messages and behaviors spread like viruses do." I believe this is true, and that this contagious quality can help you gather support and enthusiasm for your Level 3 goals. I am confident that when you learn how to communicate your vision of the best possible future in a compelling, memorable way, your vision will inculcate itself deeply within the minds and hearts of the people you want most to join forces with you. People like to feel needed, and everyone craves the chance to contribute to worthwhile goals. So often we feel like we are being asked to bail water just so the boat doesn't sink. Surviving can be motivating, too, but not very inspirational. Trust me, you will be a real hero when you invite others to join you in creating the next best version of yourself, of them, and of the world. They will thank you for asking them to come on board, and you will be thrilled to have them with you—whether it's rough water or smooth sailing that you encounter together along the way.

I hope you believe me when I say that other people will jump at the chance to help you achieve your Level 3 goals. Even if you're a bit skeptical about this, I'd like you to consider some ideas about creating the ideal conditions that will foster highly contagious communication.

For your vision to become a highly contagious one, you need to communicate on multiple levels, so your message is heartfelt and compelling. The best way I know of doing this is to engage in private, one-to-one dialogues with the people you want to bring on board. In intimate conversations you will be better able to screen out the noise and hurry of the faster-harder-smarter world. Private conversations also allow you to tell each listener why you have chosen him or her, in particular, to help you. This offer of appreciation on your part is a powerful motivator for other people. When you communicate your esteem, respect, and gratitude, your listener will gladly join forces with you.

A private conversation also allows you to delve

This is the true joy in life, being used for a purpose recognized by yourself as a mighty one. Being a force of nature instead of a feverish, selfish little clod of ailments and grievances complaining that the world will not devote itself to making you happy. I am of the opinion that my life belongs to the whole community and as I live it is my privilege—my "privilege" to do for it whatever I can. I want to be thoroughly used up when I die, for the harder I work the more I love. I rejoice in life for its own sake. Life is no brief candle to me; it is a sort of splendid torch which I've got a hold of for the moment and I want to make it burn as brightly as possible before handing it on to future generations.

George Bernard Shaw

deeply into the whys and wherefores of your Level 3 agenda. Take the time to share the details of your vision and show how important and valuable it is. Your listeners will see that without it, rapid-fire life is a roller coaster of ups and downs going nowhere.

As you articulate why you have selected your particular goals, how much they mean to you, and how you envision achieving each one to shape the best possible future, the person you are speaking to will start to identify with you. The more self-revealing you are in the conversation, the more your listener will be attracted to the depth of your commitment and desire. When you let people come in touch with your deepest motives and intentions, they can begin to see themselves in what you say. As they see themselves in your vision, they appreciate the person you are, the conversation you are having, and the future you want most. You will have their undivided attention.

At that point in your conversation when your listener begins to identify with you and the importance of what you are communicating, it's your turn to shower your listener with attention. Take time to explore the thoughts, feelings, and insights that your vision of the future has triggered in your listener. Ask as many questions as you can think of to draw the person out:

"How do you see the future?"
"What aspirations do we share?"
"Do you have any experience achieving similar goals?"
"What can I learn from you?"
"What am I missing?"

This is the moment to reward each listener with *your* undivided attention. Your attentiveness and curiosity will show how much you appreciate and deeply value your listener's responses. You want your vision to instill itself in the minds and the hearts of the people with

The important thing is not to stop questioning. Curiosity has its own reason for existing. One cannot help but be in awe when he contemplates the mysteries of eternity, of life, of the marvelous structure of reality. It is enough if one tries merely to comprehend a little of this mystery every day. Never lose a holy curiosity.

Albert Einstein

whom you discuss it—those whom you have chosen to help make your vision a reality. Communicating how much you appreciate your listener's input creates the best possible conditions for this.

There is one final element essential to creating the contagious atmosphere necessary for others to be inspired to join you in pursuing your Level 3 goals: your unwavering belief in the value of their moral support and their efforts on your behalf. The people you want to help you must feel your unequivocal belief in the value of their presence and the contributions they can make. If your Champions don't experience your total belief in them, they will never really come on board.

Behold the power of beliefs

The beliefs you hold about people actually influence their view of you and your goals, and ultimately their effectiveness in helping you realize your vision. Believing in a person's worth and value is the most fundamental way you can express your deepest appreciation for the very existence of that human being. When you have an image of this individual as an intelligent, helpful, resourceful partner, he or she will become intelligent, helpful, and resourceful.

The power of positive images to influence the effort and effectiveness of other people has been proved in scientific studies. For example, teacher expectations are more predictive of actual student achievement than almost any other single predictive IQ achievement measure.* Their strong influence holds true whether the teachers expect students to perform exceptionally well or expect below-average performance. The impact of teachers' positive expectations creates a halo effect that encourages outstanding performance, while the impact of teachers' negative expectations casts a shadow effect that retards student achievement. Our biggest question associated with these findings should be, "Why? Why do images that teachers hold of students have such a powerful effect?"

This phenomenon is often referred to as the Pygmalion effect. I've always been fascinated by the fact that images people

---

* Teacher expectations are highly correlated with student achievement. Studies report that correlation coefficients range from .5 to .9.

hold of us can affect how well we perform because they profoundly influence how we actually view ourselves. If someone we respect holds us in high esteem, we are more likely to hold ourselves in high esteem and perform accordingly. If someone we hold in high regard is dismissive about our value and competence, we are more likely to underrate ourselves and underachieve.

With this in mind, before, during, and after every conversation and communication you have with those you want to join you, remember to express your positive expectations. Tell the listeners, as specifically as you can, what you value about the contribution you expect them to make. For example, you might say something like this:

> "You make it so easy for me to express what keeps me awake at night. I can tell you anything and it doesn't blow you away. I'm looking forward to having you as a sounding board and sanity check while I'm in the process of achieving these tough goals."

Or, something like this:

> "You are able to see through the complexity of a situation and come up with completely practical solutions. I'm going to need this kind of help from you so I don't get mired in the deluge of demands and can continue to make progress."

Or, maybe you could express a contribution like this:

> "The ideas you come up with are bold and full of imagination. Your creative thinking is a terrific complement to my more analytical mind."

Once your listeners are able to understand the particular contributions they each can personally make, they will feel strongly motivated to help you. They will trust you and respect you for being astute enough to see the essence of who they are and what they have to offer as you set about achieving your Level 3 agenda. As an added bonus, what you learn from your constituents will help

> *Every moment is a golden one for him who has the vision to recognize it as such.*
>
> Henry Miller

you manage the pressures of Level 1 and Level 2 demands as well.

Without a shared identity, there can be no shared vision.

Companies have self-images, too. Corporate cultures run from bloodthirsty to warm and fuzzy. Employees come to expect certain types of behavior, and the expectation becomes the reality—whether it's 80 hour work weeks, or on-site child care and flex time.

Now I'm going to tell you about an organization whose top brass knew that if the company were to survive, they needed to set a Level 3 agenda and generate an inspiring shared vision among all employees. The problem was, this company's culture was so divided that before they could achieve Level 3 goals, they had to find a way to turn a culture of conflict and mistrust into a culture with a strong sense of community and deep mutual appreciation. They did, and the transformation was nothing short of miraculous.

The company was a high-profile biotechnology corporation. So far it had been very successful, but to stay competitive the company needed to stay lean and to keep a sharp focus. The immediate task was to unify several functions around a shared vision of success three years into the future.

The two middle managers who had been appointed to lead the visioning process asked us for help. Tony represented the research and development unit of the company, while Deborah worked in the sales and marketing side of the business. When our consulting team met with Tony and Deborah to discuss the project, we realized that this job was going to be extremely demanding. Achieving a shared vision among all employees across all departments would be difficult, if not impossible, under the divisive conditions that existed. It was going to be hard to get all the areas of the company on the same page for one day, let alone unite them behind a common vision for the future.

> *The thing always happens that you really believe in; and the belief in a thing makes it happen.*
>
> Frank Lloyd Wright

We discovered that each department had its own little vision of what would constitute success, and that each vision was so different from the next that the company was in gridlock most of the time. For example, the sales managers held the view that new products had to be introduced to the market almost immediately following the earliest phase of product validation. They believed this was the only way to encourage customer confidence and penetrate new markets. As you might imagine, the people in research and development felt very differently. The research scientists believed that the success of the company hinged on highly reliable, well-tested products. They wanted to be cautious in the promises made to customers, new markets, and Wall Street. They felt that since the burden of inventing high-quality, state-of-the-art products fell on them, the company should be more conservative than liberal in deciding when to announce and release new products.

It's as easy for you as it was for me to see the merit of both points of view in making the company successful. What was unusual in this situation was the degree of conflict and animosity that had developed between these two departments. The deep divisions and mistrust had been building for years. At the point when we met with Tony and Deborah, the sales and marketing professionals barely spoke at all with the scientists from research and development.

Reminding ourselves of how important it is to build a shared vision on a foundation of mutual appreciation and trust, our consulting team made the recommendation that employees from all parts of the organization begin to build a shared identity immediately. We imagined the sales and marketing department talking to the research and development team much like a private conversation between two people. Deborah and Tony agreed with our approach, and to that end we formed a design team made up of representatives from all parts of the organization. What we created together turned out to be one of the most intriguing and amazingly successful projects I've ever participated in.

Under our direction, the design team invited volunteers from all parts of the organization to participate in a three-phase process aimed at encouraging people across the company to identify with each other and to build a shared vision of the best possible future for the company. Each participant was asked to think about the following deceptively simple questions:

Phase 1: Who am I?
Phase 2: Who are we?
Phase 3: Who in the world do we want to be?

I especially want to share with you the details of Phase I. In this phase, we recruited volunteers from across the organization and formed nine cross-functional teams made of up 10 to 15 people each. The volunteers did not know what they would be asked to do, and probably expected some kind of brainstorming session with the white board and smelly Magic Markers. Instead, we taught the members of each team how to write stories that would capture their most memorable experiences. We encouraged people to write about what had been most personally meaningful, either before or during their tenure with the company. We asked them to include experiences from all aspects of their lives, not just work-related memories.

The stories that were written told of miscarriages and marathons. There were stories about children playing baseball, about parents dying, about winning international research awards, and about FDA legal challenges. People wrote about learning to ski and climbing mountains in Nepal. After the stories were polished and read within each team, one story from each team was selected to be performed on stage by a professional actor or actress during a company production entitled *Who Am I? People in Our Company Tell Their Stories*. On the day these stories were performed, more than 400 of the company's 600 employees filled the community college theater we had reserved for the performance. One by one the actors stepped forward to read a story that had been written by someone from the company, who at this point was anonymous to the audience. Since the readers did not reveal the names of the original authors, the audience listened without prejudices or preconceptions. Everyone was wide-open to being touched and influenced by the message of each story. As I sat watching each performance, I reflected on the fact that the entire theater full of people was engaged in the most intimate type of dialogue possible—the sharing of personal identity stories.

At the end of the performance, the original authors of the stories walked onto the stage and stood by the actors who had read their stories. Audience members gasped in disbelief as they saw individuals they knew mostly by reputation—in most cases, reputations that were not flattering—claim authorship of stories they had just heard and admired and identified with. The cast of actors and authors received a standing ovation that marked the beginning of a brand new sense of community that permeated the company culture and made it possible to create a deeply held shared vision of company success.

Communicating with substance, sizzle, and soul

Now that you have seen the importance of laying a foundation of trust, respect, and mutual appreciation, it's time to focus on how you communicate your vision so it is as meaningful and motivating as possible. In order to get others on board, you need to know how to motivate the mind, heart, and spirit of those you need and love.

> *Be still when you have nothing to say; when genuine passion moves you, say what you've got to say, and say it hot.*
>
> D. H. Lawrence

Substance. You have to know what you're talking about, but communicating your vision is not like presenting an ad campaign. I believe that most high achievers attempt to win support for their vision by emphasizing the substance of their Level 3 goals and the benefits that will be realized as those goals are achieved. We learned in higher education and in management development always to present our facts and figures, the rationale behind our proposals, and an exacting, logical description of our plan of action whenever we seek to persuade other people to join our cause.

When it comes to communicating with substance, most of us are well schooled and well seasoned. Like the well-versed, substantive communicators we are, we prepare our logical arguments, our white papers, our PowerPoint presentations, our pro formas and business plans, and off we go to convert those we need to get on our side. Even in our personal lives we follow similar patterns of preparation. When we want to convince a spouse or friend or parent or neighbor to see things our way and work toward accomplishing goals that are important to us, we come to the conversation prepared to prove our case. We offer substantive evidence of the wisdom and benefits of our vision in hopes of gaining the moral support and assistance of those we need.

Communicating with substance is a good thing, of course. But I'm here to tell you that, although the substance of your message is necessary, it accounts for only seven percent of why a person will follow you. Presenting the substance of your vision is like paying a mandatory fee, in that your supporters and followers do require that your goals and vision of the best possible future be carefully conceived and communicated. But substance accounts for only a small part of others' interest in your vision.

Sizzle. Let your vision of the future excite others as it has excited you. Part of my job is to prepare the most persuasive presentations possible. In my firsthand experience, working with both individuals and groups, I have found that people will feel motivated to sponsor your vision only if you provide them with a compelling story about why your goals should be accomplished and how your vision will create the best possible future. By "story," I mean a narrative. You don't need a lot of props to back you up—tables, charts, slides, and so on—because you will hold your listeners' attention with your description of your vision and how excellent it is. The way in which you support your conclusions counts, but people are persuaded more by your conviction and excitement as you tell them the story of their future.

In this part of your talk, explain how you intend to achieve your vision, and let your listeners see the passion you have for your pursuits. Let them hear your heartfelt desire to achieve your goals. If you can, describe recent examples of your goals coming to fruition. For instance, describe how your partnerships have moved in the direction you are striving for, and express what you have felt as a result (thrill, pride, exuberance, surprise, deep satisfaction, etc.). Relating a recent story of your progress, expressed with deep emotion, will motivate your listeners to identify with your progress and your positive feelings. This identification is precisely what I mean by motivating the "hearts" of other people to join you in the pursuits that excite you and please you most.

To build enthusiasm about your ideas, show your listeners how they figure into the story, too. Use the same emotion and enthusiasm you used to describe your recent accomplishments to express how you feel about their future contributions. Because you have designed your vision to contribute to the greater good, your listeners will have a place in the big picture, and will reap the rewards of your vision alongside you.

Soul. Let your listeners hear the innermost reasons why your Level 3 goals are so personally meaningful for you. When it comes to getting others on board, few things are as persuasive as your own belief in the importance of what you are doing. You've already given your supporters the substance they need to take you seriously, and the sizzle they need to get excited about your plans. Now share with them your personal conviction about your vision of the future. When you speak from the heart, others will sense it immediately. They will know that you are in earnest, and that you are 100 percent committed to your goals.

Some of my clients choke when they get to "soul," particularly if they are making a presentation at work about their Level 3 goals. For years they have believed that being "professional" means being crisp, curt, and unflappable. Aside from a couple of discreet family photos in their office, they have left their private lives at home. They are convinced not only that no one cares, but also that being self-revealing shows weakness.

It is not only undesirable, but also impossible, to separate your life—your family and feelings, for example—from your vision for the future. Communicating with soul is all about being authentic. People *do* care, if they are given the chance, so don't be afraid to be candid about how much your vision of the best possible future means to you.

I have described substance, sizzle, and soul as if you will address them one at a time, in sequence. This actually is an effective way to plan your remarks, but there's no need to be so tidy. Substance, sizzle, and soul will overlap as you communicate your vision and generate enthusiasm for what lies ahead. Remember that only seven percent of your impact on your listeners (positive or negative) can be ascribed

> *Live each season as it passes; breathe the air, drink the drink, taste the fruit, and resign yourself to the influences of each.*
> Henry David Thoreau

to the words you use to get your message across. Some of the best, earliest research on effective communications revealed that a whopping 93 percent of the impact of spoken communication is attributable to the nonverbal aspects of the interaction—for example, body language, facial expressions, tone of voice, eye contact, etc.

Think with me about this for a moment. Our nonverbal communication is profoundly shaped by the degree of trust and appreciation we have established as the foundation for the conversation. The more trust and appreciation we have, the more comfortable and at ease we feel. Our nonverbal communication also is driven by the degree of sizzle and soul in what we say. You know from your own personal experience as a listener that this is true. You, like almost anyone, are moved to join forces with someone who not only is able to communicate the worth and purpose of his or her ideas

Imagination grows by exercise, and contrary to common belief, is more powerful in the mature than in the young.
W. Somerset Maugham

(the substance), but who also is clearly energized by the process of achieving important goals (the sizzle), and deeply moved at the prospect of being able to realize such a meaningful, rewarding vision (the soul). If you don't include all three aspects of communicating in your conversation, you will remain distant, unconvincing, and disconnected.

BEST PRACTICES

The Best Practices that follow will help you put *communicate to motivate* into action. Remember that reading for understanding is only the first step. Your real learning will come from putting each Best Practice to the test in your everyday life. This is especially true for Best Practices like these, which involve communicating with other people. You will know they have moved you closer to achieving your Level 3 goals when you're able to motivate others to join you, to coach you, and to help you sustain your enthusiasm along the way.

BEST PRACTICE #18
THE THIRD IDEA

Whether you are building strong alliances with groups or with individuals who will be your Champions, Endorsers, Supporters, or Companions, you need to ensure that each person under-stands your Level 3 goals and, at least in a general way, how you see those goals coming together to form your vision of the best possible future. You want your allies to internalize your vision and make it their own so they can fulfill their specialized roles. You also want different groups of particularly gifted individuals to work together to help your vision come true. Of course, you already have an idea of how others can be helpful, but in this Best Practice, you'll learn how to solicit terrific ideas from your con-stituents that you may not have thought of yourself. Your goal is to achieve more collaborative approaches to decision making and problem solving among your constituents. Finding out how other competent people see themselves helping you requires an excit-ing give-and-take that should leave everyone enthusiastic. This kind of collaboration is effective whether there are two people involved or twenty. This Best Practice could be aimed at improv-ing a marriage or a friendship, but here your concern is strength-ening partnerships in a team, a department, a company, or even a whole community.

Step 1: Communicate your vision

It is best if you work with your constituents in homogeneous groups. If you are recruiting allies, use self-contained groups of Champions, Endorsers, Supporters, or Companions. It is helpful to combine people with similar interests because they will play a similar role in reaching your Level 3 goals. Remember, although you want everyone to understand your vision, you aren't asking all of your constituents to understand every aspect of your Level 3 agenda.

Before you start, remind yourself that people actually want you to touch them deeply enough so they cannot resist getting on board to help you achieve such worthwhile goals. Whether you are talking to an individual or a group, remember to communi-cate your vision with substance, sizzle, and soul. As you recall, this type of communication is designed to motivate the minds, hearts, and spirits of your constituents. You can think of it as if each indi-vidual is silently saying to you:

(Substance) *Talk to my mind. What does your vision look like for you and me?* Example: "I see the possibility of sharing

The Third Idea

Idea for Action #1	Idea for Action #2	The Third Idea
Benefits	*Benefits*	*Added Benefits*

ideas and developing new ways of brainstorming together so we can work collaboratively to make decisions and solve problems."

(Sizzle) *Appeal to my heart. How will we create the future together?* Example: "We've been operating independently for too long. This has taken its toll on our relationship. Sometimes the right hand doesn't know or care what the left hand is doing."

(Soul) *Speak to my spirit. Why is achieving your vision important to me, to you, and to the world?* Example: "If we are able to think together and act together, we will each feel valued and part of something bigger than ourselves. We will be able to make things happen that serve multiple agendas at once."

Step 2: Give everyone a part in the play

Remind those you are talking to about the role you would like them to serve in getting on board with you and your Level 3 agenda. You have already separated your visionary leaders (Champions), advocates (Endorsers), grassroots leaders (Supporters), and peers (Companions). If your listeners don't catch on right away, it might help to inspire them if you express your vision in the form of a story, such as the "hero's journey" motif (see pages 170–172).

Step 3: Ask others for their bright ideas, and prepare to be amazed

Invite each person (whether you are interacting with one individual or many) to jot down one idea about something he or she could do to help make your vision come true. For example, you might say, "I see you as a Supporter of this vision. What action can you take to help make this vision come true?" Ask your constituents to be brief, and be sure people work privately (not out loud) if you have a group. Some sample responses might be, "At least once a week we could jointly surface decisions and problems that need to be addressed," or "We could select one new collaborative problem-solving technique and apply it to a top priority."

Step 4: Finding the third idea

Now ask the members of your group to pair off. (If you are communicating with only one other person, you will work with each other.) Each person in the group will share his or her idea with a partner, then respond to the other's ideas, blending them together into a third idea.

Ideas must work through the brains and arms of men, or they are no better than dreams.

Ralph Waldo Emerson

Each partner must be sure to understand the benefits of the other's response so that together they can create a new idea for action that incorporates the benefits of both of the original ideas, plus added benefits that neither original idea had.

Step 5: By folding ideas together, you form an inspiring action plan

If you are working with a group, ask two sets of partners (four people) to work together to blend their joint thinking into another action idea. Repeat this step as often as you need to in

Idea for Action #1	Idea for Action #2	The Third Idea
"We could jointly surface decisions and problems that need to be addressed at least once a week."	"We could select one new collaborative problem-solving technique and apply it to a top priority."	"Let's each take responsibility for learning and teaching one new approach to collaboration. We can take turns showing the group how to apply it to the issues we address every week."
Benefits	*Benefits*	*Added Benefits*
By surfacing joint decisions and problems regularly, we can more easily see the scope and patterns of issues that matter to all of us. Right now we are in the dark.	This would give us a variety of tools, and as we apply them we will build our repertoire and discover which techniques are most effective for our application.	Each person in the group takes responsibility for increasing the group's collaboration and for addressing issues on a timely basis.

order to end up with one final idea for action that is a blend of the creative thinking of everyone in the group.

I have witnessed this process many times, and I am always amazed by the sensational ideas that are generated. If your previous experience with groups or committees is that ideas get more and more diluted with discussion, you will be pleased to discover that in this Best Practice, the final Third Idea expresses the depth and richness of all the separate conversations that took place in order to reach it.

BEST PRACTICE #19

HOW TO USE QUESTIONS TO MOTIVATE THE MIND, HEART, AND SPIRIT OF THOSE YOU LOVE AND NEED

As I've already discussed, the three aspects of communication that touch your listeners deeply in mind, heart, and spirit are substance, sizzle, and soul. Even when you are communicating with all three, however, it's possible for your listeners to misunderstand you or to miss the point. I have found that it is essential to monitor whether my listeners are following me by stopping to ask them questions, even when I think I am being crystal clear. In addition, I ask questions about their opinions, facts, figures, theories, ideas, and experience, since their contributions will enrich my vision and add to its appeal.

Step 1: Communicating with substance

Your initial focus is designed to motivate your listeners mentally. After your substantive presentation (see page 194), ask your listeners questions like:

- As I have described my Level 3 agenda, which of my goals seem most important to you?
- Which goals do you value the most?
- Which goals meet the deepest needs?
- What evidence do you see that supports my goals?
- When you think about your own agenda, how do your goals dovetail with mine?
- Can you think of another way to get on board?
- How can your expertise contribute to this cause?

When you value what your listeners think, they will want to think with you, and when you value their contribution, they will want to contribute—both now and later on in your Level 3 pursuits.

Step 2: Communicating with sizzle

In Step 1 you explained the substance of your Level 3 agenda, and you showed your listeners where they fit in. Here you want to generate more excitement, so others will see how excellent the future can be. To capture their enthusiasm, ask your constituents questions like:

- What part of the success story excited you? Surprised you?
- When's the last time you really felt galvanized by something?
- What is it about my Level 3 agenda that stirs your imagination? Your hopes? Your dreams?
- Where do you see yourself playing a part in the story of how these Level 3 goals were accomplished?

Step 3: Communicating with soul

Let's assume that during your presentation you are self-revealing, and make yourself unusually vulnerable and appealing in the process. This is where you delve deeply into your own personal motives and meanings. You express why you are striving for your goals, and you are candid about how you will benefit personally from achieving your vision. Finished? Not yet.

Ask your listeners about the goals they are most committed to achieving, and why those goals are so meaningful and important to the essence of who they are and what they bring to the world. As you connect with your listeners on a soulful level, ask questions like:

- What is the most meaningful part of this Level 3 agenda in your personal life?
- How does this agenda inspire you?
- Which of your values are supported by achieving these goals?

- How do you identify with why these goals are meaningful to me?

Getting people on board with you and your Level 3 agenda will launch you full-swing into creating the best possible future you have imagined for yourself personally, for your partnerships, and for your productivity. As you lead the way, your allies will follow. Those who join you will be motivated by your deep, persuasive communication. Their excitement and creative approaches to supporting your success will be all the encouragement you need to keep going, even when you mind, heart, and spirit are weary. In Step Five, which follows, you'll learn how to maintain your momentum even when obstacles and conflict come your way. Stay tuned!

Guiding Principles: Communicate to Motivate

- Your vision of the best possible future will captivate others if you create trust and mutual respect between yourself and each of your constituents.
- Substance, sizzle, and soul are the secret to authentic, contagious communication.
- Communicating the substance of *what* you are trying to achieve must be accompanied by your rendition of *how* to reach your goals in story form and revealing *why* your agenda is so meaningful and rewarding to you.

JOHN'S STORY, CONTINUED

By the time John reached Step Four in achieving his Level 3 goals, he was much better able to ask questions and honor the ideas of other people in his company. He told me that every single time he called upon his own desire to support and encourage others, he could almost see his relationships developing before his very eyes.

People were responding differently to John. Instead of keeping their talks "all business," he noticed that his direct reports had started bantering back and forth with him and interjecting humor into their conversations. For John, who had always seemed somewhat remote, this was a big—and welcome—change. In addition, leaders in other companies he had acquired were beginning to seek him out as a sounding board—not just an answer man, but someone who would respond thoughtfully. Best of all, everyone on John's executive team was on board with his vision of fostering the most creative corporate culture ever documented in a company of their size.

In this step, John demonstrated the power that communicating with substance, sizzle, and soul can have in actively motivating other people to join a good cause. Once he let all of his constituents know how much their support and encouragement meant to him personally, they doubled their efforts to help the vision come true.

Stack the Odds in Your Favor

How to Build Momentum

- Overcome Obstacles
- Have Courageous Conversations

This is the follow-through. Here you implement your plan, watch your progress, overcome the obstacles that present themselves, and learn how to capitalize on conflict.

> *Do, or do not.*
> *There is no "try."*
>
> Yoda

GEORGE SOLTI

Solti wanted to be a conductor ever since he heard Beethoven's Fifth Symphony as a musical child prodigy in Hungary. "That concert made my life," he said. This crystallizing experience sealed his fate.

In an interview conducted by the conductor D. Polkow, Solti described his view of what it takes to achieve excellent performance: "A first-class conductor is a combination of intelligence, psychology, and intuition, or knowing how to ride the possibilities of the moment—being able to feel the hearts and minds of your players." Solti also believed that determination and drive are key to achieving what you want.

"You must have talent and determination, or endurance. The really first-class conductors have these qualities. You must be able to suffer through all of the obstacles, and work very hard. You have to pursue conducting as your single ambition and know that somebody, somewhere, someday, will give you a chance. And when you get that damn chance, you must be ready. Go and do it. Go and pester people. I did the same. And get whatever experience you can get, however you can get it. I am quite certain that true talent does not go unnoticed."

Overcome Obstacles

What you need to DO	Watch Your Progress
What you need to BE	Resilient and Resourceful

I can't remember which famous sage first said, "Genius is one percent inspiration and 99 percent perspiration." Maybe you can remember. Was it Einstein? Edison? Churchill? Vince Lombardi? No matter who it was, what I do know for sure is that my father said it, and said it, and said it. Over and over again as I was growing up. I could hear that phrase spoken in my father's voice, ringing in my ears. Before every final exam, every piano recital, every swimming meet, and every backyard leaf-raking assignment, my dad would call me over to his armchair for a pep talk.

First dad reminded me of the goal. "Remember Kathy, I want to see an A on that algebra test ... no more glitches in "Fur Elise" ... 100 meter freestyle under 30 seconds ... leaves raked neatly curbside before dark." And then, without fail, as I started to dash off to climb whatever mountain was before me, Dad would say, "Hey, wait a minute, where's my kiss?" I'd reach up as he leaned forward and we'd rub noses for what dad called an "Eskimo kiss." Then, as I ran off but was still within earshot, my dad would say in the loudest, most parental voice he could muster, "Remember Kathy, genius is one percent inspiration and 99 percent perspiration!"

To this day, every time I create a Level 3 goal for myself, or address a situational setback of Level 2 magnitude, or even juggle competing demands of the generic Level 1 variety, I expect that *perspiration* will be part of the deal. So much so that I feel guilty if success comes too easily. More often then I care to admit, my tolerance for strain and struggles extends well beyond healthy limits.

"No pain, no gain" is the faster-harder-smarter corollary to the "99 percent perspiration" philosophy. I feel confident that the phrase "no pain, no gain" has been shouted by all manner of athletic coach and boot camp drill instructor in America. Phrases like these two are the mainstay of the Industrial Age work ethic and the mantras of Olympic athletes since the games began in ancient Greece.

I am writing this to assure you that you don't have to nearly kill yourself in order to overcome the barriers and setbacks that pop up in the course of pursuing your Level 3 agenda, or in the process of coping with Level 1 and Level 2 pressures. There is no doubt that the willingness to struggle and suffer, and hang in, and hang on, is in fact worthy of praise (in measured doses). Yet in our rapid-fire world, pain, strain, and perspiration are *not* the only ways to overcome obstacles. In fact, in a rapid-fire world, the propensity to take on struggle and strain can be downright dangerous. With so many more demands exerting pressure on you, it becomes easier and easier to overdose on stressful effort.

Since I have no doubt that you already know how to overcome obstacles the hard way (perspiration included at no extra charge), here I want to call your attention to using more creative approaches than those involving blood, sweat, and tears. This is related to "Scout for Opportunities," where you learned how to cultivate your optimism and how to find unexpected buried treasure in setbacks. In "Overcome Obstacles," however, you will learn how to actually create an action plan that will help you manage any setback advantageously.

I believe that the main difference between people who thrive and those who barely survive in a rapid-fire world is the ability to "dance" with whatever happens. Instead of trying to dominate or eliminate or control the inevitable obstacles that come their way, the hardiest among us invent ways to avoid, sidestep, learn from, push off of, and otherwise capitalize on them. When you are able to expand your awareness to perceive the hidden or subtle advantages associated with setbacks, you'll manage them with your inner resources, such as intuition and optimism, instead of depleting your stamina and endurance. Occasionally you will be able to use your ingenuity to simply sidestep an obstacle, but more typically you will need to deal with it. Just when you feel like taking a stick of dynamite and blowing an obstacle off the face of the earth, it's time to get resourceful.

If you get to the end of your rope, tie a knot in it and hang on.

Thomas Jefferson

The secret to overcoming obstacles is alchemy. When you are able to grasp the nature of a problem on deeper levels, you can apply your insights and imagination to transform it into gold. Working with problems causes you far less strain than bucking them head-on, using the brute force of your wit and will. And, if your experience in fighting demons and slaying dragons is anything like mine, a futile battle leaves you feeling angry and powerless. Rather than squandering precious time, effort, and energy on situations that are completely out of our range of influence or control, why not focus on what is working and amplify that?

It is with your richer, deeper, wiser Creative mind-set that I invite you into Step Five to explore how to stack the odds in your favor and actually build your momentum as you encounter the inevitable obstacles that come your way.

From flow to frenzy: revving the engines

I crave the thrill and experience of being so close to life that it supercharges my every move. Then I am in the ideal zone called "flow." I've already described the flow experience in the Introduction and in "Feel What You Feel." It is relevant here, too, because there is a fine line between flow and frenzy. Especially for high achievers, it is a very, very short trip from excitement to frustration, and you can travel that route in lightning speed without realizing you are on your way.

Take my usual path forward to holiday experiences, for example. Before Thanksgiving, my life is full. Like most people, I move into high gear in September after a brief Labor Day respite in some quiet, off-the-beaten-track retreat, submerged in warm, soothing water and late summer sunshine. I count on the fact that September and October offer prime time for being in flow. I am clear. I am focused. I am at my creative best. No mountain too high, no river too wide. I am traversing whatever terrain I encounter with keen awareness of the possibilities and of the way I can play to my strengths to take advantage of them. I'm living life in the smooth, rich, rewarding lane of flow. No faster-harder-smarter traps for me. I'm pursuing my Level 3 agenda and thriving on doing so.

Then, like clockwork, comes the invitation to create celebrations of thanks for the friends and family that generate the love in my life. I take Thanksgiving preparations in stride, as if they will make no impact on my already flowing commitments. After all, enhancing and deepening partnerships of all kinds fits right into my Level 3 agenda. Friends and family are of first priority in living a richer, deeper, wiser life.

Since I have years of practice, I am capable of working until six or seven, then zipping by the grocery store. There I select the freshest, free-range turkey Kansas has to offer, complete with Pepperidge Farm croutons, store-made gourmet cranberry and orange sauce, the requisite Yukon Golds, already mashed to perfection, and of course a green bean casserole I handpick with great care from the deli case. I know in my heart I would make it all from scratch were it not for my book deadline creeping closer and the ever-mounting assortment of meetings, keynote speeches, and coaching sessions I've taken on to keep my Level 3 pursuits on the front burner.

Because I am blessed with large reserves of energy, Thanksgiving comes and goes without a hitch. I've managed to stay in flow in spite of the extra Level 2 demands brought on by the welcomed traditions of the holiday. This is the good news and the bad news for a high achiever like me. The good news is the fact that I have managed to integrate the warm, inspiring moments of the Thanksgiving holiday into my Level 3 pursuits. I feel full of fond family memories, news of what's on the horizon for nieces, nephews, stepchildren, moms and dads and cousins. The bad news is the fact that I've gotten away with not slowing down or letting go of any other priority in the process. This just reinforces my belief that "I can do it all."

When the "I can do it all" approach works for a high achiever, its like falling off the wagon for a recovering addict. Just the experience of merging extra holiday activity into the flow of other Level 3 challenges lures me into adopting the Reactive mind-set of faster-harder-smarter. So when December festivities come around the next corner, I deceive myself into believing that my Christmas preparations can rival those of Martha Stewart's. With this false image of what is possible in mind, I put myself on a collision course where my Christmas challenges run head-on into my business and professional challenges and I begin to suffer the consequences of binging on the faster-harder-smarter diet.

If you are a male reader, you probably have never been tempted to imitate Martha Stewart, but you still have seasonal obligations—family gatherings, the office party, gifts to buy. If you're not Christian, surely you have been seduced by some of the pressures of the Christmas season. No one, not even the most placid, contemplative person you know, is immune from getting caught in the throes of dealing with Level 2 challenges while pursuing Level 3 challenges at the same time. Pick your poison. Maybe you get caught by trying to do it all for your children, or your customers, or your spouse or best friend when he or she is confronted with special challenges that could benefit from your help. Almost everyone is seduced into saying yes to more demands then they have the creative energy to meet. As a result, overload, hurry, worry, and all manner of frenzy are only one short obligation away.

> *Freedom means choosing your burden.*
> Eudora Welty

Even if you are the rare person who lives in serene circumstances, as you work your way closer and closer to achieving your Level 3 goals you are more and more likely to overextend yourself. It is in the very act of extending yourself beyond your own limits that you become your own self-imposed obstacles to be overcome. Just like me at Christmas, you are likely to find that your fuse is a tad shorter than usual, your chances for mistaking a simple statement for a critical comment increases in proportion to the added strain in your effort, and responding to your e-mail feels like an impossible burden and imposition.

So what's a high achiever to do when the thrill and excitement of flow turns into frenzy as a result of Level 2 demands colliding with Level 3 challenges, or as a consequence of ever-escalating Level 3 demands? The answer, you can probably guess, is to catch yourself early. Do what is necessary to observe yourself and register your reactions. Through simple acts of self-awareness, you can avoid the self-sabotage that the reactive, faster-harder-smarter approaches are bound to bring. When you run the risk of burning out, get a smoke alarm.

I have prepared a checklist of Early and Advanced Warning Signals that you can use to estimate how much of an obstacle your faster-harder-smarter habits have become in dealing with

Level 2 and Level 3 demands. As you review the chart on page 209, think of how important it is for you to get out of your own way in pursuing your long-term goals in the Personal, Partnership, and Productivity domains. It's difficult enough to reach your next, best level of effectiveness without inserting yourself as an obstacle. Assessing yourself is the first step to overcoming this obstacle to progress.

Last week when I added up my own scores, I scored a 6 on Early Warning Signals (enough to burden me) and 3 on Advanced Warning Signals (enough to isolate me). In my case, I reflected on what pressures in my life were most closely linked to my ultimate experience of feeling burdened and isolated. As I examined the range of pressures that could trigger faster-harder-smarter reactions, I narrowed the cause to an unexpected, major request from one of my firm's best clients. In response to a pending strike, the client company asked our consulting firm to design a four-day leadership training program in less than two weeks.

In retrospect I saw that I had agreed to the request without much discussion about whether the deadline could be extended. Instead of stepping back to imagine how my team and I could achieve this objective more creatively, we jumped in to help save the day. We ended up following the same process to design the course that we would use under circumstances with a much longer time frame. As a result, everyone on our team (including me) began to operate on fast-forward, feeling we had to do it all, and eventually we started feeling resentful instead of galvanized. Just recognizing the source and pattern of my reactions gave me some ideas about how to reduce the burden I was experiencing.

You gain strength, courage and confidence by every experience in which you really stop to look fear in the face. You are able to say to yourself, "I have lived through this horror. I can take the next thing that comes along." You must do the thing you think you cannot do.

Eleanor Roosevelt

My first thought was that if I was operating in a state of frenzy, the rest of the team must be, too! I called a team meeting and asked everyone who was working on this project to consider how we could operate differently to lessen our burden and to be more creative in response to the Level 2 challenges before us. The whole group was relieved to be stepping back so we could find more

Early and Advanced Warning Signals

Does This Sound Like You?

These warning signals emerge when we rely too heavily on faster-harder-smarter approaches. Check those that apply to you.

Early Warning Signals	*Advanced Warning Signals*
• Lack of thinking time necessary to be proactive instead of reactive	• Over-the-top reactions to relatively minor frustrations or mistakes
• Constantly struggling to juggle priorities	• Preoccupation with putting out fires, which prevents focusing on important, long-term goals
• Feeling like you have to do it all	• Achieving goals at the expense of people, or taking care of people at the expense of goals
• Preoccupation with completing your never-ending "to do" list	• Strained relationships with those you love and/or those you need
• Operating on fast-forward more often than not	• Nostalgia for the past or focus on the future, with disdain for present circumstances
• Nagging sense of unrest, dissatisfaction, or monotony	• Pervasive sense of resignation or helplessness
• Anxiety over how to quell the relentless demands of work and home life	• Seeing decisions as life or death when they are not
• Atypical lack of energy, enthusiasm, and motivation	• Feeling like a victim, or like you have no control over circumstances
• Focusing on everyone else's needs at the expense of your own	• Lack of desire to achieve Level 3 goals

Review the Early Warning Signals you have checked off and think about the type of frustration, burden, or sabotage you are experiencing. What aspects of your life—work, home, productivity, personal needs, relationships—are most negatively affected?

Now review the Advanced Warning Signals and consider the circumstances under which you have felt derailed, isolated, or out of commission. What pressures provoke your faster-harder-smarter habits?

What can you do to find your way to a life that is richer, deeper, and wiser?

proactive, productive approaches. Within 10 minutes we had come up with the following, to become richer, deeper, and wiser in our ways of delivering a quality leadership program on time:

- Provide the client with sample work we had already designed for other companies so we could modify existing programs rather than start from scratch
- Through our network of alliances, recruit extra freelance professionals to work on the project to lighten the workload
- Consider reducing the number of days of training from four to three days, or provide the training in two-day segments conducted six weeks apart to allow for more design time

It was simple to bring my Reactive mind-set to my own attention and to the attention of the group. I wondered, why had I waited as long as I did? I answered my own question by remembering that once anyone steps onto the escalator of faster-harder-smarter, your reactive habits take over. That's why it is so helpful to pause, check for reactive symptoms, and do what's necessary to ease yourself into other ways of responding. Intuitively I also knew that because we worked together to think of new approaches, the ideas were better and more diverse.

Make your own interpretations (with or without the help of others) and use these Early and Advanced Warning Signals as your "burning platform" for change. Remember, you don't have to live life in a frenetic, frenzied way. As you clarify and consider the trouble caused by your faster-harder-smarter habits, your motivation to do what's necessary to overcome these self-imposed obstacles will increase. You will know that it's time to tap into your creative, inner resources so you can give up the frenzy and get back into the flow.

From frenzy to flow: regaining serenity and optimism

Once you've recognized that you're in a faster-harder-smarter mind-set, you know it's time to shift. Oddly, no matter how motivated you may be, the path back to the excitement and thrill of the flow is not always clear, and rarely is it direct. I highly recommend taking a counterintuitive, creative route back to flow.

The surest, most rewarding way to reinstate a sense of exciting (not frustrating) challenge is by becoming aware of the glimmers of flow that already exist in your first-hand experience. We never live exclusively in either frenzy or flow, so our experience contains some measure of each. That is the way life is—a composite of opposing forces, a sea of contrasts, a blend of diverse dynamics working all at once. By channeling our attention, we can expand our awareness of nuances and subtleties that ordinarily elude us.

When creativity is in full fire, people can experience what athletes and performers call the "white moment." Everything clicks. Your skills are so perfectly suited to the challenge that you seem to blend with it. Everything feels harmonious, unified and effortless. That white moment is what psychologists sometimes call "flow."

Richard Kimball,
from *The Winds of Creativity*

For a moment, I want you to hold your head in your hands. Notice the pressure you feel from its weight. Usually we are unaware of the weight-bearing pressure, but with only a slight shift in attention we easily perceive it.

To find your way back to flow you use the same process of focusing your attention on the aspects of your experience you want to expand. In this case, you want to expand and enhance your sense of curiosity, your intuition, your optimism, your ability to be imaginative and innovative, your capacities for being reflective, persuasive, and collaborative. *These are your inner resources of creativity and they are always available to draw upon.* You may only be able to detect a glimmer of each, but you have my word that below the glimmer is a vast expanse, a veritable ocean of creative energy just waiting for you.

To remind yourself of what the experience of being effective and being in flow feels like, read the checklist on page 213 that describes in some detail the Early Effectiveness Signals and the Advanced Effectiveness Signals. My team and I reviewed this checklist immediately after our brainstorming meeting. We realized that in the process of dealing with our stressful situation, we had resurrected our sense of humor, our optimism, and our confidence in ourselves. The secret is to trace back your signals to actual situations and pressures, in much the same way as you linked warning signals to whatever was happening to trigger your Reactive mind-set.

In our case, it was easy to link signals of effectiveness to the stimulating, reflective, problem-solving session we created together so we could shift out of our state of frenzy into our state of flow. It was also important to identify other ways we may have been effective and creative, even though at the same time we succumbed to the reactive approaches that triggered our frenzy.

Have courage for the great sorrows of life and patience for the small ones; and when you have laboriously accomplished your daily task, go to sleep in peace. God is awake.

Victor Hugo

Reflecting on glimmers of creativity we may have overlooked, we discovered that immediately after client meetings we tended to relax and slip into humorous exchanges. We also realized that although we were swamped with deadline-driven work, each one of us still had a sense of being proactive on behalf of the firm's Level 3 agenda. Finally, we recognized a deep sense of trust in our partnerships with one another when we reminded ourselves that there was always someone to rely upon whenever any one of us fell behind schedule or encountered an unforeseen problem.

These new insights into our effectiveness gave us the encouragement we needed to expand on the conditions that fostered our most creative, effective responses. To that end, we made the following decisions:

- To cut back on the hours we spent meeting with our clients so we could devote more time to collaboration within our team. Without the clients present, we felt freer to exchange quips and follow tangents of thought that actually stimulated our imaginations so we could be more productive.
- To discipline ourselves to work within a specified time frame so we would not get stuck in a faster-harder-smarter crunch at the end

Early and Advanced Signs of Effectiveness

Does This Sound Like You?

When we begin to rely on richer, deeper, and wiser approaches, these signs of effectiveness begin to emerge. Check those that apply to you.

Early Signs of Effectiveness	*Advanced Signs of Effectiveness*
• Noticing opportunities hidden in daily crises and upheavals	• Having abiding faith in your own ingenuity and resilience
• Feeling confident that you can handle the pressures of the day	• Feeling a deep sense of calm in the face of major turmoil
• Progressing toward important goals while juggling immediate priorities	• Being excited about achieving Level 3 goals—and then excited about establishing new Level 3 goals
• Being optimistic that the best of the situation and of your abilities will emerge in the long run	• Trusting in your collaboration with others
• Feeling motivated and energetic	• Sensing the synergy between your personal, partnership, and productivity goals
• Maintaining your sense of humor through setbacks and tough situations	• Appreciating both the pleasures and the pains of living for the lessons they teach
• Being able to enjoy little moments of play and relaxation	• Discovering new possibilities for self-growth, new patterns in situations, and new possibilities in relationships
• Reaching out to other people for their ideas and assistance	• Bouncing back from setbacks and disappointments
• Generating novel approaches and innovative solutions to Level 1 and Level 2 demands and pressures	• Feeling capable and creative in response to any challenge

This checklist is all about what you are doing right. The Early Signs of Effectiveness show that your Creative mind-set is able to sustain, motivate, and even inspire you. When you are particularly creative, the Advanced Signs of Effectiveness indicate you are able to advance your agenda, and to be excited—even thrilled—about attaining your Level 3 goals.

- If necessary, to stop short of our ideal, focusing not on perfection but on what was most important
- To energize ourselves with confidence by tracking the milestones we had achieved, rather than emphasizing what we had not yet accomplished

I firmly believe that we never would have added these elements to our approach had we not done ourselves the favor of focusing on what had already stimulated our effectiveness. As I've said earlier, *whatever we pay attention to expands*. We used that quote as the mantra to encourage us to focus on expanding the signals of effectiveness that were already present.

Remember, moving forward is about progress, not perfection.

Obstacles show up in a multitude of shapes and sizes. Some we create ourselves, while others will be anything but self-imposed. Consider the obstacles caused by breakdowns in communication, or by slower than anticipated sales, or by processes that falter, or by erroneous information, or by miscalculated financial requirements. The list of problems, setbacks, and bad luck that can throw a monkey wrench into your best-crafted plan is as unpredictable as the weather in Oklahoma, where the wind blows swiftly down the plane. (As Will Rogers once said, "If you don't like the weather in Oklahoma, just wait a minute.")

Perfectionists need to be aware of certain typical self-created problems that make overcoming obstacles just that much more difficult. Perfectionists can be hard on people whose contributions do not live up to their expectations. This can interfere with forming beneficial alliances. Who wants to collaborate with someone who is a pain? In addition, because perfectionists are capable of doing magnificent work, they sometimes have trouble letting go of an objective. They keep finding more ways of improving upon that which is already good enough. Similarly, perfectionists can become so involved with what they're doing that they forget to look at the big picture. Staying on track requires constantly scanning the savanna for big game. Imagine a photographer taking a picture of a beetle, totally unaware that an elephant is charging at his backside, and you'll see what I mean.

It is one thing to tackle your own reactions to the vagaries of achieving your short-term and long-range goals. It is a whole other matter to engage an obstacle that is beyond your direct control. From unexpected interruptions (a Level 1 obstacle), to crises that take you off plan for days or weeks at a time (a Level 2 obstacle), to a barrier that prevents you from achieving a critical milestone of growth (a Level 3 obstacle), you are on the hook for doing whatever might be necessary to overcome each and every setback that comes your way.

Failing to recognize obstacles can harm you the most.

I met Elissa shortly after she had pursued and landed the position of Director of Leadership Development for a chain of 50 grocery stores located in the northeastern United States. Elissa initially consulted me because she wanted to be sure she handled her promotion well. If she turned in an excellent performance, she felt she could really go far with this corporation.

Elissa explained that her company faced many challenges in such a competitive, tight labor market. Without a significant improvement in recruiting, selecting, hiring, and retaining a high-caliber workforce, the profitability and longevity of her company would be severely compromised.

The senior management team Elissa reported to believed that the key to attracting and retaining a first-rate workforce was more effective leadership. They asked Elissa to establish an in-house leadership program that would groom 400 middle managers so they could establish a more rewarding and productive workplace culture. To be effective leaders, the 400 middle managers needed to learn how to inspire people to have confidence and pride in their company, how to give employees room to make decisions and try new approaches, and how to encourage workers to relate well to customers and to each other. Providing effective leadership of this type requires time and attention to learning, practice, and feedback.

What made Elissa's goal especially challenging was the fact that she was to complete the first five days worth of training for all 400 managers within nine months. To design and execute a leadership program, this time frame was incredibly tight, but the managers already were slated to attend five-day training classes in groups of 40. In addition, the senior management team was to teach the entire program. This meant they needed time to prepare and rehearse their presentations over and above their usual duties. On top of all this, Elissa was also supposed to implement other programs focused on areas like negotiating skills, time management, and personality profiling. Her first assignment was to bring in a course on project management.

The leadership training assignment qualified as a Level 3 challenge for Elissa, for the senior managers, for the middle managers, and for the company as a whole. The future of each person's career and the financial solvency of the company depended on a highly successful outcome.

Most of us have grown up with a set of expectations derived from a less tumultuous world. We still believe we should be able to create relatively airtight, obstacle-resistant plans to achieve important goals. We act on the assumption that if we are fast enough, work hard enough, and are smart enough, we can avoid encountering the boulders in the road altogether. When the inevitable problems surface, we are shocked. What happened to our perfect plan? Sometimes we are completely blindsided by problems that should have been obvious. Like Colleen, who missed her presentation rehearsal, we may go into a tailspin.

In establishing an exciting, challenging vision of the best possible future, you are setting yourself up for encountering obstacles that come with the territory of stretch goals. When you concentrate exclusively on the thrill and excitement of your challenges, you aren't prepared for the frustration and bouts of discouragement that are a natural element of pursuing Level 3 goals.

While the payoff for Elissa was enormous, there were several major obstacles built into her assignment. They were common problems, but that didn't make them any easier to overcome.

> *We are all continually faced with a series of great opportunities brilliantly disguised as insolvable problems.*
> John Gardner

Obstacle 1: Competing priorities

In this case, a leadership teaching assignment was layered on top of the other major responsibilities of senior management, while learning how to lead was added to the already full plate of middle management obligations. At one time or another every person involved in the leadership program was sure to feel the burden of having to accomplish too much.

Obstacle 2: Insufficient resources

From the start, Elissa realized that she and the project would have less than ideal amounts of time, money, and staff with which to work. The deadlines were written in stone because management needed to staunch the flow of workers leaving the company. Senior management had done what they could to underwrite the cost of the initiative, but profits were running behind the estimates. Because of full-employment work trends, especially for administrative personnel, Elissa was faced with the difficult task of finding anyone to assist her with the enormous number of logistical details of the project, ranging from word-processing and printing training manuals, to making travel and hotel arrangements, to registering participants for each class.

Obstacle 3: Steep learning curve

Clearly, the senior managers had not acquired the skills they needed to keep their workforce enthusiastic and competitive. To their credit, they recognized their shortcoming, and they each wanted to devote attention to developing their competence in these areas. In almost every case, the senior managers underestimated how much time and effort it would take for them to become proficient.

Together Elissa and I anticipated the difficulties she and her colleagues would face in the course of meeting the challenge of developing stronger, more skillful leaders. When the net effect of those three obstacles began to exert their influence, Elissa was as prepared as she could be. She saw the obstacles coming, so she was better able to respond creatively.

BEST PRACTICES

If you stop to think about each of these obstacles more deeply, you can see that the source of each one can be found in the nature of our rapid-fire world. Under the existing conditions of too many priorities, scarce or dwindling resources, and steep learning curves, it is more and more difficult to be proactive and to accomplish stretch objectives that take our capacities to the next level of effectiveness. So the question for all of us becomes: "How do we overcome the obstacles inherent to achieving Level 3 agendas that are so deeply rooted in the pressures of a rapid-fire world?"

The best way is to use your resilience and resourcefulness, rather than your intense effort and perspiration. Just when you're feeling trapped, you realize there is a back door out of any problem. We can choose to pour on intensive efforts out of the faster-harder-smarter mind-set, or choose to operate more gracefully and effectively out of richer, deeper, wiser

For a long time it had seemed to me that life was about to begin—real life. But there was always some obstacle in the way. Something to be got through first, some unfinished business, time still to be served, a debt to be paid. Then life would begin. At last it dawned on me that these obstacles were my life.

Fr. Alfred D'Souza

approaches. These Best Practices will help you overcome obstacles with the creativity that puts you back on the course toward achieving your goals.

BEST PRACTICE #20

WHEN IT'S THE BEST OF TIMES AND THE WORST OF TIMES, THE IMPACT IS UP TO YOU

Have you ever noticed that the really important things—say, qualities you love in someone, or opportunities you are thrilled about—are the best/worst things you can imagine? For example, I love my husband because he is so steady and logical. And sometimes it drives me crazy that my husband is so steady and logical. In this Best Practice, you will find the best and worst in any situation, so that ultimately you can make sure the best prevails.

Step 1: Envision the worst case scenario

When you come up against an obstacle, your first, best response is to calculate its seriousness. Does it represent a real barrier to your progress, or perhaps only a minor inconvenience? It was just the tip of the iceberg that sank the *Titanic*, so review the situation carefully. Ask yourself:

1. What is the worst possible impact this obstacle could have on my progress toward my Level 3 goals?
2. What can be done to minimize or prevent that negative impact?

You will recall that Elissa's Level 3 goal was to design and deliver a top-quality leadership training program taught by senior management to 400 middle managers within the next nine months so that the workplace culture would improve in ways to help attract and retain qualified employees. Elissa managed to put together a leadership training program that addressed the problems inherent in the assignment. She made sure the program did not overburden senior management (obstacle 1), that it met her restrictions of time, money, and staff (obstacle 2), and that it brought senior managers up to speed as quickly as possible (obstacle 3). However, in the course of implementing the initiative, Elissa encountered other obstacles.

Setbacks inevitably occur at all levels. A Level 1 obstacle could be a traffic jam that makes you late, a misunderstanding that causes a mistake, or a flash of temper that halts teamwork. Although unpleasant, Level 1 obstacles are relatively insignificant in the long run. They belong to the "someday we'll look back at this and laugh" category.

A Level 2 obstacle can range from minor to major. The minor variety includes distractions that consume your attention and effort for days or even weeks at a time. These obstacles are like brush fires or mechanical breakdowns—inconvenient but manageable. More intense Level 2 obstacles have no set time frame or standard resolution. These stop you in your tracks, and can be debilitating enough to curb your progress for a significant amount of time. Without question, there are Level 2 obstacles that can have a severe, deleterious impact on achieving your Level 3 goals.

Level 3 obstacles always pack a wallop. They differ from intense Level 2 obstacles because they are more closely related to your Level 3 agenda, or they represent major life stressors such as divorce, illness, job loss, moving to another part of the country, and so on. If you spent several months working on an initiative that mattered greatly to your Level 3 agenda, and suddenly everything fell through, that would be a Level 3 setback.

Elissa's *Level 1 obstacle* was that her husband was required to travel extensively on short notice, making Elissa's schedule for picking up her children from school unpredictable. This obstacle's worst impact on Elissa's Level 3 goals was the interruption of her productive work time at the office. To minimize the negative impact, she scheduled telephone and e-mail communication toward the end of the afternoon so it could be accomplished by car phone and at home on her computer.

Elissa's *Level 2 obstacle* was that the project management course she brought in received extremely poor evaluations in the pilot session. The worst impact of this failure was that it distracted her attention from progress on the leadership course. Elissa also felt that the situation reflected poorly on her, just when she wanted to show how competent she was. To minimize the negative impact, she sought input from senior managers to determine if it was feasible to postpone the course or to hire a different vendor with a better program.

Elissa's *Level 3 obstacle* occurred when a senior manager left the company. Because all senior managers were expected to participate in the leadership program, this created a sudden vacancy. The worst impact of this setback was that the effectiveness of the leadership program was diminished. Also, the absence of the senior manager was highly visible, which created some embarrassment for the company. To minimize the negative impact, Elissa needed to either recruit another senior manager to teach the segment, to give the responsibility to a key middle manager as a stretch assignment, or to step in herself.

You may be wondering if this is the end of this Best Practice. Not so. In fact, the next step is essential, and often surfaces the most amazing creative ideas.

Step 2: Envision the best case scenario
When you have finished asking and answering questions about the worst case scenarios, it's time to ask these next two questions:

1. What is the best possible impact this obstacle could have on my Level 3 agenda?
2. What could be done to maximize that positive impact?

No, I'm not kidding. Even when you face Level 3 obstacles, your Level 3 agenda can benefit. The benefits of obstacles are obscure at best. That's why asking yourself these questions and requiring yourself to answer them is so helpful. Don't censor your answers. Let yourself be spontaneous.

Elissa's *Level 1 obstacle* was that her husband was required to travel extensively on short notice, making Elissa's schedule for picking up her children from school unpredictable. The best impact this had on Elissa's Level 3 goals was that picking up her children ensured that she kept her daily focus balanced among all areas that were part of her Level 3 agenda, including being a mother who stayed closely connected to her children's lives. To maximize the positive impact of this complication, Elissa made a point of devoting at least one hour of attention to her children's needs when she picked them up before resuming a focus on work priorities.

Elissa's *Level 2 obstacle* was that the project management course she was responsible for received extremely poor evaluations in the pilot session. The best impact of this failure was that it drew attention to the fact that she was overtaxed and did not have enough resources to do her job well. Although Elissa initially was horrified that the course bombed, it turned out to be a blessing in disguise. To maximize the positive impact, she persuaded senior management to step up efforts to identify and hire a qualified training administrator.

Elissa's *Level 3 obstacle* was that a senior manager responsible for teaching a major segment of the leadership course left the company. The best impact of this unexpected event was that the remaining senior managers were able to explain, during the leadership program, why their colleague had left. This kept negative, erroneous rumors from infiltrating the ranks. To maximize positive impact, each senior manager took the opportunity to speak with substance, sizzle, and soul about the reasons for the departure of the senior manager.

Step 3: Create a summary chart for actions you can take
I have two reasons for suggesting that you create a summary chart of best and worst consequences. First, I want you to see

clearly the paradoxical qualities associated with any obstacle. Whether large or small, all obstacles can make best and worst contributions to your Level 3 agenda. Viewing every demand, pressure, windfall, or obstacle through the lens of your Level 3 agenda will enable you to effectively direct all of your effort in ways that benefit you in the long run. It is your responsibility to minimize the worst case potential and to maximize the best case potential. I am continuously amazed at how easy it is for almost everyone to neglect the best case scenarios associated with obstacles. We seem almost incapable of seeing the potential benefits of obstacles unless we discipline ourselves to do so with the help of a Best Practice like this one.

Obstacles cannot crush me. Every obstacle yields to stern resolve. He who is fixed to a star does not change his mind.
Leonardo da Vinci

The second reason I believe a summary chart is so helpful is that you can see that as a result of dealing with your obstacle you have generated at least two concrete actions you can take to protect and enhance your Level 3 agenda. This is in itself motivational. You may even feel a twinge of gratitude for having encountered an obstacle. In a strange, powerful way, the obstacle can lead to deeper understanding and wiser actions.

BEST PRACTICE #21

LOOKING BACKWARD SO YOU CAN MOVE FORWARD

A Level 3 agenda always exists within a context. You will have alliances and partnerships, supporters and confidants. Family, friends, and colleagues will help you in your efforts and share in your successes. Because your vision for the future is designed not only for you, but also for the greater good, your actions will benefit other people, even those who are at a distance from you.

The flip side of this principle is that when setbacks occur in one part of a system, the whole system is affected—and it isn't possible for you to do all the reparations single-handedly. When something goes wrong, the best solutions are generated by all members responsible for the whole, rather than by those only responsible for the part.

I have developed a specific Best Practice to use whenever a group of key stakeholders needs to address a setback. This Best

Summary Chart and Action Plan for Overcoming Obstacles

Level 1 Obstacle Elissa's husband was required to travel extensively on short notice, making Elissa's schedule for picking up her children from school unpredictable.	**Worst Case** Interruption of productive work time at the office. **Best Case** Picking up her children created a more balanced daily focus across all areas that were part of Elissa's Level 3 agenda (including being a mother who stays closely connected to her children's lives).	**Minimize Negative Impact** Schedule telephone and e-mail communication toward the end of the afternoon so it can be accomplished on car phone and at home on computer. **Maximize Positive Impact** Devote at least one hour to meeting the children's needs before resuming a focus on work priorities.
Level 2 Obstacle The project management course Elissa was responsible for developing received extremely poor evaluations in the pilot session.	**Worst Case** Distraction of time and attention away from progress on leadership course. **Best Case** Poor results draw attention to the fact that Elissa is overextended and does not have enough resources.	**Minimize Negative Impact** Seek input from senior managers to determine feasibility of postponing course or hiring a better vendor. **Maximize Positive Impact** Expand the efforts to identify and hire a qualified training administrator.
Level 3 Obstacle A senior manager responsible for teaching a major segment of the leadership course left the company.	**Worst Case** Effectiveness of course is diminished. **Best Case** Other senior managers use the leadership course as a vehicle for explaining why their colleague left, so negative, erroneous rumors do not infiltrate the ranks.	**Minimize Negative Impact** Recruit another senior manager to teach the segment, assign a key middle manager, or have Elissa herself step in. **Maximize Positive Impact** Use a portion of each senior manager's segment to speak with substance, sizzle, and soul about the reasons for the departure of the senior manager.

Summary Chart and Action Plan for Overcoming Obstacles

Level 1 Obstacle	Worst Case	Minimize Negative Impact
	Best Case	Maximize Positive Impact
Level 2 Obstacle	Worst Case	Minimize Negative Impact
	Best Case	Maximize Positive Impact
Level 3 Obstacle	Worst Case	Minimize Negative Impact
	Best Case	Maximize Positive Impact

Practice is derived in part from a strategy used by the United States Army to debrief and learn from the results of an engagement. I also borrowed elements of a group process invented by the Quakers called the "Clearness Committee," which is used to help an individual solve a personal problem that is affecting the group. The Clearness Committee is convened to support and encourage the individual who has the problem, and the meeting is conducted in a way that honors the individual's goals and wisdom.

At the heart of this Best Practice is a neutral approach to determining the facts associated with setbacks, failures, and mistakes. Assigning blame is not the point of this exercise. When I've used this Best Practice in response to a failed project, people were relieved when they found that the process asks for a reflective, comprehensive review of the sequence of events that led up to the failure.

> *In the middle of difficulty lies opportunity.*
>
> Albert Einstein

Step 1: Assemble your power circle

Invite the appropriate stakeholders—your Champions, Endorsers, Supporters, Companions, customers, etc.—to participate in a wisdom session. Before the meeting, draft a one page description of the obstacle or setback. Be sure to include a clear statement describing the obstacle, a brief background sketch of the circumstances that led up to it, and a summary of the problems you see on the horizon if this obstacle is not overcome. Stating your fears and concerns for the future will be highly motivational for your stakeholders. If they see the same consequences you see, they will be actively on board.

Two of the ten parts of the leadership program Elissa assembled needed revamping after the results of the pilot showed that participants had not understood the subject matter. Although this problem appeared to be limited to a small part of the overall program, Elissa called a meeting of all the senior management faculty so the group could collectively advise her about dealing with this setback. When she wrote her one page invitation to the group, she was careful to finesse the part about the two individuals whose modules had faltered.

The point of the meeting was not to call attention to any incompetence on their part, but to use the combined wisdom of the group to rework the program so it was 100 percent successful.

Step 2: Host your wisdom session
You will be the facilitator of this meeting. Allow two to three uninterrupted hours. Use the following agenda:

a.   Determine the nature of the obstacle. Everybody already knows why they are there, so you don't need to spend too much time describing the circumstances of the setback. Instead, invite participants one at a time to ask questions that will clarify and deepen the group's understanding of the obstacle. All of the questions should be addressed to you, in order to avoid any appearance of assigning blame. Proceed slowly, and allow time to elapse between each question and answer. To make sure everyone shares the same understanding, pose simple, matter-of-fact questions to the group, such as, "What happened?" and "What did we learn from what happened?"

b.   Generate potential solutions. Invite participants to offer potential solutions by stating their ideas with curiosity. The intention of this part of the agenda is to stimulate alternatives, not to arrive at a perfect solution. You are looking for responses like, "I wonder what would happen if we … ?" or "I'm imagining that … would be helpful."

c.   Narrow the approach. Respond to the prospective solutions by pointing out themes, and ask the members of the group to offer their opinions about which solutions they feel are the most promising. If solutions can be eliminated, discard them. Only emphasize those solutions that you, as the focus person, see as most promising. Give your reasons why you see merit in those particular solutions.

d.   Finish with group feedback. Ask the participants to give you, the focus person, feedback about your own responses. People rarely do this, yet it can be very illuminating to hear what solutions you seemed most enthusiastic and optimistic about. Your stakeholders might say, "The tone of your voice had the most energy when you talked about Solution X" or "You smiled and seemed confident when you told us why you liked Solution Y."

Wrap up the meeting by letting everyone know you will follow up with a communication that focuses on one solution and explains the details. Be sure to take time to thank the members for their input and feedback.

Step 3: Broadcast the solution

Write a one page response in which you describe the solution, who will be involved in implementing it, and how you will keep track of the progress and apprise the stakeholders of the results. A written document signifies the value of the meeting and also avoids any misunderstandings. I also encourage you to leave a voice-mail message or to have a brief conversation with each member of the meeting to express your appreciation, acknowledging what this person offered to the process.

Elissa found her wisdom session to be a rich, rewarding experience for all involved. Not only did the senior managers come up with creative ways of upgrading the two troubled modules, but they also boosted the confidence of the two managers responsible for the effectiveness of these sections of the program. This kind of success had never happened before. In the past, joint problem-solving left those most closely associated with the setback feeling demoralized and publicly humiliated. Elissa was able to keep everyone focused on the big picture—the Level 3 agenda—and to weave together the best solutions offered by the group into one coherent approach for overcoming the setback in question.

Guiding Principles: Overcome Obstacles

- Obstacles are overcome through inspiration, not perspiration.
- The biggest obstacle you may ever encounter is yourself. Whenever you see signs that a faster-harder-smarter Reactive mind-set is harming your effectiveness, it's time to shift into a Creative mind-set.
- Remember, obstacles come with the territory when you strive for Level 3 goals.

JOHN'S STORY, CONTINUED

There is a big difference between striving to make progress on Level 3 goals and striving for perfection. This difference was brought home to John in a recent team-building session I led to help bring the newest members of his executive team on board. As part of the session, John and I decided to take the whole team to a high-ropes course so they could get to know each other on a more personal level. The activities we pursued that day were both mentally and physically challenging. In effect, we undertook a tangible set of stretch goals, complete with processes that were fraught with unexpected obstacles.

What struck me about the obstacle course was an incident that occurred to Tom, one of the executive participants. Tom was an expert climber with many years of experience walking on tightropes. As we watched him climb to the pinnacle post on the first tree, everyone in the group marveled at his agility and fearlessness. We were spellbound by his grace in moving across the first set of perilous wires.

Then, without warning, he fell. My heart leaped into my mouth, and the group yelled for someone to help. The ropes held Tom safe, but he was dangling in midair. As the class gazed up in amazement, they received a powerful lesson. Tom was scrambling up the ropes and back onto his perch on the high-tension wire faster than we could visually track him. He performed his recovery with almost the same speed with which he'd fallen.

Everything costs and costs the earth. In order to win, we pay with energy and effort and discipline. If we lose, we pay in disappointment, discontent, and lack of fulfillment. So, since a price will be exacted from us for everything we do or leave undone, we should pluck up the courage to win, to win back our finer and kinder and healthier selves.

Maya Angelou

"What fabulous presence of mind and self-confidence Tom has," one of the participants said. It was true. No sooner had he failed than he recovered. He accomplished his midair reversal with the same confidence he'd had at his starting point.

Tom's behavior indicated to everyone that he treated his failures with the same positive attitude as his successes. In fact, it seemed to matter very little to him whether he was failing or succeeding at the moment. He had been intently concerned with striving. He had given himself a tremendous edge over the long haul of his challenge course by reacting to momentary failure as if it were simply part of what happens in striving for anything important.

In our debriefing session, John applauded the leadership Tom exhibited in his response to his own setback on the tightrope. He and the executive team discussed ways they could imitate Tom's resistant attitude and actions in response to the missteps and failures they were sure to encounter in their pursuit of business goals. John suggested that they adopt Tom's "positive attitude, positive action" as a motto going forward and that they each remind themselves of how Tom looked when he needed to climb back on course.

Have Courageous Conversations™

What you need to DO	Speak the Truth
What you need to BE	Fearless and Authentic

One of my favorite clients telephoned me the other day, just to touch base. When I asked Gary how his merger with a company that was once a competitor was progressing, he said, "Everything would be just perfect—if it weren't for the people!" He laughed, then I laughed, then we both took a deep breath and groaned. What Gary and I know, you know, too. How people respond to new visions, new goals, and new strategies for creating the best possible future means everything to your success. When people are with you, you can accomplish more then you ever imagined possible. When people are against you, your momentum can come to a screaming halt.

Now it is time to learn how to stack the odds in your favor when other people try to block your momentum. It's somewhat comforting to keep in mind from the start that you are destined to encounter resistors, naysayers, and detractors of all types in the course of pursuing your Level 3 agenda. It's guaranteed that you will, at some point, sabotage yourself by getting off track. As with anything else, you get up, brush yourself off, and try again. It's also guaranteed that there will be people who will resist the changes you desire most. You won't be able to escape these individuals, so you must find the courage to quell their divisive, subversive power, and summon the creativity to release their positive potential.

A Courageous Conversation is not a catfight.

As I write this, I am remembering one of my clients who was extremely capable but rather meek. When meetings became disagreeable, Anne would want to hide. She would feel her neck turning hot and blotchy, and was certain her cheeks were burning red. Anne was horrified if someone asked for her opinion, and when she was put on the spot like that, she seemed to lose her ability to be articulate. After the meeting she would make herself miserable thinking of all the things she should have said.

On the other hand, another one of my clients enjoyed nothing better than a good argument. Tony came from a large and boisterous family where everyone seemed to have a personality that was larger than life. Tony was loud and cantankerous and liked to prove himself right. When a setback presented itself, Tony would say, "No problem, no problem. I'll eat those guys for breakfast!"

A Courageous Conversation is not a win/lose situation. In order to participate in productive Courageous Conversations, Anne needed to stop worrying about being seen as a loser, and Tony had to curb his preoccupation with being seen as a winner. The conversation is about something bigger than any one individual in the room. The focus is on the play, not the players.

Here you will learn how to speak honestly and authentically with others about issues that are difficult to discuss and tough to resolve. Few skills are as important. If you pay close attention to the concepts, and put the Best Practice I will show you to work, you will be doing yourself and your Level 3 agenda a great service.

People have the power to make or break your Level 3 goals, and are your most important resource. The only way to break

> *Courage is the price life extracts for granting peace.*
>
> Amelia Earhart

down a large or longstanding barrier between yourself and others is to speak the truth with humility and compassion—that is, to have a Courageous Conversation.

How I survived a case of group resistance

Not long before I started writing this book, I accepted the assignment of creating a strategic plan with a group of scientists. Their company held some extremely lucrative patents that were about to expire, and management was turning up the heat on new product development. These scientists were charged with designing strategies that would maintain a high level of quality but reduce the time required to develop new products by 50 percent. I knew that was going to be a tough assignment, but it was a Level 3 goal for the company—a top priority that was not open to negotiation.

I went to the first meeting grateful for the chance to facilitate a strategic planning session with such talented, accomplished professionals. Facilitating a creative think tank is as exciting to me as any work I know. But I came home that evening wondering whether I would ever be able to break down the resistance that undermined our collective intelligence that day.

For the first hour, the 14 scientists were as silent as fish. Nothing I said or did sparked conversation. The sound of my own voice was practically all I could hear, and I soon started second-guessing myself. I thought: I must be really off track, because I seem to be silencing this group of otherwise lively and talkative scientists. Only moments before they had been buzzing with chatter at the coffee bar.

In the second, third, and fourth hours they did start talking, but the discussion mushroomed into a complaint session. They accused the senior leadership team of setting an impossible time limit. They claimed that a 50 percent reduction in cycle time would stifle innovation, not promote it. They talked about burnout and retention problems in the already lean ranks of the engineers. Intermittently they swapped bashing senior management for sneering at me for being too naive and too optimistic.

I'm not immune to self-sabotage. My mind raced with undermining thoughts: How was I ever selected for this assignment? What on earth made me believe I could be successful? How will I help this group of highly competitive and skeptical scientists develop a strategic plan to achieve any goal, let alone one they seem to find so impossible and even damaging?

I've facilitated many hundreds of team meetings, I've given courses in strategic planning and conflict resolution, and I've spoken and published extensively on the topics of change management and leadership skills. My stockpile of methods to handle discord is substantial. But when I walk into any group of people who resist working toward a positive goal the way the scientists did, sometimes their resistance debilitates me. Without realizing it, I let myself be sucked into their downward spiral.

The storm before the calm

On the way home that evening I reflected on the day and realized that I was starting to harbor negative judgments about the scientists. I found myself holding them personally culpable for the difficult session. I caught myself mentally accusing individuals of committing verbal crimes against their company and me. I pronounced two of the scientists blowhards who just loved to hear themselves expound on the stupidity of senior management. I blamed another scientist for her arrogance, and another one for his stern, condescending demeanor, and called them both incorrigible.

My mind was swirling with negative images. I played and replayed moments of conflict and argument and oppressive debate from the day's experience. My impulse was to turn the scientists over to their boss, the Senior Leader of Technology, to pay for their rampant dysfunction which was almost too powerful to contain.

As I pulled into my garage I saw my dog Shadow prancing toward my car. His tail was wagging as he jumped on the driver's side door with unbridled excitement to welcome me home. At least somebody still thought I was okay! His playfulness broke my preoccupation with the difficulties of the day. I promised myself I would revisit the tough situation with the scientists after a short run and a bite of dinner. I knew I needed some space to unwind and to disconnect from my strong desire to step in and correct the destructive, upsetting results of the strategic planning session as soon as I possibly could.

That evening, and for several hours the following morning, I focused on putting myself in a more neutral position. I made the shift by asking myself, "If I were to behave in such an arrogant, condescending, superior, and resentful manner, what would I be feeling?" Answering my own question, I had to admit that there had been times when I behaved ungraciously—when I felt apprehensive about my own ability to live up to a standard being imposed on me, or when I truly believed a course of action would be detrimental to

> *Courage is being scared to death—but saddling up anyway.*
>
> John Wayne

the desired results. This realization reminded me that it is a natural (not constructive, but natural) human tendency to wield intellectual superiority as a power play to protect the Status Quo out of a sincere fear of failure. Once I put myself in the scientists' shoes, I could welcome them (and myself) back to the human race. I knew instantly that if I looked at the scientists with more compassion and understanding, I could begin creating a new path with them.

Then I examined my own contributions to the fiasco. I had to face the fact that I had become unnerved when the scientists refused to value my ideas and efforts. I had interpreted their resistance to the agenda as if they were discrediting me personally. The sneering was unpleasant, but I took many comments personally when in fact they were directed at the objectives for our meeting. Feeling personally attached triggered my episodes of self-doubt.

You can rebuild momentum by speaking the truth.

I was ready to mend the fences and move forward. I asked for a meeting with three of the scientists who had participated in the strategic planning session. I singled out participants who represented the full spectrum of opinions and concerns: one scientist who was vocal and vehemently opposed to the cycle-time reduction goal, another scientist who was moderately opposed, and one more who had not yet made a final decision. They all agreed to a mini-meeting to give me feedback and advise me about what the next steps should be.

In our mini-meeting, we each took turns expressing our true opinions and feelings toward the cycle-time reduction goal and the disturbances that had occurred in the strategic planning session. I saw brilliance, creativity, and commitment to the company in all three of these scientists. I began to feel much more optimistic and confident that together, this talented, diverse group of scientists and I could devise a way of resolving the conflict between them and senior management. When one of us spoke, the other three listened and asked clarifying questions until we each fully appreciated what was said and why it was said. This conversation took over an hour because we needed time to understand each other's points of view deeply enough to be able to weave them into one coherent agenda going forward.

Next, without getting hung up on time cycles, we explored the contributions product development could make to the success of the company. We used our different interests to form an expanded vision of the best possible future for the product development division. The Level 3 goals we generated in that session included focusing on innovation, retaining engineers, and team-work. Now the scientists were interested and excited. In effect, our conversation to resolve the conflicts actually expanded the breadth and depth of what the scientists wanted to accomplish for the good of the company.

People grow through experience if they meet life honestly and courageously. This is how character is built.

Eleanor Roosevelt

We agreed that our next step would be to pro-pose this expanded Level 3 agenda to the rest of the team of sci-entists for their review, editing, and endorsement. We would clar-ify a revised Level 3 agenda and take it to the chief scientist serv-ing on the Senior Leadership Team for approval. We also agreed that strategic planning would be a welcomed, enjoyable task for the scientists if they were working toward their Level 3 goals.

When the entire team reconvened, the steps we devised that day worked well. Everyone viewed the Level 3 goals for Product Development as a significant improvement over the original, more narrow focus on cycle-time reduction. Now management's timing issue was placed in a larger context, and the scientists thought they could probably reduce cycle times by as much as 40 percent without sacrificing quality. The three scientists with the divergent interests who had met with me ended up developing strong professional ties with one another. As a bonus, the other scientists on their team supported their leadership throughout the entire course of the revision and approval process.

As for me, ever since that fateful day when the interest of the scientists collided with mine, I have become a trusted ad hoc member of the scientific community in that company. On a regu-lar basis they ask me to work with individuals and groups within that product development division whenever they want coaching or need to think and plan collectively. This is a prime example of how the willingness to speak the truth, and to honor the value of multiple angles on the truth, can lead to strong, productive rela-tionships that enhance productivity and benefit the greater good.

"You're mean and I'm leaving!"

You, too, can unleash the same authenticity and creativity in a group where conflict resides, as I ultimately was able to unleash it with the scientists. The Best Practice on page 238 is so robust that it can be applied not only to group discussions, but also to one-on-one conflict and disagreements, as this next story shows.

One of my long-term clients, the Chief Operating Officer of a large, local community hospital, asked me to help him resolve the conflict he had with the president of the hospital over how to increase market share and profitability. The COO favored growing market share and profits by making relatively bold changes in organizational structure, processes, and culture. He wanted to institute these changes quickly to avoid the inertia that sometimes accrues from slower, more methodical approaches. The president, on the other hand, believed strongly that gradual, incremental improvement was the surest path to building a sound, viable future for the hospital.

When it came to their Level 3 goals, these two individuals were in complete agreement. However, when it came to how to achieve those goals, they were completely at odds. They had come to what seemed to the COO to be an insurmountable impasse. It was as if each of them had identified so strongly with either "slow" or "fast" that they became the very embodiment of their extreme point of view, and compromise appeared impossible.

I remember leaning forward and tensing up as the COO picked up a white envelope from his desk. "This," he said, "is my letter of resignation." My heart started to race. I couldn't believe he was giving up so soon. "I've had it with debating and justifying and convincing my way through an endless series of attempts to persuade Cheryl to see things my way. I have a vision of what is best for this hospital, and I don't see why I always have to be the one to give in." The COO paused, glanced out of the picture window to his right, and then blurted out, "I'll do anything for Cheryl but fail."

I felt a strange sensation in my stomach, butterflies almost. In an odd way, I realized I was starting to feel encouraged that the COO felt backed into a corner. I realized that his resignation letter meant that he would go to almost any length to break the impasse. This doesn't mean I agreed with his decision to resign, but it was a sign to me that the stakes had just become so high that he was ready to go to whatever extreme necessary to settle the dispute.

Over the next hour, we reviewed the COO's range of options and the consequences of each. Eventually he agreed to one more round of discussions with the president. We agreed that he would tell Cheryl from the beginning that he would be willing to resign if an agreement could not be reached. I felt it was vital that she know that their discussion could end in a fight to the death, or a tremendous joint victory.

When losing ground means gaining ground

Before the next scheduled encounter between them, I had several coaching sessions with the COO and one with the president. My first recommendation was that they immediately cease any counterproductive behavior—ranging from hardheaded, no-win debates, to backstabbing—aimed at creating converts to one position or the other among the executive team. During each session, I examined the deeper reasons for the impasse. Both executives had made the common mistake of investing too much of their personal identity in their position. Losing ground in the argument meant losing face and self-esteem in the process. To further intensify matters, both were well-versed in the art of debate, but knew little about how to collaboratively solve conflict. In essence, what started out as a rational difference of opinion had escalated into a high anxiety conflict riddled with major liabilities for whoever lost.

I explored this conundrum thoroughly with each executive separately, so we could peel back the fears that were fueling the conflict and stalemate. As is often the case, they had gotten to the point where they were just repeating themselves. They needed to let light and air into their same old stuffy arguments.

Both the president and the COO came to realize that they saw any opposition as a threat to their credibility. Each one wanted to possess "the truth" about the hospital and how the health-care industry works. When they weren't locked into adversarial positions, they each recognized that there could be more than one "truth."

Both executives acknowledged that they were so deeply entrenched in their conflicting opinions that whoever lost the argument risked losing his or her identity. Eventually they saw that they each feared that the persuasive capabilities of the other would win out, and the loser would have to admit that the winner was more articulate, more powerful, and more competent.

The fact is, we all find it difficult to tell the truth at times. Not because we want to be deceitful, but because we fear we'll hurt, offend, expose or make others—or ourselves—uncomfortable. Ironically, this well-intentioned sheltering never serves your relationships. It inhibits your potential growth and prevents your ability to effectively collaborate.

Judith Dubin, coauthor,
Courageous Conversations

Over the next couple of weeks, the COO and the president had several Courageous Conversations. To their credit, and their amazement, they found the courage to overcome their fears. With this newfound courage, each entered the other's thought process. From this vantage point they each saw merits in the opposing viewpoint and integrated those merits into their own thinking. This is how they found a way to forge their differences into a united front of leadership, an approach that took advantage of both positions. They jointly sponsored a new strategy of *speeding up* and *slowing down* simultaneously in an experiment to test the validity of each.

What's important here is that both executives agreed to loosen their hold on their opposing positions just enough so they could each venture into and explore the territory of the other. In the process, each of them traded defending and promoting their personal position for becoming curious about how and when the other could be right. While their mutual respect made this possible, their curiosity is what saved the day. Curiosity vanquished competition—something that never would have happened without the willingness to let go of their entrenched positions and enter into the opposite point of view. Eventually, they were both able to buy into a third point of view that blended the best of each into a single positive force for change. This solution was more than a compromise that would never fully satisfy either side. The answer was not to slow down one executive's vision and speed up the other's. Instead, they transcended the paradox and found a way to honor the truths in *both* positions.

BEST PRACTICE

This Best Practice will show you how to be skillful in speaking openly, honestly, and persuasively about issues that are difficult to discuss. It is derived from a more detailed, comprehensive process called Courageous Conversations (coauthored by Judy Dubin and Elizabeth Page) that has been taught by our consulting firm to thousands of people. You can use the simplified version of this process to help you clear up confusion, promote cooperation, and capitalize on differences of opinions and misunderstandings so you can more easily achieve the goals that are most important to you.

In general, the speed, intensity, and intellectual demands of work and of everyday life mitigate against having any type of deeply satisfying conversation. How often have you discovered at the end of a busy day that you've hardly said "Hello," much less had a real conversation with anyone? If even casual conversation is rare, imagine how difficult it is for all of us to find the time and make the effort to have a conversation that is deep enough and thorough enough to help us resolve our differences.

Although our rapid-fire existence may not encourage conversations, nonetheless we must create the opportunities to have them. If we don't communicate our thoughts and feelings that reside below the surface, especially when we are at odds with someone else, we will always be at the mercy of smoldering resentment and unresolved tension.

To help you identify situations that are prime opportunities from promoting more authentic, proactive, Courageous Conversations in your life, review the checklist on pages 240–241 that lists some of the most common people problems you could encounter in pursuit of your Level 3 goals—situations that could well improve after having a deep, thoughtful, creative exchange. I've made this list somewhat corporate in nature, but you can easily see how these situations could crop up in other work situations and even your personal life. As you check off your interpersonal challenges that could be improved by being more honest, authentic, and persuasive, put a star by those that are linked to any of your Level 3 goals.

Now that you have determined which of your situations call for having more Courageous Conversations, you are ready to prepare yourself for entering into those conversations so you promote the most creative, effective resolutions.

I recommend that you plan and rehearse as much as you can *before* the conversation. Your rehearsal will help you ground

Courageous Conversations Checklist

This is a checklist of situations in which increased honesty and authenticity could be beneficial. Check all of the difficult-to-discuss issues that pertain to you.

☐   1.   Someone is not fulfilling a promise made.

☐   2.   You know that a close friend or colleague is doing something unethical.

☐   3.   Roles and responsibilities on projects are unclear, leading to misunderstandings.

☐   4.   You feel ignored, underutilized, unappreciated, manipulated, or disappointed by someone you value and respect.

☐   5.   You feel overburdened by the amount of work you have because someone else slacked off.

☐   6.   You believe the processes or strategies for achieving a goal need to be reconfigured but you know others will not agree.

☐   7.   You work with someone who has annoying habits you can't stand, but that person makes valuable contributions.

☐   8.   You believe there is a lot that is NOT being said that, if surfaced, could move the work forward.

☐   9.   You find yourself criticizing and complaining about others rather than working to resolve a setback.

☐   10.   You experience a contradiction between what others say and what they do, and you're losing out as a result.

☐   11.   You find it difficult to bring up bad news you've heard for fear of demotivating someone.

continued on next page

☐ 12. You believe certain kinds of behavior are inappropriate, but are reluctant to confront others about it because they are loyal to you.

☐ 13. You want or need assistance in certain areas, but are reluctant to ask for help for fear of looking incompetent.

☐ 14. You want honest feedback, but are reluctant to request it because you don't want to appear uncertain.

☐ 15. You think positive thoughts about others, but don't feel comfortable expressing appreciation very often.

☐ 16. You need to give negative feedback to someone, and are not sure how to provide this information while maintaining hope.

☐ 17. You believe one of your allies has a problem with substance abuse that is affecting his or her judgment and reputation.

☐ 18. You attend meetings that are unwieldy and unproductive, but it's not up to you to change them.

☐ 19. You'd like to intervene on behalf of a colleague, but fear it might make matters worse.

☐ 20. You believe you could add a lot to a project, but are not in a leadership role on that project.

☐ _____

☐ _____

☐ _____

☐ _____

☐ _____

yourself in the many layers and complexities of the situation. Imagine what your partner (or partners) in the conversation might think, feel, and say. Conducting a kind of internal role-play as part of your rehearsal process is a great idea.

Sometimes, after rehearsing, people find weaknesses in their own opinions or motives, and as a result decide not to go forward. However, most of the time they discover that a thorough rehearsal gives them a reality check and the confidence they need to move forward in a richer, deeper, wiser way.

Step 1: Reframe

We call Step 1 "Reframe" because if you are like most people, your initial frame of reference on this interpersonal challenge is more negative than it is positive. A negative frame of reference can put the kibosh on the success of your whole encounter. I suggest you follow the ABC's of reframing so you can shift mentally from a negative to neutral zone, and then into a positive mindset about the person (or people) involved and the eventual benefits you will create together.

A Is for Assess.   What are you bringing to the situation? Ask yourself:

- What are my sensitivities—triggers that would cause me to react in ways that might *interfere* with the successful outcome of this conversation?
- What are my strengths and capacities, hopes and expectations? How will these aspects of my involvement *promote* successful outcomes of this conversation?

On my way home from the disastrous meeting, I realized that my sensitivities to criticism and resistance had provoked me to feel personally attacked when I wasn't. Then my own downward spiral had added fuel to the fire, and I had begun to blame and harbor negative judgments about the scientists. Before continuing, it was important for me to move into a more positive view of myself and my ability to resolve the impasse.

B Is for Be Positive.   Think about several things you appreciate about the person (or persons) involved in the difficult issue or situation. Describe to yourself, truthfully, what you appreciate most about them. Most people aren't actually hateful. Chances are, somebody, somewhere, likes them for some reason. However, if you have to grasp at straws, do so. Shake off the blame or frustration you're feeling. Move yourself into a discovery mode.

I once was so annoyed with a CEO that the only thing I could find likable about him was his necktie. So I started with that. I wondered where it had come from. Did he have good taste in neckties? Or perhaps his wife had lovingly chosen it for him? Was he really so bad? Was there more to him than I realized?

When the scientists threw me off track, I had to purposely reframe my experience of the meeting. Once I got out of my own way, I was able to remember and appreciate the diversity of opinions and the creative brilliance of the scientists. I also applauded some of them for their commitment and loyalty to the company.

C Is for Change Places. Even if the shoe doesn't fit, wear it. Put yourself in the other person's shoes. It's a cliche, but it works! What factors might be contributing to the situation for him or her?

As I thought about the scientists, I was able to relate to the fact that we all get defensive if we are afraid that we won't be able to achieve a goal that is set too high. Reducing their product development cycle times by 50 percent was a drastic request. No wonder they weren't cooperative! We all block progress when we fear that achieving the goal will do more harm than good. It has happened to me, and it happened to the scientists in our planning session.

Step 2: Tell the truth fast

You must rehearse how you can clearly and concisely express your version of the truth about the situation so that your opinions, feelings, and positive intentions for the outcome come through loud and clear. Your opening statement in the conversation should have four components:

State your intention. Start your statement with phrases that frame your positive intentions, such as:

"Here's what I hope to learn."
"Here are my intentions for our relationship."

"Here are the opportunities I think will open up as a result of having this conversation."

"I am trying to be open and appreciative."

Describe what happened when. Describe the behavior or event in a neutral and precise manner. Give a specific, nonjudgmental, factual description of the situation.

"When ..." (Not a global, blaming statement such as "You always ..." or "You never ...")

Then, *recall the results.* Describe how you have experienced the result of the above, such as consequences, thoughts, and feelings. This is your experience, so use "I" statements. And, tell the whole truth—your reasoning, your assumptions, what worries you, what feels unfair.

Share your positive vision of the future. Now describe what you believe could be the best possible future. Explain the positive point of view for the ultimate solution or resolution. This is the place to express your optimism. You can't explain all the details, however, because you haven't figured them out yet.

In my mini-meeting with the scientists, my Courageous Conversation opened something like this:

State your intention: "I've had something on my mind since our strategic planning session, and because our working relationship is so important to me, I want to discuss it with you."

Describe what happened when: "... when your group found fault with the cycle-time reduction goal and complained about the meeting ..."

Then, recall the results: "... then I felt frustrated and worried about getting the strategic plan in place."

Share your positive vision of the future: "... I believe we can resolve the problems you have with the goal itself—and I have every expectation that we will—because I believe that all of us are working for the good of the company."

After our initial exchange, I said, "It's important to me that we find a way to mesh all our interests into a succinct agenda for Product Development so we can build coherence within the department and speak with one voice to senior management. I'd like to do that today so we can take our agenda forward as rapidly as possible and avoid any further discord."

In the actual mini-meeting, I taught the scientists the four elements of Tell the Truth Fast so they could each express their own truth about our conflict and their hopes for resolution. The scientist who was on the fence about the wisdom of the goal actually mirrored my steps. He said:

(Intention) "Ever since you called me about coming to the debriefing session I have been worried about this issue tearing our group apart...."

(When) "When I saw how polarized our thinking was in the meeting and afterward ..."

(Results) "Then I started trying to help people talk to one another privately so they could air some of their concerns without going public...."

(Positive vision of the future) "I believe we still have a long way to go, but I'm glad the four of us have agreed to tackle this issue together."

You can see that telling the truth fast got our conversation off to a great start during our mini-meeting. The three scientists and I were amazed at how much we learned from each other and how much we agreed with each other's positions. Everyone was willing to be open to the influence of the others once we saw the sound reasoning behind our differing points of view on the truth of our quagmire.

As you know from the details of this story, which I gave you earlier, the three scientists and I were able to expand the vision of the best possible future of the product development division. Before the next meeting with the full complement of scientists, we distributed some materials. We noted each of our areas of agreement and then suggested a time line to review our vision with the rest of the scientists, the senior VP of technology, and the senior leadership team. We also added a brief version of our new

Level 3 agenda to spark interest. Meanwhile, the three scientists—my new best friends—were creating a lot of enthusiasm because they couldn't help talking about their new goals.

To recap the process of preparing to have a Courageous Conversation, I have prepared guidelines for you that are summarized in the chart below.

Preparation Guidelines for Having Courageous Conversations

STEP 1: **Reframe**

To shift from a negative frame of reference to a positive point of view:

    a. Assess: What sensitivities and strengths are you bringing to the situation?
    b. Be Positive: What do you appreciate about the person?
    c. Change Places: Stand in the shoes of a person with an opposing point of view.

STEP 2: **Tell the Truth Fast**

To rehearse your opening statement:

    1. State your intention
    2. Describe what happened *when*
    3. *Then* recall the results
    4. Share your positive vision of the future

Guiding Principles: Have Courageous Conversations

- Speaking honestly, authentically, and courageously about difficult issues restores a clear sense of direction and builds momentum.
- Until you speak the truth, no one can see who you are or know what you want.
- People want to hear the truth—your truth.
- People want to speak the truth—their truth.
- Without truth there can be no trust, no true collaboration, and no lasting success.

Celebrate Every Victory, Large and Small

How to Leverage Your Success and Wake Up to What's Next

- Don't Go Back to Sleep
- The Best Is Next!

*E*njoy your achievements . . . and do it all again!

> The important thing is this:
> to be able at any moment
> to sacrifice what we are
> for what we can become.
>
> Charles DuBois

EDGAR MITCHELL

One would think that walking on the moon is enough of an accomplishment for one lifetime. For Edgar Mitchell it was merely a prelude to his life and heart's work.

Edgar Mitchell pursued his career goals with the gusto and passion we have come to associate with astronauts like him. He was thrilled to be on a space mission to the moon. He stared out the windows of the space capsule, beheld the vastness of space, and viewed Earth as only someone in a space capsule can. He was struck by the wonder of the universe, and simultaneously asked himself, "What comes next?" After all, he wondered, what could possibly follow a successful space mission? On his return to Earth, Mitchell was surprised to find himself curiously dissatisfied. He even felt guilty for having these vague feelings of malaise.

Then it struck him: He would dedicate the next part of his life to exploring the inner terrain—the terrain of the mind, of intelligence and knowledge, of creativity and human potential, and of healing. Mitchell heeded this call, and in 1973 founded The Institute of Noetic Sciences, which now serves as a research foundation, an educational institution, and a global membership organization dedicated to living into this vision. Edgar Mitchell was still a great explorer, but now he was using his wisdom and insatiable curiosity to advance humankind through the inner journey—a journey that is not limited to the very few of us who can climb into a spaceship and walk on the moon, but open to all of us.

Don't Go Back to Sleep

What you need to DO	Wake Up to Your New Reality
What you need to BE	Passionate and Proactive

Catching up with people we haven't seen in years can be such a thrill. You arrange to meet your best friend from college between flights at the airport to find out what he or she has been doing for the last umpteen years. Your favorite cousin calls you to tell you her daughter has been accepted into medical school, and it seems like just last year she graduated from high school. When someone we care about reaches out to fill us in and share life stories, we usually find we have a lot to celebrate.

One special hallmark of overdue exchanges is how sensitive we are to how the other person has changed. It's not just differences in physical appearances that catch our attention. Often we are impressed by how much more accomplished, or gregarious, or wealthy, or influential, or humorous the person seems (in contrast to our memory of how things used to be). Our new impressions of someone we've known and loved for a long time captivate us, and we can't wait to talk about what we see.

When it comes to celebrating the lives and adventures of those people who matter most to us, we are ready, eager, and able. But when it comes to celebrating personal success—the daily, weekly, monthly milestones and escapades of our own life— rarely do we stop long enough to take stock of how far we've come and how much we've grown. If we are not careful, when we finish one project, we move quickly on to the next. So that in the process of living minute by minute, hour by hour, day by day, we lose sight of our progress, our accomplishments, our learning, our personal growth, and, in the end, our very selves. In essence, we fall asleep at the wheel as we travel through our own lives.

Don't let this happen to you. Call yourself up and see how you and your life have changed for the better. Have an exchange with yourself so you don't forget to *celebrate every victory, large and small*, and to become richer, deeper, and wiser in the process.

Take stock of your creative resources— again, and again

Taking stock of your internal creative resources is the single, best investment you can make in achieving what you want in a rapid-fire world. This is true because your ability to shape the future depends upon the reserves of creative resources you have at your disposal. Achieving what you want in a rapid-fire world is an inside job from start to finish (and of course by "finish" I mean reaching a milestone or achieving a goal in service of an ever-expanding and evolving best possible future).

The breeze at dawn has secrets to tell you,

Don't go back to sleep.

You must ask for what you really want.

Don't go back to sleep.

People are going back and forth across the doorsill

Where the two worlds touch.

The door is round and open.

Don't go back to sleep.

Rumi

Like best friends, you can embrace the creative resources you have developed within yourself. Making direct contact with your curiosity and intuition, with your optimism and vision, with your resilience and passion, will remind you of who you are and how you've been able to make good progress. When you have a chance to meet these very real and alive aspects of who you are, the encounter will inspire you to keep on growing.

When you are ready to have this conversation with yourself, be sure you connect with the innermost regions of your mind, heart, and spirit. This will take some contemplation, so pick a time and place where you have some solitude, whether you're on a 12 mile run or sitting in the corner of a coffee shop. It is only in these deeper, less visible zones of your heart, mind, and spirit that you can discover what's available from the farthest reaches of your creativity. It is there, in the silence of your imagination, that you will be able to reacquaint yourself with the most creative aspects of yourself that have been the real secrets to your success.

To get started, I recommend that you review the work you did for Best Practice #3, "Taking an Inventory of Your Creative Resources: The Do's and Be's" (see pages 51–52). The first time you completed that inventory, you identified the creative resources that you thought would be most essential to achieving the Level 3 goals you had just set up for yourself. At that early juncture, I asked you to put a check next to each creative resource that was a strength for you at that time, and to mark with an X each resource that was underdeveloped, dormant, or untapped. Finally, you circled the creative resources you believed would be most valuable to you in achieving your Level 3 goals— presumably some that were your strongest, most well-developed resources, and some that were not.

It's time to take an inventory of your creative resources again, although this time you begin by looking backward instead of forward. The assessment you make will help you see how much you've grown in creative capacity since you began pursuing your Level 3 goals. I've included a fresh chart of the Be's and Do's again for your convenience (see pages 252–253).

Which resources helped you handle the generic stress of your Level 1 obligations?

Think about the various times when you were most creative and effective in dealing with Level 1 pressures as you pursued your Personal, Partnership, and Productivity goals. For example, recall the times when you were able to delegate a task, or pace yourself to ensure stamina, or ask others for help, or use your discretion in selecting which demands you agreed to take on and which ones you did not. Place the number 1 by those creative resources you relied upon most often in response to Level 1 pressures.

Which resources helped you handle your Level 2 stresses?

Now reflect on when you were most creative in responding to the countless Level 2 situational crises, setbacks, windfalls, and surprise turns of events that you surely encountered in pursuit of your Level 3 agenda. Recall the times when you were able to see the opportunities hidden within the turmoil, or use windfalls to accelerate your progress, or maintain momentum in spite of obstacles, or bounce back quickly. Place the number 2 by each creative resource you relied upon to be effective in response to Level 2 pressure. You will most likely place a 2 next to resources you relied upon in response to Level 1 pressures also. It is common and very desirable to rely on the same creative resources in dealing with multiple levels of pressure.

Which resources did you tap into and rely upon in pursuit of your Level 3 agenda?

Think about how you took your blinders off, stayed outrageously optimistic, made the future happen inside you, got others on board, and stacked the odds in your favor. Place the number 3 next to each creative resource you activated to achieve your Level 3 goals. You can place a 3 by any and all creative resources you tapped to be effective in meeting Level 3 demands—even by the ones you tapped in response to Level 1 and Level 2 pressures.

Your Inventory of Creative Resources

What You Need to Do:	*What You Need to Be:*
Step One: **Take Your Blinders Off**	
See the big picture	Curious and committed
Access your internal landscape	Intuitive and aware
Step Two: **Be Outrageously Optimistic**	
Use upheaval to fuel your creativity	Calm and reflective
Become energized	Optimistic and responsive
Step Three: **Make the Future Happen Inside You**	
Challenge the Status Quo	Imaginative and visionary
Give up your old habits	Observant and innovative
Step Four: **Get Others on Board**	
Consolidate your relationships	Influential and collaborative
Lead the way	Articulate and persuasive
Step Five: **Stack the Odds in Your Favor**	
Watch your progress	Resilient and resourceful
Speak the truth	Fearless and authentic

continued on next page

Your Inventory of Creative Resources (continued)

What You Need to Do:	What You Need to Be:
Step Six:	
Celebrate Every Victory, Large and Small	
Wake up to your new reality	Passionate and proactive
Realize untapped potential	Inspired and confident

Give yourself a promotion.

Now it's time to celebrate by letting the extent of your creativity sink in. Take a few moments to dwell on how frequently you relied on certain creative resources. Note those you marked with more than one number. Compare the creative resources you tapped most often with the resources you marked as strong (✔) and those you marked as weaker (X) on your initial inventory. Celebrate the creative resources you have reinforced and strengthened since you took the initial inventory. You can be particularly proud of the ones you have just begun to rely upon. These newer, less

> *To keep a lamp burning we have to keep putting oil in it.*
> Mother Teresa of Calcutta

well-engrained resources form your growing edges, the frontier of your ever-expanding capacity to achieve what you want in a rapid-fire world.

Appreciating your allies

When is the last time someone expressed his or her heartfelt thanks to you? I don't mean "Thank you for holding the door open" or "Thanks for picking up the dry cleaning." I mean sincere gratitude for a difference you made in their life.

When someone thanks you in this way, it makes you feel 10 feet tall. There is no better gift than to be praised for who you are and what you've meant to someone else's life. Most human beings want others to thrive and be successful, so we like nothing more than knowing we've played a positive role in others' lives.

Interestingly, many of us have more difficulty giving people positive, appreciative feedback than we do giving them negative feedback. We keep our positive thoughts in our heads, making it almost impossible for others to know how thrilled and thankful we are for the talents and gifts they have offered us in the course of meeting our Level 3 goals. Sometimes words fail us, and we just don't know what to say or how to say it. Sometimes we may be concerned that others will think we have an ulterior motive, as if we are flattering or complimenting them so they will give us something we want in return. Insecurity or competitiveness can prevent us from voicing our appreciation because we fear that shining light on another person's competence makes us look less effective in comparison. And sometimes we are so worried about what could go wrong that we forget to talk about what is going right. But mostly we simply take each other for granted.

It's time to flex your "appreciative" muscles. Never before has it been so crucial to be articulate and passionate about expressing your deep appreciation for the way your allies have aided your progress and success every step of the way. When you are able to express what you sincerely appreciate and admire about them and how grateful you are for their support, you build mutual trust in a way that no other type of interaction can.

When you provide your appreciative feedback, it is helpful to your ally if you specify how and in which circumstances he or she contributed a particular gift or talent. For example, let's say you appreciate one of your allies for his steady support and quiet efficiency during a recent uproar. You could slap him on the shoulder and say, "Thanks, buddy." You could even add, "I couldn't have done it without you!" This kind of encouragement is fine, but it doesn't show your ally what he really did to help you—and what you hope he'll do again. What if you said:

> "Russell, whenever people on our team begin to fall apart at
> the eleventh hour of meeting a tough deadline, you always
> offer to take them aside, to reassure them, and to show them
> exactly how we will be able to make the deadline. You are
> always honest and reasonable, so people trust you and take
> you at your word. I want to thank you for stepping in and tak-
> ing charge to calm people and get us all back on track. Last
> week, you helped keep me calm when the shipment of supplies
> we needed didn't arrive on time. Thank you for making your

confidence contagious, especially when we are working under chaotic conditions."

Who in the world trusts you and relies on you most? If you think about it, they are people who know and value who you are. They see your values, your character, your virtues, your shortcomings, your sensitivities, your foibles, your blind spots, your competencies, your hopes, your dreams, your genius—the whole person you are. They are people who thank their lucky stars that you are in their life. They know you have made and will continue to make a positive difference when they need you, and they let you know it. So give your allies one of the best gifts they could ever receive: the gift of praise, of appreciation, of thanks for the positive difference they have made in your life.

> *I realize that living well is an art which can be developed. Of course, you will need the basic talents to build upon: They are a love of life and ability to take great pleasure from small offerings, an assurance that the world owes you nothing and that every gift is exactly that, a gift. That people who may differ from you in political stance, sexual persuasion, and racial inheritance can be founts of fun, and if you are lucky, they can become convivial comrades.*
>
> Maya Angelou from *Wouldn't Take Nothing for My Journey Now*

It is particularly important as you near the completion of a particular Level 3 agenda to express your appreciation to each and every ally, constituent, and stakeholder who has made a positive contribution in shaping the best possible future you have pursued. Let your enthusiasm and gratitude shine through every spoken or written message you send. Communicating with substance, sizzle, and soul is essential to creating a real celebration of those who have helped make your achievements possible.

Don't forget to celebrate your own success.

I want to emphasize how important it is to your sense of personal accomplishment, your self-esteem, and your future effectiveness for you to confirm and celebrate your Level 3 successes. Early on you sowed the seeds of your success. As you have moved further along in this process of creating the next, best version of yourself and your world, those seeds you planted so carefully have taken root and are blossoming throughout the landscape of your life in subtle and breathtaking ways.

If you want to reap the full benefits of all you have accomplished, it's your job to celebrate the vibrancy of each of your achievements. Just as you might find the time to stop and celebrate a majestic field brimming with the first yellow jonquils of the spring, let yourself pause to take a longer look at the surprising beauty of your own success. I promise you it will be a pause that will inspire and refresh you—a pause that you will be glad you didn't miss.

Like the jonquils, evidence of your success will begin to appear across your Level 3 agenda. Of course, you will see the results of your perseverance, but your efforts will also be validated in other ways. People who don't even know about your agenda will notice that things are moving more smoothly, or that you seem happier, or that working with you is a pleasure. Someone might even give you a glimpse of the impact your goals have made on him or her directly. When this happens—and for sure it will—it's a great moment to celebrate.

In December, almost 11 months to the day after I began to coach John, he received a letter from his vice president of marketing. As he read it out loud to me, I was pleased that it gave John a chance to celebrate how the seeds of creativity that he had planted in his quickly growing company had in fact taken root and were flourishing.

To outgrow the past, but not extinguish it;

To be progressive, but not raw;

To be free, but not mad;

To be critical, but not sterile;

To be expectant, but not deluded;

To hear, amidst the clamor, the pure deep tones of the spirit.

William L. Sullivan

"John," he read. "I see that we are becoming an executive team that thrives on dialogue—honest, open, hard discussions of the issues—and that takes swift action to resolve these issues. This group is creative, driven by our ability to look at any situation from myriad perspectives while always holding the company's best long-term interests in mind."

John stopped to appreciate the part about being "creative," then continued, "Our team is now willing to try new things. We are always challenging ourselves first, and then the organization as a whole. We never know what will be next—but we are always willing to step up with our team because we are trusted and trustworthy."

John paused again, and I took the opportunity to point out to him that being called "trustworthy" is the highest praise.

He continued reading. "I see that our whole organization is energized, fluid, flexible, and responsive. We are pushing ourselves to understand emerging situations and to act on them. We have a clear understanding of what we are trying to accomplish, and there is a spirit of the highest level that is noticeable throughout the company. A desire to be counted on is clearly evident. There is an appreciation that the organization as a whole is committed to creating an environment that enables each individual to contribute to their highest potential and calls forth the best in everyone."

This is exactly what John wanted to accomplish all along, so he was smiling broadly as he finished reading the letter. "Thanks again for all you have offered me this year—your support, your encouragement, the bold challenges you've given me, and most of all, your friendship. I look forward to the future we are creating together. Signed, jsd."

John told me that Jerry had always been a quiet supporter of his, but that Jerry rarely gave him specific feedback on anything. Actually, John was shocked that Jerry would be so articulate and so positive about how the executive teamwork had contributed to building a culture of creativity and excellence. It was out of character for him to focus on the human being side of the equation.

I asked John, "What do you make of the fact that Jerry, someone who rarely if ever registers the value of teamwork, would spend the time and energy to put his thoughts in writing and send them to you?"

John paused and said, "I guess he wanted to really make an impression on me that even a guy as silent as he has been has noticed a big improvement, and thinks what is going on is good for the company."

Left to his own habitual faster-harder-smarter reactions, John would have simply read Jerry's letter and gotten a momentary buzz out of the positive message, then written a quick "Thank you" back to Jerry and moved on to the next subject.

Instead, he stopped to recognize that Jerry's letter validated his agenda and his efforts. Then he noted the links between his Level 3 goals and the changes Jerry specifically mentioned.

After helping John celebrate his accomplishments and the recognition from one of his most trusted allies, I posed a question I'd been dying to ask:

"So, John. What are you going to do next?"

The Best Is Next!

What you need to DO	Realize Untapped Potential
What you need to BE	Inspired and Confident

I am constantly amazed by how creative we can be. There are days when everything works and flows together like the confluence of great rivers. People are communicating well with each other, important work is getting done, and although the day is hectic, we are energetically and enthusiastically in pursuit of our Level 3 goals.

My partners and I meet for a hallway conversation at 8:15 A.M. to set the week's agenda for our project managers. We think together, we plan together, we speak with one voice. Our day opens on that harmonic chord and we're off and running.

At 9:00 A.M. I meet with our director of marketing to brainstorm business development ideas that will take our firm's impact in the world to the next level. There is nothing I enjoy more than creating a path forward where we've never been before. I leave that conversation energized, more convinced than ever that we can broaden our reach and touch more people's lives.

We're due at a client's office by 11:00 A.M., where we will propose a new performance management coaching process for an insurance company. My partner Terri meets me in the lobby. We have one more quick conversation about our roles in the forthcoming meeting. Terri agrees to take the lead.

In the elevator on the way up we exchange ideas about where Terri can take her family for spring break, and express our satisfaction at how quickly we were able to help another business identify why so many employees had left lately.

Terri and I sit across from each other at one end of a large mahogany conference table, waiting for the meeting to begin. I look up at Terri. She is thumbing through the proposal one more time. She looks calm and sure of herself. I think about how much our firm relies on her expertise in showing large companies how to give people the direction and motivation they need to excel. I remind myself how much I admire Terri for the strong commitment she has to developing people. As a partner, a coach, a wife, mother, and friend, Terri's Level 3 agenda is to help people see who they are born to be and what they do best.

I notice that my energy and enthusiasm are rising. The pace of the morning, my focus on the growth of our firm, and my deep appreciation for Terri have all buoyed my expectations for this meeting.

The highest reward for a person's toil is not what they get for it but what they become by it.

John Ruskin

I see our client at the door, and realize I am sitting on the edge of my seat as I rise to shake his hand. I'm full of anticipation for what can happen next.

Can you feel the vibrations? It's the rhythm of talented, successful people on the verge of achieving what they want.

In today's rapid-fire world there is always something we can be doing to move forward on our Level 3 agenda. We all have the Creative mind-set we need to turn the pressures of the hour into the fuel we need to succeed tomorrow. Our responses to shifting priorities, escalating demands, crises, setbacks, surprises, windfalls, and leaps forward can be stepping-stones to the future we most desire ... if we know the secret to becoming richer, deeper, and wiser in the process.

Often people attempt to live their lives backwards; they try to have more things, or more money, in order to do more of what they want, so they will be happier. The way it actually works is the reverse. You must first be who you really are, then do what you need to do, in order to have what you want.

Margaret Young

To have what we want, we have to know what we want. We have to be willing to capitalize on every pressure, large or small. It is simply a matter of resonating with the rhythms of whatever happens so we can move in the directions of our deepest desires and fondest hopes.

As a person who is now very familiar with *The Six Steps for Achieving What You Want in a Rapid-Fire World*, you have already tasted what life can be like if you view whatever happens through the lens of your Level 3 agenda. A canceled appointment becomes your found time, an interruption turns into a welcome diversion, a setback is a shortcut in disguise. Windfalls signal amazing opportunities, and surprises and downturns transform themselves into wake-up calls. Situation by situation, looking through your Level 3 lens illuminates the glory of what is possible every step of the way toward achieving what you want.

Becoming the next, best version of yourself never stops.

From a richer, deeper, wiser perspective, your new opportunities to grow will never run out. When you delve into the recesses of your desire, you find out which aspects of yourself are most ready to emerge. You take a good, solid look at those capacities and potentials that are now ripe enough to flourish *if* you give them the attention and intention that brings them forth.

Devoting yourself to becoming the next, best version of who you can be means that from now on you are willing to live your life out of desire, not obligation or sudden impulse. It means that today and tomorrow and each day after that you are willing to taste whatever it is that you long for and ache for. It means that in every waking moment to come you are willing to call yourself back from the promises and requirements and distractions of the world to be true to who you really are and what you really want out of living.

> *It is to what you aspire rather than what you attain that brings into being even what you do attain. Never set your sights too low.*
>
> Miriam Allen deFord

When you devote yourself to the pursuit of growing for the good of yourself, for the good of your relationships, and for the good of the world around you, your agenda becomes irresistible. Like a magnet, your vision of what you can bring to life pulls you toward a future worth living into. With this vision of the best possible future and the next, best version of yourself in mind, you will never mistake effort for accomplishment, frantic activity for progress, or empty dialogue for learning. This is your only way out of faster-harder-smarter living.

You are a pioneer.

Anyone who risks living life on creative terms is a true pioneer. Because you have set your Level 3 goals out of an intuitive sense of who you really are—out of your passion for growth, out of your dedication to making the most important contributions you believe are possible—you have accepted the responsibility for achieving what you want without falling into the traps of convention or obligation. This is what makes you a pioneer in your own life and in this transition generation of ours.

Today our parameters of success require, more than ever before, that we be proactive, not reactive. Given the context of today's rapid-fire world, if we react to the ever-escalating demands by trying to keep up, engage them more intensely, or outsmart them, we are setting ourselves up for implosion. Without the inner sense of direction our Level 3 agenda provides, we lose our way. We get caught up and chewed up by the grinding, relentless, insatiable demands of the moment.

As a pioneer in richer, deeper, and wiser, you know it doesn't have to be that way. When you are living out of your center, out of what you want, you always can find your way home if you get lost. You know what sustains you and what your life is dedicated to so you can move in the direction of your deepest hopes, dreams, and desires.

> *The greatest thing in this world is not so much where you stand as in what direction you are moving.*
>
> Goethe

Being a pioneer is never easy. You've learned that. You've found out that you have to stretch yourself and expand your capabilities to be able to embrace all of what comes your way—the good, the bad, and the unexpected. You've learned to move with life and through it so you can reach your next destination. You have learned to trust the fullness of every moment of confusion, of disappointment, of pressure, of thrill, of excitement, and of surprise for what can be made of it. There is no better way. *There is no other way.*

> *Hold fast to the Great Image, and all the world will come.*
>
> Tao Te Ching

As a pioneer, you know that operating in a rapid-fire world out of a Creative mind-set is revolutionary. You are rare in the world, and you are scouting new terrain. That's why the lessons you've learned are so easy to forget *if* you don't remind yourself to remember. You are not following a blueprint or a road map. You are charting your own way.

Practice is all you need to keep you going and growing.

Throughout your Six Steps for Achieving What You Want, you have made your way by following Best Practices. They have been tried, tested, and proven. They are "practices" because they must be done regularly and frequently to be effective.

Think back over how far you've come and how much you've learned. Stepping into the Best Practices helped you understand life better and yourself better. They helped you recognize and absorb the wisdom that the story of your life is offering the world. Completing each Best Practice allowed you to be more enthralled with every day and even more passionate about living each moment of your life authentically. You learned how to step into sweet moments of stillness where you could dwell on your experience, not control it. You saw how even brief exchanges can affect people for better or for worse. You are careful now to pay more attention and to imagine what the best possible impact of every conversation can be. You've lost your tolerance for deception, masks, or white lies. You've found the courage to step up, speak out, and demand honesty for the sake of making something brand new possible.

It is in the practice of what's best that you've been able to deepen your appreciation of the moment and use what you've found as motivation to move forward or reason to sit still. With practice, you've found out what boons and blessings an impossible sense of hope and an outrageous dose of optimism can bring.

Although the sea is alive with waves that

Waking Up doesn't turn people into something they're not—it merely opens the door to what they can become. The exciting thing is, once that door has been opened, it opens another, which opens another, which opens another. Soon, fears and constraints lift, individuals become aware of their ingenuity, imagination arises from dormancy, and potential is unlocked so it can be developed and brought forth.

Terri Goslin-Jones, partner,
The Cramer Institute

charge the shore, endlessly smashing to spray on the black and slippery rocks, beneath the surface of the water the ocean floor is calm. Seaweed trails gently along the sand, and silvery fish rock gently back and forth as above their heads the waves hurl themselves into oblivion. Our surface reactions to the winds of change and the torrential demands of the rapid-fire world can never be fast enough, hard enough, or smart enough to keep us afloat. To survive and thrive in the throes of a rapid-fire world, we must dive beneath the struggle, down to the core of who we really are. When we operate out of the deeper aspects of ourselves, we tap into the currents of our desires and creativity that run silent and run strong.

Success

To laugh often and much;

To win the respect of intelligent people and affection of children;

To earn the appreciation of honest critics and endure the betrayal of false friends;

To appreciate beauty, to find the best in others;

To leave the world a bit better, whether by a healthy child, a garden patch, or a redeemed social condition;

This is to have succeeded.

Ralph Waldo Emerson

As we join forces with those currents, move with them, and let them guide us, the chaos on the surface can never harm or deter us. We continue forward, flowing with the desire and creativity that carries us toward the shores of the best possible future and the next best version of ourselves.

Bibliography

Abram, David. *The Spell of the Sensuous: Perception and Language in a More-Than-Human World*. New York: Vintage Books, 1996.

Albom, Mitch. *Tuesdays With Morrie*. New York: Doubleday, 1997.

Angelou, Maya. *Wouldn't Take Nothing for My Journey Now*. New York: Random House, 1993.

Apatow, Robert, Ph.D. *The Spiritual Art of Dialogue: Mastering Communications for Personal Growth, Relationships, and the Workplace*. Rochester: Inner Traditions International, 1998.

Bateson, Mary Catherine. *Composing a Life*. New York: The Atlantic Monthly Press, 1989.

Bellman, Geoffrey M. *The Beauty of the Beast: Breathing New Life Into Organizations*. San Francisco: Berrett-Koehler Publishers, Inc., 2000.

Bezold, Clement, Rich J. Carlson, and Jonathan C. Peck. *The Future of Work and Health*. Dover, Mass.: Auburn House Publishing Company, 1986.

Bock, Kenneth, M.D., and Nellie Sabin. *The Road to Immunity: How to Survive and Thrive in a Toxic World*. New York: Simon & Schuster, Inc., 1997.

Branden, Nathaniel. *The Art of Living Consciously: The Power of Awareness to Transform Everyday Life*. New York: Simon & Schuster, 1997.

Capra, Fritjok, David Steindl-Rust, and Thomas Matus. *Belonging to the Universe*. San Francisco: HarperCollins, 1991.

265

Carpenter, Siri. "Future-Oriented Thinking Is a Staple for Infants and Toddlers," *Monitor on Psychology,* October 2000, 36.

Champy, James, and Nitin Nohria. *The Arc of Ambition: Defining the Leadership Journey.* Cambridge: Perseus, 2000.

Childre, Doc Lew. *Freeze Frame: Fast Action Stress Relief.* Boulder, Colo.: Planetary Publications, 1994.

Cooper, Robert K., Ph.D., and Ayman Sawaf. *Executive EQ: Emotional Intelligence in Leadership and Organizations.* New York: Grosset/Putnam, 1997.

Cousins, Norman. *Human Options.* New York: Berkley Books, 1981.

Covey, Stephen R. *The Seven Habits of Highly Effective People: Powerful Lessons in Personal Change.* New York: Simon & Schuster, 1989.

Cramer, Kathryn D., Ph.D. *Roads Home: Seven Pathways to Midlife Wisdom.* New York: William Morrow and Company, Inc., 1995.

Cramer, Kathryn D., Ph.D. *Staying on Top When Your World Turns Upside Down: Turn Your Stress Into Strength.* New York: Penguin Books, 1991.

Cray, Dan. "How Do You Build a Pyramid? Go Fly a Kite," *Time,* December 6, 1999, 8.

Csikszentmihalyi, Mihaly. *Finding Flow: The Psychology of Engagement with Everyday Life.* New York: Basic Books, 1997.

Davis, Stan, and Jim Botkin. *The Monster Under the Bed.* New York: Touchstone, 1994.

Drucker, Peter F. *Innovation and Entrepreneurship.* New York: Harper and Row, 1985.

Dubin, Judith A., and Melanie R. Keveles. *Fired for Success.* New York: Warner Books, 1990.

Dubin, Judith A., and Elizabeth Page. *Courageous Conversation.* St. Louis: The Cramer Institute, 1998.

Field, Joanna. *A Life of One's Own.* New York: Jeremy P. Tarcher/Putnam, 1981.

Fields, Rick, Peggy Taylor, Rex Weyler, and Rick Ingrasci. *Chop Wood, Carry Water.* New York: Tarcher/Putnam, 1984.

Fox, Matthew. *The Reinvention of Work: A New Vision of Livelihood for Our Time.* New York: HarperCollins, 1994.

Bibliography

Frankl, Viktor E. *Man's Search for Meaning*. New York: Touchstone, 1959.

Fritz, Robert. *Creating*. New York: Ballantine Books, 1991.

Gardner, Howard. *Extraordinary Minds*. New York: Basic Books, 1997.

Gardner, Howard. *Leading Minds: An Anatomy of Leadership*. New York: Basic Books, 1995.

Gish, Jen. "Coming into the Country," *New York Times Magazine*, May 7, 2000, 27–28.

Gladwell, Malcolm. *The Tipping Point: How Little Things Can Make a Big Difference*. Boston: Little Brown, 2000.

Gleick, James. *Chaos: Making a New Science*. New York: Viking, 1987.

Gleick, James. *Faster: The Acceleration of Just About Everything*. New York: Panthcon Books, 1999.

Goldberg, Natalie. *Writing Down the Bones*. Boston: Shambhala, 1986.

Goleman, Daniel. *Emotional Intelligence*. New York: Bantam Books, 1995.

Goleman, Daniel. *Working with Emotional Intelligence*. New York: Bantam Books, 1998.

Goleman, Daniel, Paul Kaufman, and Michael Ray. *The Creative Spirit*. New York: Dutton, 1992.

Hammarskjold, Dag. *Markings*. New York: Knopf, 1965.

Hampden-Trevor, Charles. *Maps of the Minds: Charts and Concepts of the Mind and Its Labyrinths*. New York: Macmillan Publishing Co., 1981.

Henderson, Hazel. *The Politics of the Solar Age: Alternatives to Economics*. Indianapolis: Knowledge Systems, 1988.

Hendricks, Gay, Ph.D., and Kate Ludeman, Ph.D. *The Corporate Mystic*. New York: Bantam, 1996.

Hillman, James. *The Force of Character and the Lasting Life*. New York: Ballantine Books, 1999.

Hollister Presents. *Why Didn't I Think of That?* New York: Dover Publications, Inc., 1970.

Jaworski, Joseph. *Synchronicity: The Inner Path of Leadership*. San Francisco: Berrett-Koehler Publishers, Inc., 1996.

Jensen, Bill. *Simplicity: The New Competitive Advantage in a World of More, Better, Faster.* Cambridge: Perseus Books, 2000.

Kimball, Richard S. *The Winds of Creativity: Finding Fulfillment Through Creative Act.* New York: Green Timber Publications, 1996.

Koestenbaum, Peter. *Leadership: The Inner Side of Greatness.* San Francisco: Jossey-Bass Publishers, 1991.

Kotter, John P. *Leading Change.* Boston: Harvard Business School Press, 1996.

Land, George, and Beth Jarman. *Break Point and Beyond: Making the Future—Today.* New York: Harper Perennial, 1992.

Levering, Robert. *A Great Place to Work: What Makes Some Employers So Good (And Most So Bad).* New York: Avon Books, 1988.

Levine, Rick, Christopher Locke, Doc Searls, and David Weiberger. *The Cluetrain Manifesto.* Cambridge: Perseus Books, 2000.

Levine, Stewart. *Getting to Resolution: Turning Conflict into Collaboration.* San Francisco: Berrett-Koehler Publishers, Inc., 1998.

Lewin, Roger. *Complexity: Life at the Edge of Chaos.* New York: Macmillan Publishing, 1992.

Lightman, Alan. *The Diagnosis.* New York: Pantheon Books, 2000.

McLagan, Patricia, and Christo Nel. *The Age of Participation: New Governance for the Workplace and the World.* San Francisco: Berrett-Koehler Publishers, Inc., 1995.

Mendelsohn, Jane. *I Was Amelia Earhart.* New York: Vintage Books, 1996.

Miller, William C. *Flash of Brilliance.* Reading: Perseus Books, 1999.

Naisbitt, John, Nana Naisbitt, and Douglas Philips. *High Tech, Soft Touch: Technology and Our Search for Meaning.* New York: Broadway Books, 1999.

Ogilvy, James. *Living Without a Goal: Finding the Freedom to Live a Creative and Innovative Life.* New York: Doubleday, 1995.

Olson, Robert W. *The Art of Creative Thinking: A Practical Guide Including Exercises and Illustrations.* New York: Harper and Row, 1980.

Page, Elizabeth. *Courageous Conversation.* St. Louis: The Cramer Institute, 1998.

Palmer, Parker J. *The Courage to Teach: Exploring the Inner Landscape of a Teacher's Life.* San Francisco: Jossey-Bass Publishers, 1998.

Bibliography

Piirto, Jane, Ph.D. *Understanding Those Who Create.* Scottsdale: Gifted Psychology Press, Inc., 1998.

Powers, Richard. "American Dreaming: The Limitless Absurdity of Our Belief in an Infinitely Transformable Future," *New York Times Magazine,* May 7, 2000, 66–67.

Profoff, Ira. *The Dynamics of Hope: Perspectives of Process in Anxiety and Creativity, Imagery and Dreams.* New York: Dialogue House Library, 1985.

Radin, Dean, Ph.D. *The Conscious Universe: The Scientific Truth of Psychic Phenomena.* San Francisco: Harper Edge, 1997.

Restak, Richard, M.D. *The Brain—The Last Frontier.* New York: Warner Books, 1979.

Rico, Gabriele Lasscr. *Writing the Natural Way: Using Right Brain Techniques to Release Your Expressive Powers.* New York: St. Martin's Press, 1983.

Rilke, Rainer Maria. *Letters to a Young Poet.* New York: Vintage Books, 1984.

Root-Bernstein, Robert, and Michele Root-Bernstein. *Sparks of Genius: The Thirteen Thinking Tools of the World's Most Creative People.* New York: Houghton Mifflin Company, 1999.

Rothschild, Michael. *Bionomics: Economy as Ecosystem.* New York: Henry Holt and Company, Inc., 1990.

Ryan, Kathleen D., Daniel K. Oestreich, and George A. Orr III. *The Courageous Messenger: How to Successfully Speak Up at Work.* San Francisco: Jossey-Bass Publishers, 1996.

Schlain, Leonard. *Art and Physics: Parallel Visions in Space, Time, and Light.* New York: William Morrow, 1991.

Schwartz-Salant, Nathan. *The Mystery of Human Relationship: Alchemy and the Transformations of the Self.* London: Routledge, 1998.

Sinetar, Marsha. *The Mentor's Spirit: Life Lessons on Leadership and the Art of Encouragement.* New York: St. Martin's Griffin, 1998.

Smith, Deborah. "What Makes a President Great?" *Monitor on Psychology,* October 2000, 45.

Srivastva, Suresh, and David L. Cooperrider. *Appreciative Management and Leadership.* Revised ed. Euclid, Ohio: William Custom Publishing, 1999.

Star, Alexander. "Questions for Dr. Antonio Damasio, What Feelings Feel Like," *New York Times Magazine*, May 7, 2000, 31.

Stone, Douglas, Bruce Patton, and Sheila Heen. *Difficult Conversations: How to Discuss What Matters Most.* New York: Viking, 1999.

Toffler, Alvin, and Heidi Toffler. *Creating Your Own Civilization: The Politics of the Third Wave.* Atlanta: Turner Publishing, 1994.

Trout, Jack, and Steve Rivkin. *The New Positioning: The Latest on the World's #1 Business Strategy.* New York: McGraw-Hill, 1992.

Vaughan, Susan C., Ph.D. *Half Empty Half Full: Understanding the Psychological Roots of Optimism.* Orlando: Harcourt, 2000.

Waldrup, M. Mitchell. *Complexity: The Energy Source at the Edge of Order and Chaos.* New York: Simon & Schuster, 1992.

Weisbord, Marvin R. *Discovering Common Ground: How Future Search Conferences Bring People Together to Achieve Breakthrough Innovation, Empowerment, Shared Vision, and Collaborative Action.* San Francisco: Berrett-Koehler Publishers, 1992.

Wenger, Win, Ph.D., and Riland Poe. *The Einstein Factor: A Proven New Method for Increasing Your Intelligence.* New York: Pima Publishing, 1996.

Whyte, David. *The House of Belonging.* Langley: Many Rivers Press, 1997.

Wilber, Ken. *The Marriage of Sense and Soul: Integrating Science and Religion.* New York: Random House, 1998.

Wolf, J. Rinke, M.D. *Winning Management: Six Fail-Safe Strategies for Building High-Performance Organizations.* New York: Achievement Publishers, 1997.

Zander, Rosamund Stone, and Benjamin Zander. *The Art of Possibility.* Boston: Harvard Business School Press, 2000.

INDEX

Index

Index

Index

Index

Index

Please visit the Web site for this book, www.fasterhardersmarter. com. Submit your thoughts; complete a Personal Potential Profile; assess your Wisdom Quotient; learn new approaches to building resilience, unleashing potential, and creating the next best version of yourself, your team, and your organization. Read tips and timely advice from the author and find out about Dr. Kathryn Cramer's schedule of appearances.

Dr. Cramer is the managing partner of The Cramer Institute in St. Louis, Missouri. If you would like to learn more about The Cramer Institute's keynote addresses or the consulting, training, and coaching programs we customize for leaders, teams, and organizations, please visit our Web site, www.cramerinstitute.com. Or you can contact us directly at:

The Cramer Institute
7800 Maryland Avenue
St. Louis, Missouri 63105
(314) 725-0500 (phone)
(314) 725-3000 (fax)
www.cramerinstitute.com
www.fasterhardersmarter.com

ABOUT THE AUTHOR

Kathryn D. Cramer, Ph.D., is a licensed psychologist and founder of The Cramer Institute, a consulting firm that offers customized change management, leadership development and coaching processes, keynote addresses, and signature programs found nowhere else. The Institute works with clients including MasterCard, Monsanto, The United States Air Force, DuPont, Earthgrains, Bank of America, as well as with many major hospitals and associations. For more than a decade, The Cramer Institute has been inspiring individuals, teams, and organizations to find creative ways of forging satisfying, successful, and sustainable futures.

Dr. Cramer is a popular keynote speaker at conferences and corporate events around the world and the author of *Staying on Top When Your World Turns Upside-Down* and *Roads Home: Seven Pathways to Midlife Wisdom*. In addition to these books, Dr. Cramer is published extensively in her field and has produced two films on stress, one of which earned an Emmy Award.

Dr. Cramer earned her master's degree in psychology from De Pauw University and her doctorate in psychology from St. Louis University. She founded the Stress Center at St. Louis University Medical Center and served as its director for 9 years. Dr. Cramer is a member of the American Psychological Association. She resides in St. Louis with her husband, John Davis, and their dog, Shadow.